Community Prevention of Alcohol Problems

Edited by

Marja Holmila
Senior Researcher
Social Research Institute of Alcohol Studies
Helsinki
Finland

Foreword by Sally Casswell
Professor, Director of Alcohol and Public Health Research Unit
University of Auckland
New Zealand

Consultant Editor: Jo Campling

  in association with
THE WHO REGIONAL OFFICE FOR EUROPE

First published 1997 by
MACMILLAN PRESS LTD
Houndmills, Basingstoke, Hampshire RG21 6XS
and London
Companies and representatives
throughout the world

ISBN 0-333-64839-0 hardcover
ISBN 0-333-64840-4 paperback

A catalogue record for this book is available
from the British Library.

This book is printed on paper suitable for recycling and
made from fully managed and sustained forest sources.

10   9   8   7   6   5   4   3   2   1
06   05   04   03   02   01   00   99   98   97

Printed in Great Britain by
The Ipswich Book Company Ltd
Ipswich, Suffolk

Contents

List of Tables

List of Figures

Acknowledgements

This book is a product of extensive teamwork. The action part of the Lahti project involved a great number of people in Lahti, both professionals and lay people, both adult and young. All these persons whose names cannot be mentioned here are warmly thanked. Special appreciation belongs to Sirkka-Liisa Mäkelä, the project's local coordinator, without whom the work could never have been accomplished. Her commitment, experience and boundless imagination made her the leading force in the project. Among the other important project members in Lahti were Hannu Hyvärinen, Risto Kajaste and Ritva Teräväinen in the city's health bureau. Also the youth workers Lealiisa Kämäri, Kirsi Malola and Lasse Kantola, as well as Rauno Haahtela at the restaurant and hotel school (Fellmanni Institute) and Ritva Piispanen and Sirkku Blinnikka at the city library had a major role in making the project happen. The deputy mayor Kari Salmi gave the project his support from the very beginning.

The Lahti project was a collaborative project between the Finnish Foundation for Alcohol Studies and the World Health Organization's European Office. Peter Anderson at the WHO's European Office was from the very beginning one of the most active promoters and supporters of the project. He also formed the link between this project and the European Alcohol Action Plan, thus setting the project in a wider action perspective.

The Alcohol Policy Planning and Information Unit in Alko Ltd gave both financial resources and professional know-how for the educational events in Lahti. Pekka Olkkonen and Leena Warsell were both members of the project team, having an indispensable role in the project.

The research component of the project was made possible by the support of the Social Research Institute of Alcohol Studies, the Finnish Foundation for Alcohol Studies and the Biomedical Research Centre of Alko Ltd. Many of our colleagues supported and encouraged this work. Klaus Mäkelä read the entire manuscript and gave useful comments. Raija Ahtola and Marjaana Seppänen deserve special thanks for carrying out qualitative interviews among the heavy drinkers' family members. Göta

Friman did the painstaking work in finalizing the literature list, and Eeva-Liisa Tuovinen drew the figures. Lynn Green-Rutanen checked the English language.

Marjatta Montonen, a research fellow at the Finnish Foundation for Alcohol Studies, was the principal researcher for the education component of the project, and the Liquor Weeks were her own invention. She also commented extensively and with great acuteness on the early versions of this book. Many chapters have benefited greatly from her work.

As the editor of this volume, my special thanks belong to Jo Campling, whose perceptive and clear advice led me through the most crucial phases in the making of this book.

Notes on the Contributors

Kari Haavisto is a Researcher at the Social Research Institute of Alcohol Studies, Helsinki, Finland.

Marja Holmila, PhD, Docent of Sociology in Helsinki University, is a Senior Researcher in the Social Research Institute of Alcohol Studies, Helsinki, Finland.

Pekka Sillanaukee, PhD, Docent of Medical Biochemistry, Tampere University, is Scientific Director of Pharmacia AB, Diagnostics, Alcohol Related Deseases, Uppsala, Sweden.

Jussi Simpura, PhD, Docent of Social Politics in Helsinki University, is a Senior Researcher in the Social Research Institute of Alcohol Studies, Helsinki, Finland.

Pekka Sulkunen, PhD, Docent of Sociology in Helsinki University, is a Senior Researcher in the Social Research Institute of Alcohol Studies, Helsinki, Finland.

Jukka Törrönen, BSc, Sociology, is a Research Fellow with the Finnish Foundation for Alcohol Studies, Helsinki, Finland.

Foreword

In the words of its editor, Marja Holmila, this book sets out to 'increase knowledge on two interlinking issues: local community as a system of preventing alcohol problems and the art of planning and implementing community prevention projects'. It succeeds in this aim by providing a detailed and thoughtful description, not only of the activities of the Lahti project and the community response to these, but also of the bigger picture of which this research exercise based in a small community in Finland is a part.

This bigger picture described is to some extent specific to Finland's social, economic and political history, and to some extent is the global change of which we are all a part. The chapters by Pekka Sulkunen and Jussi Simpura do an excellent job of contextualizing the project. We are reminded of the globalization that is occurring in relation to commodity production and communication and which impacts on all aspects of our lives, not least in the way we create meaning around alcohol issues. The changes in the role of the state have created a window of opportunity for more local action. The environmental activist's slogan: 'think globally, act locally' will be increasingly acted out in relation to public health issues, and, as the authors point out, alcohol is now more likely to be framed as a public health issue than as a unifying moral crusade.

Changes in the role of the state in relation to alcohol in Finland are particularly profound because of the dismantling of the state monopoly which previously controlled the production and distribution of alcohol. Withdrawal of the state from regulation of business has been found generally to lead to a greater emphasis on the role of public interest groups and the private interests in such regulation; the interaction between the community, the private interests and the state in defining and implementing such regulation is a topic of considerable interest for public health practitioners and researchers. The story of the Lahti project describes the very early stages of such a process, with community sectors and researchers feeling their way in an arena which has been until recently very much the responsibility of the Finnish state.

Although the state withdrawal from alcohol issues in Finland has been relatively recent, the speed with which the construction of other ways of viewing the role of the state in relation to alcohol can become prominent is illustrated in the insightful analysis of the opinion leaders' discourse around alcohol issues. The neo-liberal view of the media informants in Lahti constructs drinking as an important site for the acting out of individual competence and willingness to show self-control; in this construction any interference by the state in people's access to alcohol is viewed very negatively.

It is in this context of changing discourses that the project set out: in uncharted waters, with no clear objectives, but with some resources to deploy 'when people seemed to enjoy themselves or had passionate views on the issue'. The project engaged in some innovative strategies to increase people's attention to alcohol issues, using the Finnish people's very high level of involvement with public libraries, for example. Preliminary excursions were made into the issues of the sale and distribution of alcohol but much of the focus was on providing assistance and insight to those individuals already involved in a risky way with alcohol. These were strategies which received considerable positive local media attention, as would be expected. Given this, it is not surprising that the project succeeded in what came to be seen as a primary aim: to increase the importance given to alcohol in people's construction of social problems.

This book is not, however, simply a recounting of a community action project. It is a scholarly work in which a range of theoretical perspectives, 'new paradigm' research methods and the data gathered are clearly described and skilfully interwoven into a readable narrative. The reader of this book will not only learn about the Lahti project but also understand its location within the constructionist approach to social research. The book stands not only as the tale of a relexive response to alcohol-related harm in the community but as a reflexive report on the research project itself.

SALLY CASSWELL

1 Introduction
Marja Holmila

1. HARM PREVENTION IN TRANSIENT COMMUNITIES

Talking about community often raises critical questions. It is claimed that communities no longer exist, and that modern life consists of autonomous individuals living in fragmented realities, surrounded by quickly changing environments and free from the stable social structures of local communities. The importance of local communities has indeed been diminished in various ways. Mass migration to new localities and even to new countries has been breaking the communal ties for several generations. Today's international media and commodity markets create a feeling of global citizenship. The same products can be bought in supermarkets worldwide, the same television programmes can be watched all over the world.

Community prevention faces a double dilemma; not only is community claimed to be absent, but the prevention of alcohol problems is often understood as influencing separate individuals, not social entities. The ideas behind prevention of health problems are strongly influenced by the Enlightenment idea of rational and independent individuals. Health promotion thus relies upon the model of rational, unified self, consciously making decisions about one's conduct in everyday life in the quest for self-improvement, social success and integration. Public policy in the area of health promotion faces a legitimacy crisis, as it is felt to interfere with individuals' freedom of choice (Lupton 1995).

According to Giddens, disentangling the different kinds of communal relations from each other will produce a new insight into the concept of community. He writes: 'The sociological accounts have mostly juxtaposed the communal character of traditional orders with the impersonality of modern social life. In capturing this conceptual distinction, Ferdinand Tönnies's contrast of *Gemeinschaft* and *Gesellschaft* is the classic source;

1

whether they have used this specific terminology or not, others have drawn a very similar opposition. One of the difficulties with this debate concerns the terms in which it has been conducted. The "communal" has been contrasted with the "societal", the "impersonal" with the "personal" – and, from a somewhat different perspective, the "state" with "civil society" – as if these were all variants of the same thing. But the notion of community, as applied either to pre-modern or to modern cultures, comprises several sets of elements that must be distinguished. These are communal relations *per se*; kinship ties; relations of personal intimacy between peers; and relations of sexual intimacy. If we disentangle these, we can develop a standpoint different from any of these referred to above' (Giddens 1990, p. 117). Defined like this, communities have even in the modern world a place in peoples' lives.

In the sense of kinship ties, friendships and relations of sexual intimacy or family, community has not lost its meaning in the modern world. In the sense of an embedded affinity to place, community has to a great extent been destroyed, although one could argue about how far this process has gone in specific contexts. An ordinary citizen acting as an advocate of any issue will usually start by influencing the people in the locality where he or she lives. As Robert Sacks observes: 'To be an agent, one must be somewhere' (Giddens 1990, pp. 115–19).

According to Bauman, local communities involve not only networks of people, in contrast to the hierarchical and bureaucratic organization of nation-states. They also involve 'community' in the sociological sense: feelings of being and acting together, sentiments of making choices spontaneously and responding to local needs, a sense of acting with, and not only acting for or because of others (Bauman 1993, pp. 145–85).

Even in present-day societies, the concept of community includes cultural aspects of history, lifestyles and identities. It is an emotional concept, too. One might have positive thoughts of home, family and security, or negative thoughts of suffocating repression and small-minded control – depending on one's life situation and experiences. Realistically, community means all these things at the same time. It is, after all, a system of everyday life.

The environment also influences the individual's behaviour. The daily messages one receives on alcohol and drugs from the media, during discussions with friends, on walks through the city's entertainment areas or shopping malls all have an impact. More indirectly, the lack of opportunities, insufficient leisure activities, sad architecture and atmosphere around one can have a negative influence on one's well-being and mental health and thus create the need for drinking.

A special feature in local communities is that they provide a security-net of social ties. When everything goes well, individuals tend to form their closest relationships with their families, work colleagues or interest groups, and have fewer contacts with their local environment. But when employment or health problems arise, work-related and interest-group-related ties are first to break. In the end also family can be lost. Welfare agents in one's local community are the remaining, crucial social ties for help and support. Awareness of the existence of this 'security network' defines people's relationships to their localities in the welfare societies.

The international and state organizations have taken precedence over localities in decision-making over a great many issues affecting marketing of alcoholic beverages, of social and health policies, and so on. However, embeddedness in a given geographical place is in the end the final test of the applicability of these decisions. The decisions need to be implemented at the local level, and the local agents become crucial actors in this process. Welfare services, for instance, are ruled by state legislation, and to a great extent implemented by experts 'raised' within the state structures. Yet these services are provided within an organized local community in a geographical area. A structure for making decisions about the environment and collecting and using public money is required. Local government organizations provide a range of services which are central to the social and economic wellbeing of their citizens. They are large-scale spenders of public money and have a role in representing the concerns and views of the ordinary people (Blair 1991). The local policy processes have, in democratic societies, their impact in government policies, and pressures for legislative changes can be created through local political bodies. Alcohol policy regulations need to be supported by the majority. Local preventive action has a role to play also in influencing people's alcohol policy opinions and in informing the decision-makers of the norms and attitudes prevalent in communities.

2. PREVENTING OR PROMOTING?

In spite of sceptical comments concerning the diminishing role of communities, community-based work has increased in the practice of health education during the last ten years or so. This development has been further encouraged by the fact that health education has been shown to be likely to have an impact only when efforts to change the individual's behaviour are connected with changes in the wider community. The need for development of the prevention field has become more pressing as the harmonization of European Union regulation policies has limited the scope of national policies in controlling and regulating the sales of alcohol and other drugs. At the same time, health and social policies are being decentralized in most European countries. The local actors are responsible for treating the harms caused by excessive use of substances, as the state's role is diminishing both in financing and planning these services.

Some of the best-known examples of community projects on alcohol and drug use are, however, from countries outside Europe. Such are the Midwestern Prevention Project (Pentz *et al.* 1989), the Tri-Community Prevention Project in Ontario (Giesbrecht *et al.* 1990) and the Community Action Project in New Zealand (Casswell and Gilmore 1989). There have not been many European community projects aiming at prevention of alcohol-related problems. Scotland was involved in the World Health Organization study on community response to alcohol-related problems (Ritson 1985). The WHO/Euro study on community response was carried out in 13 countries (Hannibal *et al.* 1995). In Oxford a community public policy has been developed to create a balanced alcohol strategy (Mathrani 1993, pp. 95–101). Two projects are presently being carried out in Sweden (Romelsjö, Andren and Borg 1993, pp. 130–7; Hanson *et al.* 1993, pp. 147–57). Also in Italy and Denmark similar initiatives have gained ground (Allamani 1995, Elmeland and Nygaard 1995).

The North American and the European approaches to community action differ most, perhaps, in their attitudes towards the role of authorities on one hand and citizens' grassroots activities on the other. Europeans and in particular Scandinavians have a greater tolerance towards the role of the state in one's

life. Thus the European definition of a community is more likely
to acknowledge the role of the professionals and bureaucrats
in one's life.

Both the terms 'harm prevention' and 'health promotion'
have been used in the literature describing community programmes. One of the strengths of the prevention terminology
is that it immediately requires exact use of language. Because
one needs to know what to prevent, action is easily translated
into specific goals and targets. Such a 'problem', 'threat', 'dan-
ger', or, more recently, 'risk' can either be health-related, or
it can also be, for instance, a social evil, crime or violence
(Albrecht and Otto 1991).

The challenge within the discourse of prevention is in defining which are the most relevant problems to prevent. But
what is a problem, and who is to say that it is one? Many actors
in the community (e.g. the police) see alcohol primarily as a
source of public disorder or crime or as a moral problem (as
does the church), or as financial loss (as do employers and city
officials). At its worst, prevention terminology encourages processes which lead into labelling some individuals as deviant
and their isolation as the 'remedy' of the problems.

Two extreme approaches here can be called the objectivist and
relativist or constructionist approach (Simpura and Tigerstedt
1992, p. 9). Objectivist thinking sees certain social conditions
as objectively and intrinsically undesirable, and therefore, as
'social problems' independent of any definitional process. Constructionists, on the other hand, maintain that social conditions
such as poverty, crime or ill health are not social problems by
virtue of their mere existence, but become such only in a permanent process of defining and redefining certain conditions
as problematic. To become social problems, social phenomena
need to be collectively defined and managed. This happens in
a continuous negotiation or struggle between social actors.

In contrast to the constructionist approach, a fairly clear objectivist attitude towards problem definition has been taken in
many community programmes: the problem to be tackled is a
health hazard depicted in epidemiological studies (Jacobs 1986;
Farquhar *et al.* 1990; Institute of Medicine 1992). According to
Puska, a central role of the carefully designed community programme is to form a link between the basic health research and
the large-scale public health programmes and governmental

policies. A community programme thus forms a 'pilot', 'demonstration' or 'model' for testing the approach for nationwide use. It applies at the same time epidemiological knowledge to identify the health problems and the action priorities, and behavioural and social knowledge to design the actual programme contents and activities (Puska 1993, p. 5). The evaluation research reveals the effects and usefulness of such programmes.

As will be argued by Jussi Simpura in Chapter 3, the construction of alcohol problems in a locality is not likely to happen as a 'natural process'. Community activists are likely to need to engage themselves in participation in the problem definition. Due to the character of alcohol problems, activists have to initiate a constant remaking of alcohol problems as social problems.

The language of 'health promotion' instead of problem prevention has some advantages. Health promotion is a positive term: one is attempting to promote something good. This 'good' means not only absence of a disease but it stresses the positive aspects of life (wellbeing) rather than the negative aspects. WHO launched the Ottawa Charter for health promotion in 1986. It gives the following definition: 'Health promotion is the process of enabling people to increase control over and to improve their health' (Ottawa Charter 1986), and highlights the social determinants of health, the crucial role of social and economic environments and process and the relationships and system influences that create health. Importantly, the Ottawa Charter focuses on the need for public policies (Kickbusch 1993, p. 50).

The advantages of the health-promotion perspective are probably most evident in all activities which involve direct contact with individuals, and which aim at activating their own resources. For instance, if community work with young people concentrates on problems, the right kind of encouraging and future-oriented relationships with youth may be impossible to obtain. Also, in supporting heavy drinkers or their families, the idea of promoting the positive sides of their lives (or enabling) is often more rewarding than the concept of preventing harm.

Health promotion understood like this is exciting and inspiring. Its weakness is in its being very general and spreading over nearly all aspects of life. It may run the risk of becoming the well-meaning and feeble communitarianism which some writers have been very sceptical about. Albrecht and Otto (1991, p. 6) write: 'strategies that are only or primarily directed toward an artificial recreation of community and network commitments instead of performing controlled, problem-oriented prevention and intervention should be viewed with extreme scepticism'. Even if one wouldn't accept this demand for controlled action in all its strictness, it is likely that community actors also need specified goals. There is a need to define the order of importance, too: not everything can be done at the same time, and resources need to be allocated by setting priorities.

3. THE SURFACE LEVEL AND THE DEEP STRUCTURE OF COMMUNITY LIFE

A city, even a medium-sized one, is a complex structure. It contains a multitude of social networks in different levels and it is comprised of many organizations. Its borders are unclear, and many networks and organizations stretch over the city's boundaries. What are the elements of the community we are studying in the preventive action? From the practical perspective of the community action study, the most apparent way of defining the city consists of looking at the institutional arenas relevant for problem construction and problem management.

Firstly, a city is the unit of organizing and implementing the welfare services. Decentralization of health and social policies is taking place in Finland as in most European countries, and local authorities are given more responsibilities for treating the harm caused by excessive use of substances (Blair 1991). In Nordic countries the municipal authorities have always had a central role in providing local services, and now their role in the decision-making concerning these services has increased.

A community is also the forum for cultural life. Educational establishments can be seen as one part of the welfare services provided by the city, but a great part of cultural life is based on citizens' own creativity, interests and their collective memory of cultural history and heritage. Schools, adult education and free libraries as well as numerous cultural institutions support the local culture. The media are a means of contact and information in the community, and an influenzal opinion leader.

The voluntary sector is the institutional expression of the non-governmental part of social life. The church, voluntary organizations and leisure-time organizations meet and influence mostly within their own home town.

The city is also a unit for drug policy planning, discussion and influence. The present changes in the Nordic alcohol system increase the importance of local action. The monopoly system has to a great extent been dismantled, and national alcohol control policies have been loosened as a result of a liberal trend in the alcohol policy climate. The city is also a geographical and architectonic unit, comprised of streets, buildings and parks where people walk or drive. It has a space and an environment which need to be collectively maintained and supervised, so that the citizens are safe and comfortable when moving around. This element in community life involves the action and decision-making of e.g. the city council, the police, and the liquor-licensing authorities.

Last, but perhaps most important, a city can be seen as a conglomeration of neighbourhoods and homes. Family institution and informal networks are perhaps the strongest elements of community life.

These five elements are all on the surface level of community life. They carry and organize the experience of citizenship. The ties of belonging, of reciprocity and togetherness are the deep structures of community life. In the context of getting on with a community action project, it is not necessary to first sociologically analyse those emotional and mental bonds between individuals, but to trust in their existence and positive energy. We hope to be able to show in this book that their real potential can be discovered in the process of action research.

4. REFLEXIVE PROBLEM PREVENTION

The approach taken in Lahti can be called reflexive problem prevention. The overall setting is described in Figure 1.1. The upper line of the figure describes the project's elements, which include both action and research. The lower line describes the relevant community institutions. In the middle of the circle is the living and changing community life, containing a deep structure which for ever escapes exact analysis.

- Taking part in action
- Process analysis

- Taking part in public discourse
- Analyzing the discourse and social conditions

ACTION AND RESEARCH

- Interventions
- Evaluation

PROBLEM CONSTRUCTION

COMMUNITY LIFE

PROBLEM MANAGEMENT

- Local elites

COMMUNITY INSTITUTIONS

- Welfare services

- Cultural life

- Local administration and politics

- Media
- Voluntary organizations
- Neighbourhoods and homes

Figure 1.1   Reflexive community prevention

The alcohol-related problems to be prevented cannot be taken as given, but are constructed in a continuous collective process. All community institutions mentioned in Figure 1.1. took part in the problem construction, but the input of public discourse, the local elites, the media and the cultural life are particularly relevant for problem construction. Corresponding forms of research were the analysis of forms of discourse and the examination of social and cultural conditions.

The other side of problem prevention is the practical work in managing observed problems. Among the community institutions, the welfare services, the local administration and the homes and neighbourhoods are closest to the problem management aspect of the process. Within the project, planned interventions and the evaluation part of the research are closest to the problem management.

The two opposites of the circle require each other and make

each other possible. Managing problems presupposes their definition, and the process of definition is possible only in the context of practical attempts to manage the problems.

The close connection between action and research in all parts of the project is the reason for calling it reflexive problem prevention. Data for analysis were collected in connection with the action. Continuous feedback on the research results gave the action and research interpretations new directions. The methodologies used included both quantitative and qualitative methods, and data were gathered in various different ways.

In order to be able to place the gathered information in some conceptual framework, the action-related research needs to be grounded in the social and historical context of the action. A look at the Nordic welfare state and the history of their alcohol policies is required. The following chapter will take this historical perspective.

5. THE LAHTI PROJECT

History

The intitiative of starting the project came from the researchers at the Research Institute of Alcohol Studies. Independent of that, local work had been carried out for writing up a drug policy plan and for forming a permanent drug policy group in the city of Lahti. Developing the idea of a community action project and negotiating the programme started in 1992. The project was officially opened in October of the same year, and then carried out during the years 1993–94. The project became a demonstration project for the WHO's European Office in 1993.

The core actors in Lahti were the welfare professionals of the city. They also supported the volunteer organizations and individuals who took part in the project. The mayor of Lahti and all the main decision-making bodies in the city supported the project. The project organization was very light. There was no separate budget, and the funds came from the annual budgets of the different cooperating partners. The work was coordinated by a project group, which consisted of the local coordinator, the researchers and two national alcohol education specialists.

The project consisted of independent modules, the most important of which were the intervention study on alcohol policy thinking, brief intervention in primary health care, setting up educational events, youth work, support for families of alcoholics and responsible service of alcohol.

Alcohol Policy Thinking

The intervention study on alcohol policy thinking aimed at analysing the local key persons' ideas on alcohol as a social problem (see Chapter 4). The study was conducted in a manner which made it at the same time an intervention into the participants' thinking. The objects of this reflexive intervention were not only the key persons, but also the researchers.

Brief Intervention in Primary Health Care

An experimental study was carried out in the primary healthcare centres of Lahti, starting from a few and spreading to cover the total patient population of the town. The aims were to increase knowledge of alcohol-related problems among healthcare professionals, to study the prevalence of heavy drinkers in primary health care, and to get experiences of brief intervention as a part of the routine clinical setting.

Setting Up Educational Events

The educational interventions during the project were based on the idea that the success of education depends more on the target groups' pre-existing interest and motivations, and their anchoring in the social and cultural environment rather than on the designs of the educational interventions as such. Most of the messages sent were rather general (with the exception of two messages aiming to increase the public's knowledge), aiming at increasing people's awareness. The concrete topics were often formulated in a process together with the local participants. The project arranged several major happenings in market-type surroundings; it spread out some printed materials, published posters in the public areas and put a lot of emphasis on media advocacy. Producing information and creating action were often connected to each other as elements of one and same process.

Youth Work

The youth-work projects included intensive group activities for heavy-drinking youngsters, face-to-face drug and alcohol education in the schools, in the Young People's Community Centres and during church activities, and also general information given during the project campaigns.

The education directed at the youth aimed among other things to increase their knowledge of the strength of different drinks and the degree of drunkenness caused by certain amounts of alcohol. The adults' attitudes towards their children's drinking proved to be ambivalent and full of contradictions. It is thus hard for the adults to give any consistent education for their offspring in these matters. Many discussions during the project reflected the need to involve the parents in defining the norms of alcohol use. It was felt that without coherent messages shared by both the professional educators and the family, it is difficult to influence the young.

Families

The counselling sessions arranged for the intimate others in Lahti avoided the image of treatment, and emphasized the cognitive, solution-oriented approach and open elements in the intervention. In order to open up the discussion around the intimate others' situation and to reduce the stigma attached to the lay notions of co-dependency, a qualitative study was carried out on the living situation of persons with close persons drinking excessively.

Sales Surveillance and the Responsible Service of Alcohol

Availability of alcohol has increased rapidly in Lahti. Especially the number of medium-beer bars has grown fast, ranging from ordinary lunch places to daily 'sitting rooms' for the marginalized heavy drinkers. Medium beer is also sold in ordinary supermarkets, and the teenagers in Lahti find it easy to purchase their own drinks, even if the law forbids serving alcohol to those under the age of 18.

Preventive intervention in Lahti focused on two interlinking issues: 1) prevention of alcohol-related public violence and 2) promotion of responsible service of alcohol. Prevention of public violence focused on influencing the ongoing changes in the system of sales surveillance, as well as on creating public discussion by publishing local data on violence. Server training courses for people working in the field were arranged together with the local restaurant school in order to promote responsible service of alcohol.

Inspiring New Networks

The project aimed at creating new types of local networks among the welfare professionals in particular, and to some but lesser degree between professionals and volunteers. The traditional way of working within the municipal structure is to follow the hierarchical procedures inside one's own administrative sector, and horizontal ties between, say, the social and the health sectors or the social sector and youth work, are difficult to create and maintain. A project such as the Lahti project can change this by arranging meetings and happenings where the sectoral devisions are overcome. Individuals who share inspiration can find each other and start cooperation with new kinds of aims and methods.

Lahti is an industrial city which grew with great rapidity in the 1960s and 1970s. The population is now 93 000 inhabitants. The city is located about 100 kilometres north of the Finnish capital. The city is best known as a centre for winter sports, and has during the last decades devoted considerable attention to developing other areas of its cultural life.

The project took place during a very difficult time in Lahti. Unemployment increased sixfold between the years 1990 and 1995, growing from 4 per cent to a record 26 per cent of the labour force (Appendix 1). This unfortunate development can be seen as a collective crisis in a community, causing a lot of social misery and also increasing health problems. It may have activated people to strengthen their community ties. The idea of working together with others in the locality may suddenly have become more attractive than it may have been during the years of busy moneymaking and competition. This could have been one of the reasons for the positiveness of the reception of the project.

The economic recession also increased the municipality's health and social professionals' worries about their future job perspectives. This threat may have acted as one more incentive to look for new methods of working and to develop the prevention approaches. Thus the fast growth of unemployment could paradoxically have worked as a motivating factor for the project, explaining some of the easiness and positiveness of getting it started.

6. RESEARCH METHODOLOGIES

Research on a community project needs to be a study on action and movement. It means understanding and evaluating efforts to change the reality towards desirable goals. How can this be achieved? Social scientists can choose between various options in describing their object: they can try to take a snapshot or a series of snapshots of a still-life object, as surveys tend to do. Or they can try to 'film' the object in motion, as is often done in observational studies analysing the moving and changing community. Research can also try and interpret the 'film' taken by others: sociology aiming at understanding people's meanings and interpretations can be based on the representations, for instance spoken or written texts, produced by the people.

The methodology for this work contains all of the three approaches, yet so that they are used in the framework of action research: case studies, action research and evaluation research.

Case Studies

Case studies can be defined as empirical inquiries that investigate contemporary phenomena within their real-life contexts, especially when the boundaries between the phenomenon studied and the context are not clearly evident (Yin 1994, p. 13). In other words, one would use the case-study method when one deliberately wanted to cover contextual conditions – believing that they might be highly pertinent to the phenomenon being studied. An experiment, for instance, differs from this as it deliberately divorces a phenomenon from its context, so that attention can be focused on only a few variables. Surveys, on the other hand, can try to deal with phenomenon and context, but their ability to investigate the context is limited. Important here is that in the Lahti project the action – the prevention project – and the context – the cultural and social structure of the community – are not to be clearly separated. The context of the action and the action itself are studied at the same time.

Action Research

Action research differs from other types of social studies in two basic ways. First, it takes an active approach to change. Action research aims at changing the social group or the society, at producing innovations. Secondly, the relationship between the researcher and those studied is different in action research than in other types of research. Traditional academic research stresses the distinction between the researcher and those studied. The researcher avoids influencing the studied persons or groups in order to obtain as objective results as possible. Action research, on the contrary, tries to break down the barriers between science and the world outside it, to make research a part of a process and to build good communication networks between different actors.

Kurt Lewin (1946) generally receives credit for introducing the term 'action research' as a way of generating knowledge about a social system while, at the same time, attempting to change it. At about the same time, Collier (1945) called attention to the need for developing an approach to generate action-oriented knowledge to understand and improve American Indian affairs. Corey (1953) had similar ideas in education. A distinctive action research thrust also developed in Great Britain immediately after the Second World War (Trist and Murray 1990). The inter-disciplinary group that pioneered this work later formed the Tavistock Institute of Human Relations in London.

The early action research work grew from the desire of researchers to discover ways of dealing with important social problems. However, shortly after these early developments, much of the action research approach began to be applied primarily to intra-organizational and work life problems, and this has been the major focus of action research since then, although wider communities have also been the focus of some action research studies (Elden and Chisholm 1993).

The main characteristic of action research is not that it has a special ability to solve social problems, as is sometimes claimed. All kinds of social science can be of help in solving social problems. Rather than its ability to solve problems, the distinctive element in action research is the way it understands the process of knowledge formation.

Action research bases its knowledge on the group's or system's characteristics on acts. It 'checks' the interpretations of the system in a straightforward manner, by engaging in action with it. It is this special dialogical and practical way of obtaining knowledge of the studied case that distinguishes action research from other kinds of studies. The action groups formed inside the system have to agree in open and dialogical atmosphere about the action, its goals and main methods. Only when the planned action corresponds with the values and understanding of the groups will something happen. Practice will thus be the ultimate check of what the system can and wants to do and how: of what it is like.

Alan Touraine uses the term 'intervention sociology' instead of action research (Touraine 1978). Touraine sees society as a field of action, where the interests of the various actors are the basis for their social relationships. Social relations are predominantly unequal; they are power or class relations. Action means active struggle over the social and cultural ownership of historicity in the common field of action. The researcher takes part in the processes of this field by making an intervention in it.

Touraine has studied mostly social movements, their ideology and the factors influencing it. The research process is based on creating confrontation, when the different partners bring forward their own ideology, and also develop it. The researcher takes part in this confrontation, and analyses it scientifically. This analytical knowledge concerning the ideology of the movement is fed back to the movement in order to develop its action. Action and movement bring forward the internal dynamics, conflicts and differences of opinions of any group, which then are more visible to the researcher.

Touraine's approach differs from the mainstream of action research tradition in how he sees the researcher's role. According to Touraine the interventionist should not get involved, or be committed. He stays outside the internal disputes and conflicts of the acting group (Touraine 1978). In real life, this usually means that one can only study systems that are already in movement. This approach does not suit situations where the whole process is started when the researcher arrives on the scene.

There is a difference between Touraine's intervention sociology and action research, then, but it is not very clear-cut. Action research processes do not start from a standstill, either, and they can never be completely novel. Action in any system is always based on what has been going on before. Researchers hop on the moving wagon and start reading the map together with the others, but it is a matter for interpretation how the studied and reported part of the journey started. On the other hand, action researchers generally tend to mediate rather than take stands in internal disputes. Yet it is very difficult to believe that interventionists could ever stay completely outside the process and be neutral to its internal dynamics, the way Touraine claims. After all, he himself maintains that sociologists should take an active part in discussion and clarification of different points of view in the confrontation.

From Outcome Evaluation to Process Evaluation

The elements of evaluation are usually divided in three parts: formative, process and outcome evaluation (Duignan, Casswell and Stewart 1992, pp. 4–5; McGraw *et al.* 1989, pp. 459–83). Formative evaluation is closest to the development of the prevention activities themselves. It ensures that the project is needed, well designed and well implemented. Evaluation input is provided to programme-planning and decision-making on an ongoing basis, through the collection and feedback of relevant information to programme personnel and management. This includes needs assessment, review of previous literature, objective-setting, pretesting of materials, and piloting. Process evaluation describes exactly what occurred in programme-planning, implementation and running. It can take place on a small or large scale depending on the resources available and the need to communicate to others the details of what occurred during the programme. It usually uses qualitative research methods, but can use quantitative. It provides those seeking to find out about a programme with a detailed description of what occurred. It also assists the interpretation of outcome evaluation results by providing possible explanations for observed outcomes. Outcome evaluation attempts to measure the programme objectives that have been achieved. Outcome evaluation is the type of evaluation social scientists are most familiar with and around which there has been a great deal of conceptual work in the past, for instance in regard to the topic of quasi-experimental design (Cook and Campbell 1979; Hoole 1978).

Researchers differ as to how much they emphasize the three areas of evaluation. Process evaluation still has the role of the newcomer: although process evaluation is discussed as an essential component to be included in any programme evaluation, there is not much discussion in the literature of how such evaluations should be designed. A remarkable exception is Michael Quinn Patton's well-known book (Patton 1980). A system of process evaluation was also developed and described in the Pawtucket Heart Health Program (McGraw *et al.* 1989, pp. 459–83).

Recently the previously heated debate between outcome and process evaluation and between quantitative and qualitative measures has turned into realization of the necessity of both, and the importance of developing multi-method approaches (Aaro 1992; Albrecht 1991, p. 419; Duignan, Casswell and Stewart 1992, pp. 4–5). Outcome questions are often the first questions posed to the evaluator, but they should be the last ones to be answered. Only if the programme seems to be operating in a satisfactory manner can the answers to outcome questions be meaningful (Pirie 1990, p. 206; Rutman 1980).

Deciding what is meant by programme 'outcomes' or 'effects' is often more difficult than would first appear. The effects of any programme can be conceptualized as a chain of events leading from the programme to the ultimate outcome. Thus the 'outcome' of the programme could be evaluated on any of these levels. The choice of which outcome to study is determined by several factors: the soundness of the scientific evidence linking the various events in the chain, the feasibility and cost of obtaining the measurement, the statistical power to detect effects at various levels and so on. The choice of which endpoint to measure is also dependent upon the needs of the audience for the evaluation (Pirie 1990, p. 205).

Qualitative studies have an important role in process and impact evaluation. One of the reasons for this is that one has to avoid taking the official programme as a true guide to action and making the goals it contains the measure of analysis. For obtaining effects, it is the daily routine of the programme, the reality of the programme implementation, that is significant. The actual treatment varies from person to person, from setting to setting, and from time-point to time-point. With the usual techniques of standardized social research it is difficult to assess; but it may be possible through systematic, quantifying observation or research techniques of qualitative social research (Albrecht 1991, p. 421).

Part I
Local Prevention in Context

2 Alcohol Policy, the State and the Local Community

Pekka Sulkunen and Jussi Simpura

1. INTRODUCTION

The historical development of alcohol policy in the Nordic countries is an integral part of their welfare-state systems. However, this monolithic structure, centred on the nation-state, seems to be eroding in two directions. First, with increasing globalization the nation-state as a sovereign actor is losing its powers to international agencies and networks. At the same time, the nation-state is becoming a fragmented localized unit, often geographical in nature but consisting of other kinds of network structures. This bifurcation of nation-state policies both upward and downward is a consequence of more general structural changes in world economies, production and information flows.

For community action the assumed bifurcation provides a double role. From the point of view of actors in local grassroot movements, community action is an opportunity for new community structures and action patterns to arise. These are independent of and even opposed to state organs and activities. For actors in the existing state-centred systems, community action may be an instrument in adapting state-centred operations to increasing demands for better accounting for local interests within a globalizing context. So community action is both a means of criticizing existing public action patterns and a means of developing them for changing social, cultural, political and economic conditions (cf. Gundelach 1994).

At the same time the legitimacy of state policy is being challenged for 'endogenic' reasons: public policy, especially in the area of public-health promotion, is thought to interfere with individuals' freedom of choice. The rise of the new public-health movement, including community action projects, is partly a reaction to this legitimacy crisis. Local communities involve not only networks of people, in contrast to the hierarchical and bureaucratic organization of nation-states. They also involve community in the sociological sense: feelings of being and acting together, sentiments of making choices spontaneously and responding to local needs, a sense of acting with, and not only acting for or because of others (Bauman 1993, pp. 145–85).

2. ALCOHOL AND CONSUMPTION RISKS

In the context of the welfare state, preventive alcohol policy has come to seem like a marginal and spasmodic occupation. Social security schemes that reach levels of 20 per cent of all incomes, huge expenses for public services, education and infrastructure, together with expenses for external and internal defence, are major fields of state activity that overshadow alcohol policy in terms of the number of people affected, in the importance of its influence in their lives, and also in the political attention they attract.

However, alcohol policy as a public issue has been and remains visible even in the most advanced welfare states. In fact, historically, the attention it receives has seldom been directly related to the dimensions of harm caused by alcohol itself. Instead, alcohol as a social problem has, especially in countries with strong traditions of state-controlled alcohol policy, originally been a symbolic issue, a means of self-assured moral superiority in ascending social mass movements: the self-asserting middle class in North America (Gusfield 1986; Levine 1983), the nationalistic movement, the peasantry and even the working class in the Nordic countries (I. Sulkunen 1985). In this sense modern alcohol policy has from its beginnings in the mid-nineteenth century been an integral part of constructing modern – industrial, urban, national – societies. The underlying social processes of modernization, the moral sentiments and cultural conflicts that it has aroused in public life have often become apparent and acquired a discursive form in debates about alcohol, both as a blessing and as an adversity.

Classic social movements have had their day but preventive alcohol policy is still with us, less as a movement than as a structure, and less as a field of mobilization or of moral battle than as a tradition. In contemporary affluent societies this tradition is now facing a break that reflects key issues in postmodern public life, and sometimes it does this with more expressive power than routine political discourse has on the major classic areas of welfare-state policy.

Alcohol is a consumer item that involves a risk both to the consumer, to the drinker's social environment and to society as a whole. Preventive alcohol policy is staged in the paradox of contemporary advanced societies, a paradox that could be called consumption risks. While these societies have reached an unforeseen degree of manageability and technical competence in maintaining healthy life, new risks appear as life becomes more complex, rich in consumer experiences but increasingly dependent on technology. The very fact that we know more about causes of troubles and ways of dealing with them is in itself important in arousing worry about threats to life, health, security and well-being. Prevention is reasonable societal response, and there is abundant scientific knowledge to insert high expectations of successful preventive policies in many areas of public-health protection.

Yet this new awareness of risks is reflected in preventive policies in a manner that is far from uniform and often confronted with serious and fundamental resistance. Tobacco in western societies is an extreme case where rational risk-awareness, based on firm scientific evidence, has won the upper hand over non-rational considerations of pleasure and symbolic meaning. But there are other consumer goods, notably alcoholic beverages, which are enveloped in a symbolic shroud too thick to surrender unconditionally to simple utility calculations. Not only the meanings attached to alcohol, but also conceptions of the relationships of individuals to society and the functions of public powers in this relationship are at play whenever alcohol is constructed as a social problem, and whenever preventive alcohol policy is considered as a means of its remedy. Nordic and North American preventive alcohol policies are breaking down; the Commission of the European Union is driving a policy of tax harmonization downward. Furthermore, in all of the cases where the preventive side has had the upper hand, this has resulted in bitter conflicts which would result in a reduction in the prices of alcoholic beverages.

Alcohol is only one instance of one of the most subtle and difficult public issues in contemporary societies. Two of the traditional issues concerning the welfare state are those of public services and income redistribution. A third has been added: the strife over consumption between different interest groups and different moralities. On the one hand, consumers need protection against risks; on the other, they construct their indentities on the basis of sovereignty as independent decision-makers for their own pleasure and satisfaction. Any attempts to regulate consumption publicly, on whatever grounds, will easily be interpreted as a disparagement of this sovereignty and as unacceptable paternalism. This is what has been called the 'public health predicament' of affluent societies (Sulkunen 1996).

3. ALCOHOL POLICY AND THE MODERN TRINITY OF PROGRESS, UNIVERSALISM AND NATIONALISM

The period during which preventive alcohol policy has evolved in the Nordic countries has been one of accelerating modernization, beginning from the first ironworks and paper mills in the mid-nineteenth century. By the late 1980s these countries had become almost completely urbanized societies based on industrial high technology, intensive agricultural production and globally integrated economies. This change would not have been possible without comprehensive ideals or doctrines that have penetrated morality, political life and even aesthetics. Three of these ideals – material technological progress, egalitarian universalism and state nationalism – have been intimately related to the way that alcohol has been treated as a social problem in the Nordic societies (Sulkunen 1991).

The ideal of material and technological progress has dominated western thinking in all areas of life. In religion, the Protestant ethic has been a progressivist one. In economy the ideal of accumulation and efficiency has dictated not only work organization but also discourses on economic policy and conflicts, however interest-based the concrete goals of action might have been. Even in everyday life the choice between a large number of options in education, occupation and family arrangements, liberated from tradition by the crushing power of modern freedom, has been justified in terms of means to an end. As Michel

Maffesoli (1994) has emphasized, modernity has tended to sacrifice the present for the future in all areas of life. Even the major political cleavage between the left of the industrial labouring classes and the conservative right has been closed in the ideal of progress; the debate has been about which of them is pursuing the politics that best serves this interest (Touraine 1992, pp. 79–108).

Egalitarian universalism has been closely – and in so far as progress has really been made – functionally related to the advancement of material life. Progress has only been possible through a rapid rise in educational levels and a transformation in working life that can be observed as the growth of the new middle class (Sulkunen 1992). The corresponding social mobility has required that individuals are rewarded for merit, and they have been encouraged to gain it especially in education. Universalism means that everyone is treated as a citizen, and even though this may not lead to equality, in the end-result it is a principle that is compatible only with the doctrine of equality of possibility (cf., for example, Titmuss 1987).

State nationalism, in contrast to simple ethnic nationalism, has been a safeguard ideology to support and maintain the ideals of progress and universalism. It has been a unifying force far stronger than the division of social class. The construction of the modern welfare states in the Nordic countries would have been unthinkable without the rhetoric of national interest.

The trinity of progress, universalism and nationalism has been the framework from which preventive alcohol policies have been developed. The postwar increase in alcohol consumption in advanced capitalist countries is related to the improved opportunities for consumption created by material and technical progress (Sulkunen 1983). In many countries the redefinition of alcohol-related problems as health hazards – or the tendency towards medicalization (Mäkelä *et al.* 1981) – reflected a change of moral codes in a modern, individual-oriented society but also a confidence in material and technical progress in treatment methods.

At the same time egalitarian individualism called for new, universalistic solutions to the prevention of alcohol problems. Nordic alcohol monopoly systems in particular were originally based on principles of social discrimination, the intention being to exclude women, young people and the working class from the world of drink (Bruun and Frånberg 1985; Järvinen and Stenius, 1985). As late as the 1970s there were still traces of discriminatory alcohol policy in many countries. In Belgium, for example, there was legislation against the serving of strong drinks in public places, and also a law stating that alcohol could be sold retail only in containers of two litres or more. The main purpose was to prevent workers from buying spirits. The well-known British rules on opening hours of public houses were also originally aimed at disciplining the working class (Harrison 1971). French working-class cafés have been subjected to similar restrictions, but here the motivation was even more explicitly political: cafés and other public drinking places have been important scenes of political agitation since the eighteenth century (Brennan 1989), even more obviously so after the Commune (Barrows 1991). The dry history of Swedish restaurants has a very similar background (Magnusson 1985).

In Finland public campaigns to promote self-restraint and hygiene (ritualistic classification of different types of drink, 'manners' as to how drinks should be served and the like) were carried out in the postwar period, but they were for a long time met with resistance by the lower classes because they were considered tantamount to discrimination (Simpura 1982). Only with the rise of the new middle class into a culturally dominant position have such table manners become generalized, but great confusion still exists on what is the proper way to serve drinks (Sulkunen 1993).

It was not until the 1960s that universalistic principles finally displaced the old tradition of discriminatory alcohol policy in the Nordic countries. The first universalistic, truly modern response to the alcohol question in the welfare state came with the theory of total consumption (Bruun, Edwards, Lumio *et al.* 1975). According to this approach alcohol control should focus on per capita consumption rates in whole populations rather than on individuals, on specific risk groups or on drinking behaviour. Price policy, opening hours and density of the distribution network were the favoured policy measures. These implied another principle of the welfare-state thinking typical of the time: moderate drinkers, too, should sacrifice some of their pleasure and comfort in solidarity with those more at risk.

As in other countries with a strong temperance tradition (Canada, USA, Switzerland), the egalitarian, solidary and uni-

versalistic preventive alcohol policy, within the political framework of the national welfare state, gained support from anti-
alcohol lobbies. For example, the Nordic Temperance Council
declared in their 1968 programme that their aim is no longer
to combat the use of alcohol as such, but to reduce abuse rates
and, in this, total consumption and availability are key factors.
This support was more important than the numbers involved
in the movement, because temperance was one of the early civil
religions around which national political structures and civil
societies were built in the nineteenth century (I. Sulkunen 1985;
Eriksen 1990).

In many countries where temperance movements have not
been part of their national civil religions, preventive alcohol
policy has been incorporated – in terms of universalism – into
the welfare-state agenda. In France, socialist Prime Minister
Mendès-France set up a governmental office to combat alcohol-
related problems (Haut Comité d'Etude et d'Information sur
l'Alcoolisme) in 1954; in Germany temperance organizations
are quasi-governmental; and all western capitalist countries have
some sort of governmental organs to monitor the development
of alcohol conditions, even though they may have limited power
actually to do anything.

4. MODERNITY, ALCOHOL AND THE STATE IN THE NORDIC COUNTRIES

Three specific characteristics in the process of modernization
in the Nordic countries are so important that they have led to
what is often called the Nordic model of the modern welfare
state (Kosonen 1995; Boje and Olsson Hort 1993). These features of modernization are: 1) it is recent; 2) it is state-driven;
3) it combines social action from above with social movements
from below. These features explain the emergence of state-
centred alcohol control systems particularly in Norway, Sweden
and Finland; and they are also important in understanding the
change they are undergoing at the present time.

1. Recent. The building of the Nordic welfare state was properly
started in the early twentieth century, somewhat later than in
the leading western European countries (cf. Kosonen 1995).

This delay was due mostly to the domination of agriculture in the production system long into this century. With emerging industrialization and increasing difficulties in maintaining a large landless agricultural population, the new questions of the working class and the landless, the pressure for welfare reforms grew both among the leading elites and among the population at large. In the Nordic countries, Sweden was the pioneer in developing the welfare system, followed soon by Norway and, on somewhat different lines, Denmark. In Finland the development was clearly delayed, because of different political developments. Finland's struggle for independence (1917) ended with a civil war, which together with a slower industrial development and slow urbanization also slowed down the building of welfare systems. By the late 1930s, all Nordic countries were well underway in providing income maintenance systems for major population quotas. After the war, the extension of social welfare systems was slowly accelerated, and in the heyday of the 1960s and early 1970s they were completed with a large-scale network of public service provision in health and social welfare. The extension was finally stopped by various economic crises from the late 1970s onward. For a long time the welfare expenditure of the Nordic countries was well behind that of many central and western European countries, but in the mature phase in the 1980s, the Nordic welfare state reached and passed most of the other industrialized countries. The relatively recent maturity of welfare-state building is most visible in Finland, which did not reach the levels of the other Nordic countries until the 1980s (see Table 2.1).

2. State-Driven.   Given the late and slow start of industrialization in the Nordic countries, it would have been possible that their fate would have been to remain agricultural and underdeveloped societies forever. The intervention of the state was necessary to accumulate capital stock for investments in basic industries (forestry, energy, traffic and communications). But industrialization required aspects other than investments. The labour force had to be educated, liberated from too much dependency on farming, mobilized to move into industrial communities near the factories, which were often dispersed in vast, sparsely populated rural areas. And finally, effective ideological and political mobilization of the population was required to

Table 2.1   Central features of the welfare state development and alcohol policy in Finland, 1930–95

	1930	*1950*	*1970*	*1990*	*1995*
Urbanization: urban population %	21	32	51	62	64
Industrialization: agricultural households % of population	61	42	18	8	..
Welfare expenditure % of state budget	3	13	20	28	25
Milestones of welfare system building	• (1937) National Pensions Act (reform 1956) • (1948) children's allowances • (1961–62) work pensions • (1963) sickness insurance • (1971) unified school system • (1972) Public Health Act • (1972) Act on daycare for children • (1985) Unemployment insurance				
Alcohol consumption (litres 100% alcohol p.c.)	1.3 (1936)	1.7	4.3	7.7	6.5
Milestones in alcohol control system	• (1932) end of prohibition (1919–32), establishing of State Alcohol Monopoly • (1969) major liberalization of the alcohol sales system • (1995) separation of administrative tasks from the Monopoly				

Sources: Urbanization: *Statistical Yearbook of Finland*, 1995 Table 25.
Industrialization: Central Statistical Office of Finland 1991.
Welfare expenditure: *Statistical Yearbook of Finland*, 1931 to 1995. Figures on expenditure on social security and health.
Alcohol consumption: *Alcohol Statistical Yearbook*, 1936–1995, Finnish Alcohol Company.

make 'sacrifice of the present for the sake of the future' understandable and acceptable.

The central role of the state in the Nordic model of modernization was not only necessary but also readily available as a
heritage from earlier periods of Swedish rule in Norway (1814
to 1905) and Finland (from the twelfth century to 1809). A
special system of central government consists of the so-called
central boards in a number of administrative branches such as
education, health, housing and agriculture. The function of
these central boards has been to assure that the same administrative standards were met in all parts of the country. Regional
administration consists of regional offices called *länsstyrelser*,
which were regional representatives of the central government.
They have been used by the central boards to inspect, advise
and supervise local authorities to assure that national standards have been applied uniformly in the whole country.

The Nordic alcohol monopolies have been based on this
model of central administration, and, respectively, the disintegration of the monopolies can be seen as part of the recent
decentralization of the whole state administration. The Swedish 'Bratt system', voted in in 1922, was an alternative to Pro-
hibition and aimed to correct distortions created by the earlier
'Gothenburg system' of local alcohol monopolies. The Bratt
system involved personal quotas per month for each consumer;
to keep a record of purchasers and of the continued eligibil-
ity of each citizen for a purchasing licence. One of the most
Byzantine national central bureaucracies was created in Stockholm to record details of each purchase, reacting to excess
and to violations of acceptable drinking behaviour (Bruun and
Frånberg 1985, pp. 74–114).

Personal purchasing control systems were also tried in Finland and Norway but they never went to the extremes of those
in Sweden. Nevertheless, national uniformity of standards was
their ideal too, and there is some fascination in the exactitude
in which liquor stores open and close each day at the same
times. The Finnish state alcohol monopoly originally covered
the production of all alcoholic beverages except beer, imports
and wholesale and retail sales of all alcoholic beverages above
2.25 per cent alcohol. Rural areas were completely dry until
1969, with the exception of a few restaurants for tourists only
in tourist areas. The first licensed restaurants were opened also

for the local clientele in rural communities in the early 1960s and the first liquor stores only in 1969. Retail sales of medium beer of up to 4.5 per cent alcohol were liberated from the monopoly stores at the beginning of 1969 (Simpura 1982; Mäkelä, Sulkunen and Österberg 1981).

The monopoly was responsible also for granting on-sale licences and for their inspection. In the 1980s the monopoly's licensing policy was relaxed and the number of on-premise outlets increased rapidly, from 1525 in 1980 to 2560 in 1990. The growth continued in the 1990s. Furthermore, the monopoly had important educational and research functions. It was administered under the supervision of the Ministry of Health and Social Affairs, but the national importance of the alcohol question was stressed also in its own administrative structure. The Board consisted of representatives of the political parties, elected by Parliament. Each year the Board prepared a report on 'the evolution of the alcohol situation' for Parliament.

Finland's entry to the European Union in 1995 ended the state monopoly on production, imports and wholesale. Inspection functions were delegated to the *länsstyrelsen* and to the Ministry of Health and Social Affairs, which also now has the licensing authority. Research and educational activities are now also separated from the monopoly.

3. From Above and from Below. The Nordic welfare states are the outcome of elitist interests from above and political pressure from below (cf., for example, Boje and Olsson Hort 1993). Besides capital accumulation through the state, elites had an interest in maintaining social order and the legitimacy of the nation-state. Also, rapid modernization required state measures to provide an appropriately educated labour force to meet industrial requirements, especially to provide sufficient nutrition (see, for instance, Jensen and Kjaernes 1996) and housing (see, for instance, Juntto 1990).

Essential, and again specific to the Nordic model, is that popular support for it was solicited from and accumulated by both the industrial working class and the small rural population with similar incentives and motives. Often on opposing sides ideologically, they united forces in their demands for social security schemes that for this reason became based on universalistic flat rates rather than being means-tested and income-related; more so in Sweden and Norway than in Finland (Olsson 1990; Kosonen 1995). In Finland, a specific additional factor in welfare development has been the struggle between workers' and farmers' interests (Haatanen 1992).

The same universalism has been the basis on which women's extraordinary participation in paid labour – in itself a necessary requirement of rapid industrialization – has been possible (Julkunen 1992, Esping-Andersen 1990).

The three particularities of the Nordic model have not coexisted in complete harmony, which is most concretely apparent in the area of alcohol policy. Elite-driven, state-directed alcohol control systems operated from above, although originally supported by active popular movements, were from the very beginning in contradiction with the principles of universal citizenship cherished from below. Especially in Finland, concerns about public order in the immediate postwar period led to particular and selective uses of the control apparatus against women, the rural population and the working class, and expressly in favour of middle-class men. The modern ideas of progress, democracy and national interest originally associated with temperance messages turned into symbols of welfare-state paternalism, and this latter symbolism dominates increasingly as advances in progress, democracy and national unity are being made. The conflict-ridden, ambivalent disparity of elitist and democratic perspectives on alcohol is still visible in the debate on alcohol policy, more so in Finland than in Sweden or Norway.

5. GLOBALIZATION AND LOCALIZATION: BIFURCATION OF NATION-STATE POLITICS

For more than ten years now, the demise of contemporary nation-states has been predicted on the grounds that they are too small for the big problems of society and too big for small problems (Williams 1983, pp. 197–9; Bell 1987, p. 116, quoted by Lash and Urry 1994, p. 279). Preventive alcohol policy in its Nordic monopoly versions is a brilliant example of the nation-state approach to a problem that is becoming too big, or globalized and internationalized, but also too small, or localized and fragmented.

The nation-state is one of the institutions from an era that

Lash and Urry (1994) call the era of 'organized capitalism'. In their view two processes in particular are producing what they call the era of 'disorganized capitalism'. First, physical and technical development has led to time–space compression, or to the shrinking of the globe in terms of communication and information networks. Second, the new world also produces new kinds of subjects who are increasingly aware of the opportunities for a new reflexive relationship toward their lives and the world around them, the world being more and more aestheticized in matters of style, taste and choice. As a consequence, the relatively solid social institutions of organized capitalism become fluid and disorganized. From the point of view of the nation-state, the disorganization goes into two directions, those of globalization and localization.

Globalization, both cultural, social, economic and political, leads to the consequence that 'no longer are nations-states obvious and legitimate sources of authority over civil society' (Lash and Urry 1994, p. 281). Of course, the nation-state is not disappearing overnight but undergoing a gradual change in its internal and external structures. As Robertson (1992, p. 184) puts it, to date there is nothing to suggest that nationally organized society, more specifically the state, is about to wither away. In the case of the Nordic countries, an important aspect of globalization is the loss of former cultural isolation and also the slowly disappearing cultural homogeneity. In such conditions it will become more difficult to formulate issues centrally as national policies.

Comparing the world today with the days of building the Nordic welfare state and the mobilization of temperance movements as a crucial civil action for preventive alcohol policies, Gundelach (1994, p. 7) points to three important social changes: 'Compared to the early industrial society the present society is marked by the following: 1) a high degree of differentiation; 2) a high degree of individualization; 3) hedonistic and self-realization values.'

Differentation is closely linked to globalization and the fate of the nation-state as a decisive source of identity. Citizenship as an automatic and significant membership is giving way to chosen membership in what are called 'invented communities'. These invented communities are more temporary by nature, and therefore, also provide a weaker basis for mobilization around problem issues than has been the case with the communities of 'modern' or 'organized capitalist' societies. New social movements, based on the weak and temporary memberships of a disorganized world, may be important in formulating new ways of thinking about social issues (cf. Eyerman and Jamison 1991; see also Maffesoli 1994), but are not likely to lead to stable political organizations and institutions like those around the Nordic alcohol policy systems.

In the direction of localization, a puzzling consequence of increasing globalization is that the scope of comprehensible action is limited. Nation-state issues turning to global ones escape the capacities of individuals, no matter how well-equipped with global networks and cultural competence they may be. What is left for civil action, then, is essentially the local forum. This is strikingly evident in the debate around environmental issues, but can be seen on other issues too. To quote Lash and Urry (1994, p. 293) once more, 'Certain aspects of the environment are only comprehensible at the local level, indeed for many people that is all of the environment that can be challenged. It is only local action that can be envisaged and sustained.' Replace 'environment' here with 'social environment', and the perspective for local action in preventing social problems, like the alcohol-related ones, is already at hand.

Globalization and localization serve both as causes and solutions in the present crisis facing the Nordic welfare-state, particularly in Finland and Sweden. Ever since the 1970s, three major dimensions of the expected crisis have been legitimation, fiscal capacity and effectiveness (see e.g. Olsson 1990, Mishra 1990). With increasing globalization and international economic integration, the fiscal capacity of small nation-states to maintain their welfare systems has been challenged. International competitiveness are the key words more than ever in small countries. Welfare expenditure is one of the few parameters that, to some extent at least, can be regulated by nation-state decisions, but international economic perspectives increasingly dictate the direction of national decision-making. In this sense, globalization is one of the explanations of the welfare crisis. But it is also a solution in two respects at least. First, political and economic integration is seen by some as an opportunity for promoting internationally coordinated welfare systems. For instance, the most optimistic proponents of the Nordic welfare system have seen EU membership as a channel for spreading Nordic welfare ideas to wider circles. Second, it is hoped that international integration, in the long run, will lead to more stable economic conditions. Such a development would help to overcome the present fiscal crisis, and much of the welfare system could still be preserved.

Localization can also be seen as a factor in weakening the basis of a unified welfare policy. Instead of universalism, tailor-made solutions for specific groups and specific geographic locations will be favoured. The interplay of localization and globalization is neatly visible in the social policy programmes of the EU (e.g. European Social Policy, 1994) where the dominant activity pattern is to focus on short-term programmes to overcome social ills within regionally limited contexts. Universalist ideas like the EU slogan of preventing social exclusion serve as broad umbrella concepts with weak links to operative action. On the other hand, localization can be seen as a solution to all of the three crises of the Nordic welfare state. It eases the effectiveness crisis in search of greater flexibility and lighter administrative structures, and in shaping pseudo-market systems for health and welfare services. Localization also helps to ascertain the legitimacy of welfare policies by bringing decision-making closer to service consumers and beneficiaries. For fiscal crises, localization provides means for better economic control on the immediate local level, without time-consuming and costly upper-level bureaucracy.

6. ALCOHOL-RELATED ISSUES IN GLOBALIZATION AND LOCALIZATION

A most visible field where increased globalization touches alcohol-related issues is the European economic integration. Some effects of integration are especially relevant for the alcohol monopoly in Nordic countries (see e.g. Holder *et al.* 1995). The idea of seeing alcohol issues predominantly as health and social issues, as has been the case in the Nordic countries, is secondary in EU policy where agricultural, industrial and trade interests dominate the alcohol scene. In Europe, a constant dispute is going on between public health interests and the advocates of alcohol production and trade. The European Alcohol Action Plan (1993) of the WHO Regional Office for Europe is the most important document supporting the public health argument. It has been challenged by the lobbying organization of European alcohol producers, the Amsterdam Group (see *Alcoholic Beverages and European Society*, 1994). Even more importantly, the opening of new channels for international alcohol trade within the EU and in central and eastern Europe also shakes the foundations of the Nordic universalist alcohol policies. The fate of the Nordic alcohol monopolies has been left, by political decisions, largely to the faceless 'market forces' of disorganized capitalism.

Localization of alcohol issues has a long tradition in the alcohol monopolies in Nordic countries. Local municipalities have been entitled to express their views on alcohol sales and on-premise serving in their jurisdiction, although the actual decision-making has long been in the the hands of centralized bodies (see Chapter 3). There have also been differences between the three monopoly countries in this respect. In Norway, local political and administrative units have traditionally enjoyed larger autonomy than in Finland, which has a stronger centralized tradition. Sweden has been an intermediate case. In both Finland and Sweden, the development of the general welfare system has gone in the direction of increased local independence, partly as a response to fiscal difficulties, but also as a consequence of changes in the political atmosphere (see Chapter 3). As a consequence, some of the control institutions of the earlier centralized system have gone through an upheaval or have been watered down (e.g. the system of municipal inspection of alcohol sales in Finland), or the former alcohol-specific tasks were moved to other local bodies in the general field of health and social welfare administration. The separation of alcohol-related administration from the activities of alcohol monopolies was completed in 1995 in Finland. In all the three countries, new central administrative bodies for alcohol-related issues were created in the mid-1990s, starting their work in 1995 in Finland and Sweden, and in 1996 in Norway. In Finland and Sweden the reform evidently strengthens the role of local political and administrative actors, whereas in Norway the reform is less radical.

7. FUTURE PERSPECTIVES

This chapter has had the double task of building a conceptual framework. First, it is aimed at presenting alcohol issues as a social construction in a change from modern to postmodern social relations. Second, alcohol issues have also served as an example of how and in what kind of contexts postmodernism is taking place in the Nordic welfare state. From the alcohol policy point of view the bifurcation of state power to global and local levels, combined with the fading out of the modern trinity of progress, universalism and state nationalism may seem like a pessimistic conclusion. International constraints reduce the possibilities of national action, and the political goodwill for preventive action within the World Health Organization seems relatively weak in comparison with business interests in the free markets of commodities.

The social alcohol question has gradually lost its central place in movements that once were important in the nation-building process; these movements have become bureaucratized and merged into the state apparatus. New middle-class individualism will not tolerate state intervention into the private areas of consumption; fewer resources will be available to support those marginalized by a drinking problem; and treatment services will have unequal standards. This means that the visibility and moral weight of the alcohol issue are not as great as earlier, but the alcohol problem itself is still there. However, it is no longer a special issue surrounded by potent ideological dogmas of national civil religions; instead, it is one typical problem area where the individual confronts the state and vice versa.

Within the bureaucratic structures of the state, alcohol problems are blending into professional interests. Nowadays we see the flag of preventive alcohol policy being waved by doctors, social workers and bureaucrats far more often than by voluntary organizations. This is the case at least in Finland, Sweden, the United States and France.

It is possible (but by no means inevitable) that other identity-structuring social forces – ethnic, national, local movements, moral crusades revolving around environmental protection or peace – will find in alcohol a holy enemy, a symbol of the negative other. It is more likely, however, that in a decentralized society the question and worry about it simply disintegrate; if state monopolies that sell alcohol are in disrepute, it is even more difficult to maintain monopolies as a measure for combating the drinking problem. The definition of all social problems is increasingly divided between the media, special interest groups and the authorities. As far as research is concerned this means that we must address ourselves not only to state authorities but also to several different kinds of actors in the field.

The new public health movement (Lupton 1995, pp. 58–76), including community work, is one reaction to this disintegration. Its rhetorics of empowerment and health promotion imply that people who are influenced and helped by research interventions are not only objects on whom policy is practised but independent subjects who themselves make choices. The agents in the field include individual citizens and invented communities of several kinds. The local bureaucracies themselves are seen as agents of change and not merely the low end of a hierarchy that executes policies designed by its higher levels. Local professionals, not only medical but also educational, are intermediary groups that have easy access to local people and have specialised capacities to influence their actions and thoughts.

3 Constructing Alcohol Problems in the Community

Jussi Simpura

1. INTRODUCTION

Community action aims not only at changing drinking behaviour and related harm and the social and physical environment, but also at influencing the public agenda and alcohol's position in it. Public opinion and attitudes toward drinking are both objects and tools of community action. In the long run opinion changes may lead to changes in drinking patterns and harmful consequences, but these typically occur through very complicated processes and are hardly predictable. Also, it may be difficult to attribute such changes to a certain community action effort. Therefore, within time frames that are relevant for policy-making on the community level, community action should be seen as participation in the processes of defining or constructing alcohol problems. This chapter is about the multitude of channels for such construction processes.

The definition of alcohol problems as social problems is different in different countries and in different times. Also, the channels of constructing problems may vary considerably. Which are the forums and arenas of problem definition, who are the central actors and what kinds of channels are available for constructing social problems? How is public agenda-setting related to everyday behaviour and which behaviours are actually the object of community action? What is local in local community action in a globalizing world penetrated by supranational media influences? We shall first strive for a schematic model of the field and channels in construction processes. After that, some alcohol-specific features of the main channels will be discussed in the special case of Lahti, in its Scandinavian welfare context.

41

2. THE MULTIPLE CHANNELS OF PROBLEM CONSTRUCTION

Taking the construction of social problems as one of the starting points in community action resembles the ideas of the so-called constructionist school of the study of social problems (see Spector and Kitsuse 1987; Schneider 1985). That approach emphasizes the view that social problems do not exist as objectively observable realities but become observed through subjective definitional processes only. The American constructionist school is loosely divided into two major factions. The strict constructionists deny completely the objective existence of social problems without the mediation of definitional processes (claims-making), whereas contextual constructionists admit that historical and social contexts should be accounted for as a kind of objective background of definitional processes. This dispute has led to extensive philosophical debates (see e.g. Woolgar and Pawluch 1985) which are beyond the scope of this presentation. For community action, the merit of the constructionist approach lies in the fact that it has raised the processes of problem construction to the status of a worthwhile research object, and at the same time to that of a legitimate object of community action.

American constructionist thinking stresses the importance of civil action, that is, the mobilization of various claims-makers on public arenas. The idea of community, and of local community in particular, is strongly present also in recent North American developments of community action in prevention of alcohol problems (Greenfield and Zimmerman 1993). The most striking feature of this line of communitarian thinking (Etzioni 1993; Anderson and Davey 1995; Gundelach 1993 on a specific Danish variant) is perhaps the implicit assumption of unlimited spontaneity in society, and consequently, the relatively weak interest in examining the role of more stable institutions such as the state in definition processes. In many European countries, the presence of the state as a central actor in problem definition would be self-evident. Also, the European state may in some countries appear as a basically sufficient and even benevolent actor in these definitional processes.

The idea of community as a central framework of action is probably different in ethnically, socially, culturally and even economically relatively homogeneous countries like the Scandinavian countries, compared to the colourful heterogeneity of the USA in particular. Such historically different thought-forms may even influence the role and nature of civil action, which is an essential feature in the constructionist model. The constructionists have extensively discussed the possibility that social problems and social movements were actually but two different names for one phenomenon (e.g. Troyer 1989). In the Scandinavian countries, much of civil action and social movements mobilize themselves with governmental support and within governmental structures. These countries could correctly be called 'state-penetrated civil societies' (an expression suggested by Mäkelä (1988)). Respectively, the American communitarian societies could be named 'sponsor-driven civil societies'. Both of these characterizations have deep implications for the prospects and nature of community action.

Hilgartner and Bosk's 'public arenas model' gives useful ideas in developing a schematic presentation of alcohol issues as social problems. The model builds on the constructionist view of social problems as products of a process of collective definition. A basic feature of the model is that potential problem issues are seen as competitors for the limited and therefore scarce resource of public attention on various arenas. The model has six main elements (Hilgartner and Bosk 1989, p. 56):

1 A dynamic process of competition among the members of a very large 'population' of social problem claims.
2 The institutional arenas that serve as 'environments' where social problems compete for attention and grow.
3 The 'carrying capacities' of these arenas, which limit the number of problems that can gain widespread attention at one time.
4 The 'principles of selection', or institutional, political and cultural factors that influence the probability of survival of competing problem formulations.
5 Patterns of interaction among the different arenas, such as feedback and synergy, through which activities in each arena spread throughout the others.
6 The networks of operatives who promote and attempt to control particular problems and whose channels of communication crisscross the different arenas.

Two important remarks must be made before entering the construction of the model in the case of community action for preventing alcohol problems. First, the idea of regarding various potential problem issues as competitors calls for an analysis of the changing order of importance or seriousness among a set of social problems. Changes in such an ordering can also be used for evaluation of a community action project (see Chapter 11). Second, the model of Hilgartner and Bosk concerns situations where various problem issues strive for more public attention. This is a kind of fight for getting issues defined as social problems proper. However, on a less publicly visible level, various actors have to try to manage problem phenomena on a day-to-day basis, within the ever-changing context produced by the public processes of problem definition. Definition of problem and managing a problem are two interconnected levels that are both important for community action thinking. Both of them are also legitimate objects of community action aiming at prevention of alcohol problems.

The list of the arenas or channels of problem construction again varies from one country to another, and from one historical period to another. Hilgartner and Bosk (1989, pp. 58–9) give the following lengthy directory: 'executive and legislative branches of government, the courts, made-for-TV movies, the cinema, the news media (television news, magazines, newspapers, and radio), political campaign organizations, social action groups, direct mail solicitations, books dealing with social issues, the research community, religious organizations, professional societies, and private foundations'. This list is admittedly very American, but still applicable as an example. Hilgartner and Bosk refer also to 'some vague locations' such as society and public opinion and point out that these, unlike those listed above, are not such concrete arenas where problem definition takes place. It seems realistic, however, to include both society (and culture) and public opinion as general background elements in the schematic presentation.

To simplify the model, let us follow the lines of a recent study on environmental issues in the Finnish media (Suhonen 1994, pp. 51–3) building on the tradition on agenda-setting studies in media research (e.g. Reese 1991; McCombs and Shaw 1993). There 'a triangle of agendas' was suggested, consisting of media, power structures and the general public, and operating with two

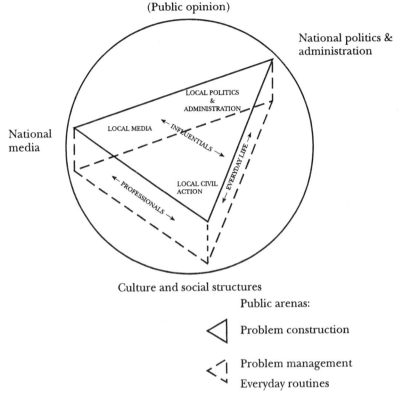

Figure 3.1   A schematic presentation of the local and general fields
of problem construction

realities, culture and the real world. For the consideration of
community action, this triangle is insufficient as it does not show
a place for organized civil action. This can be remedied by keeping in mind the two-level structure suggested above: problem
management and problem construction. On the construction
level, the 'general public' actually consists of civil action groups
working in public arenas. On the level of daily practice of welfare professionals engaged in problem management, the general public has a more passive role as recipient and interpreter
of public messages.

A further elaboration of the model was needed when thinking
about community action as local action in a national and globalizing framework. Also here a double perspective is needed, to

account for the limited but still existing degrees of freedom of specific local activity. It is important to remember that local activities do not take place in a vacuum but are closely related to national and even international processes.

Compared to Hilgartner and Bosk's list of public arenas, the role of various specific groups and arenas, such as the research community, professions and economic interest groups is simplified here. In a state-penetrated welfare society, even these groups mostly work within or through governmental structures. These groups, together with local media actors, political and administrative elites and civil activists, comprise a set of local influentials. Later in this chapter we shall propose that the core of all that is local is the people, in particular the ones who are influential, who live and work and act locally in a basically and increasingly non-local world.

The corners of the triangle in Fig. 3.1 represent the major channels of problem construction on the local level. Within each of them, a multitude of alternative sub-channels can be distinguished. These will be discussed in detail below, using materials from the Lahti Project as examples. Before that, a review of the background fields of culture, social structures and public opinion is needed, to set the field of problem construction action into a more general context.

3. THE CULTURE, SOCIAL STRUCTURE AND PUBLIC OPINION

In each country and in each local community, there are cultural conceptions about alcohol and drinking that must be taken seriously in preventive community action. Beliefs about the beneficial effects of wine have prevailed in the Mediterranean countries, even if they now are becoming less common. In many countries, ideas of alcoholic beverages and particular drinking patterns are part of national or local identity. Wine and the Mediterranean countries, vodka and the Russians, or beer and the Czechs are good examples. In Finland, the belief that the Finns are particularly prone to drink large amounts per occasion and to get heavily intoxicated has become a part of the mythical national self-identity. Indeed, the concept of 'mythical intoxication' was launched when studying the presentation of drinking in Finnish films and other cultural products (Falk and Sulkunen 1983). In most cases, empirical findings on drinking patterns support cultural stereotypes, but only to a limited extent.

Examples of local cultural peculiarities are more difficult to find in today's world of homogenized and internationalized consumption patterns. For instance, the site of the Lahti Project, the city of Lahti, lies in a region known for the traditions of a special home-brewed beer, 'sahti'. But there are no signs of a strong presence of 'sahti'traditions in local drinking patterns. It is still possible, however, that consciouness of the traditional beverage may produce a certain specific positive or negative attitude towards drinking and towards beer in particular.

In pre-industrial and industrial societies, conceptions about drinking have often been related to conflict surfaces in the social structure. The attempts of governments and the bourgeoisie to control the drinking of farmers and later, of industrial workers, were common during the last two centuries in the industrialized countries. The same pattern was repeated, for example, in the worries of landowning farmers over the drinking of the landless population of Finland in the late nineteenth century (Peltonen 1988). Even specific cultural drinking patterns may bear elements of conflicts in the social structure. For instance, the mythical intoxication of the Finns has been interpreted as another indication of a rebellion against the 'masters', or all upper classes and upper political structures. In such conditions, preventive interventions run the risk of becoming understood as an attack against some basic rights of the population. A good example of such a failure in alcohol prevention is Gorbachev's 1985 alcohol reform in the Soviet Union (see Tarschys 1993; Gerner 1995).

Post-industrial or late modern societies face new types of potential conflicts. In many countries, the continued high level of unemployment is creating a new underclass of those excluded from wage labour. Alcohol problems may be used as another label to distinguish the 'good' poor from the 'bad'. During the years of the community action experiment, the city of Lahti was hit heavily by rapidly rising unemployment that reached the unbelievable level of 27 per cent of the labour force in early 1994. Public worries about drinking did not, however, seem to be very much influenced by high unemployment, neither on the local level nor in national debate. In Europe, multiethnicity is rapidly increasing, thus shaping new challenges for preventive community action. Finally, the expected lifestyle fragmentation of late modern societies has so far seldom become linked with structural conflicts in the society. There are, however, some milder forms of critique that may still lead to serious difficulties in welfare policy. The 'new middle class' and its critical attitude towards alcohol policy is an interesting example (see Chapter 2).

4. LOCAL MEDIA AND ALCOHOL ISSUES

The study of media as a channel for problem construction should cover a wide range of operators. Newspapers, journals, local radio and local TV should all be included. For the evaluation of a community action project, it is the media coverage of the project activities that is of interest (see Chapter 11). For the preparation of a project, it is central to analyse the structures of argumentation in media. In this chapter, we shall discuss the newspapers only, because the distinction between national and local media can be effectively made there. In addition, in the Finnish conditions newspapers are perhaps a relatively more important media channel than in many other countries.

The newspapers have an active role in agenda-setting and thus may follow a long-term policy fairly consistently. But at the same time, they reflect the changes in the outer world. In rapidly changing social and political conditions, such as those in the ex-socialist countries, the repertoire of press writings may fluctuate quite dramatically (see Lagerspetz (ed.), 1994). This can be seen both in the coverage of various issues and in the ways of argumentation. In more stable conditions, the fluctuations are smoother but in the long run still remarkable.

In Finland, Matti Piispa (1994) has studied the ways of writing about alcohol issues over four decades, 1950–90. Studying the alcohol-related editorials of leading newspapers he could distinguish three different periods. In the 1950s, which were still the heyday of traditional alcohol consumption, the dominating view of problem drinking was that the problem was drinking in itself, irrespective of the patterns and beverage preferences. From the late 1950s onwards, the core of the alcohol problem was reformulated, and now it was the pattern of drinking that was the most troublesome. In particular, it was thought that it was the overwhelming popularity of distilled beverages that led to frequent uncontrolled intoxication. This argument was used to support a radical reform of alcohol control policies (1968) which turned Finland into a beer-drinking country in a few years (see Mäkelä, Sulkunen and Österberg 1981). However, the expected change towards new, moderate drinking patterns did not follow. The new milder beverages did not substitute for the old ones, but came as an addition to the traditional habits (see Simpura, ed. 1987). In the early 1970s, a new way of argumentation was adopted, called the public health perspective (see Bruun *et al.* 1975; also Edwards *et al.* 1994). As a consequence, in the press debate around alcohol in the 1970s, the core of the alcohol problem was seen in the level of aggregate alcohol consumption in the population. Finally, turning to the late 1980s, a further redefinition took place. Now the problem was seen in excessive patronizing by the state and the restrictive alcohol control policies. They were seen as preventing citizens not from problem drinking but from the right to self-control, and thereby depriving them of the opportunity to find their own ways to moderation. This form of argumentation prevailed in press debate in Finland all through the early 1990s.

Respective periodizations can be found in many countries. In press debate they are most visible in countries where alcohol issues have been an important question in overall politics for a long time (e.g. the Scandinavian countries except Denmark). For the planning of a community action project on alcohol, it is important to notice that older forms of argumentation are long lived in today's newspaper writing. The present press debate becomes understandable when it is analysed as a response to older debates, and not only as a reflection of present-day conditions.

As a consequence of technological change, there is a tendency towards more unified media content from centralized and often international sources. Respectively, the editorial input on local issues and also the newspapers' own interpretation of ready-made materials is diminishing. In the case of Finland and the Lahti project, a peculiar feature is that there is one overwhelmingly dominant national newspaper with high penetration in at least all major cities. This leaves the local press less space in nationwide issues but respectively perhaps more space in local issues.

In the Lahti project, a separate substudy was conducted on newspaper writing about social problems in the period from 1985 to 1992 (Hanhinen 1994), that is, in a period immediately before the three-year community action experiment. Three newspapers were analysed: the leading national newspaper; the only seven-day newspaper in the city of Lahti; and a weekly local paper with mainly commercial advertisements, descriptions of local events and some often very polemic editorial material. Only material that represented the newspaper's own views was included. During the studied eight-year period a remarkable shift was found in the overall framework of writing.

In the late 1980s, a positive welfare state thinking was dominant, and the public good was an acceptable basis for action in most issues. In the 1990s, with the deep economic crisis and mass unemployment, the welfare-state framework weakened and was partly replaced by arguments that emphasised economic necessities instead of the public good. The study on newspaper writing found that the local newspaper was much more critical towards the welfare state than the national paper. This may be due to the fact that the local newspaper has a more conservative background than the national one. In both newspapers, a lessened interest in the problems of the marginalized population groups was noticed. The concern about those worse off belongs to the welfare-state framework, whereas the brave new world is for the successful middle class only.

This change of framework was reflected also in writing on alcohol issues, although still rather weakly. Alcohol and drugs figured only in some 1–2 per cent of all writings on social problems in the newspaper editorials. There was no significant difference between the nationwide and the leading local newspapers in the frequency of treating alcohol issues. However, the leading national newspaper emphasized public health aspects in its alcohol-related editorials, while the local newspaper presented more remarks on various economic issues such as the societal costs of problems. The ideological change was somewhat visible in that the national newspaper largely followed the prevalent public health model of Finnish alcohol policy, although with critical tones, whereas the more conservative-minded local newspaper viewed alcohol policy often as an example of excessive state patronizing of the citizens. The third paper, the small commercial local paper, had the most local and individualized view on alcohol issues. Its writings were more dramatized and focused on suspected wrongdoings of various people. As such, it worked as a moral gatekeeper differently from the larger newspapers. In general, the treatment of alcohol and drug issues was found to be more dramatized in the local media than in the national media.

The results also suggested that the role of newspapers and other media was becoming more important in processes of problem construction in Finland in the early 1990s. The life cycle of social problems as public issues was becoming shorter, and this favours media at the expense of other public arenas as channels of problem construction. A particularly relevant finding was that in Finland, the local media are likely to gain more influence due to an administrative reform that provided municipalities with more power and responsibility in the use of public funds. The reform took place formally in 1994, but its preparation phase already opened new discussions in the local press. In the traditional welfare state framework, the local press followed and reported mostly the national issues of alcohol policy and other social policy sectors. Local perspectives or the needs and problems of the local population were rarely mentioned. In the new situation, the media's role as a public observer of local politics is likely to be stronger.

5. ALCOHOL-RELATED ISSUES IN LOCAL ADMINISTRATION AND POLITICS

The second main channel in constructing alcohol problems as social problems on the local level is local politics and administration. Again, the systems of politics and administration are very different in different countries. However, a number of general questions can be posed everywhere. First, what are the relationships between local and state actors in determining alcohol-related issues? Second, are there political forces which, from either an ideological or a professional point of view, systematically bring alcohol-related issues to the fore (social workers, medical professions, police etc.)? And third, respectively, are there systematically pro- or anti-alcohol groups in the local politics and administration? The answers to these questions require a detailed study of local politics. In the planning of a community action project, such a study should preferably be accomplished in advance of the proposed action.

In the Lahti project this advice could not be followed. However, at the end of the project a study of politics and administration was completed (Sairanen 1995), partly in the interest of finding out how the Lahti project, where the city administration was a central cooperator, was related to other alcohol-related issues in local politics. The study is based on the minutes of the City Board, the City Council and some city committees from the years 1991 to 1994.

The municipal authority's capacity to decide on alcohol-related issues is not very extensive in Finland. The City Board, which is elected from among the Council members, gives a statement on each application for an on-premise licence. Sales of beverages below 4.7 per cent alcohol content are allowed in grocery stores and the city cannot intervene there. In the rare cases when opening a new monopoly liquor store is considered, the City Board has to be the active applicant. Alcohol-related issues are treated also in connection with health and social service provision. The city provides a large number of services itself and buys them from other providers. It also supports civil organizations working in the field of treament and prevention. In addition the city has its own unit for health education and prevention of alcohol, tobacco and drug problems.

In the four-year period studied, there were three major alcohol-related issues on the agenda. Repeatedly, the Committee on Adolescents proposed a 'shelter café' with some auxiliary services to be opened for youngsters and children, and repeatedly, the proposal was rejected because of the City's financial difficulties. An initiative of the Christian Party to set up a municipal plan for preventive alcohol and drug policy was accepted in 1991. Two years later, a permanent working group on alcohol and drug issues was founded. Most of the other alcohol-specific issues in the Board and in the Council were small, routine financial decisions. Interestingly, in 1994, the economic depression had pushed alcohol issues completely aside from the agenda of the Council. The Board still had some smaller decisions in this field.

The permanent carriers of alcohol-related worries were the Christian Party, the Committee on Adolescents and later, the permanent working group on alcohol and drug issues. The

Christian Party could also be considered as the core of a small anti-alcohol group. For instance, the party annually wonders why the Board statements on on-premise licence applications are never negative. The opponents of the pro-alcohol group are not easily detected, and are most likely to be spread out among different groupings.

Another example of Board discussions on alcohol concerns the Lahti project directly. As a part of the 'On the Wagon' weeks, the project team proposed that the City would refuse to serve alcoholic beverages at its own events during those weeks. This proposal was brought to the Board by the Assistant Mayor on health and social welfare. At the end, however, the decision was made that the city 'strives to avoid serving alcoholic beverages' during those weeks.

6. LOCAL CIVIL ACTION AND ALCOHOL ISSUES

Civil action was the third main channel of problem construction in the triangle model suggested here. In the constructionist approach to the study of social problems, an ideal-type of definitional process would be people's spontaneous mobilization around a specific problem issue. In the real world this seldom takes place. Civil action is built around existing organizational structures and uses existing cultural resources (e.g. Williams 1995). This is not to say that in most cases there wouldn't be any room for spontaneous civil mobilization. But admittedly, civil action takes place in a world where it faces partners and opponents coming from highly institutionalized interest structures. In the American context, sponsor-driven civil action seems to be crucial. In the Scandinavian welfare state context, state-induced civil action is of central importance.

Traditionally, the temperance movement was strong in Finland from the late nineteenth century until the 1960s. Even after that, it successfully guaranteed its position by a close alliance with political parties. Each party had its own temperance organization which served as a channel of career-making for many politicians. This system was largely reorganized with the coming of the 1990s, and the temperance movement today has to rely more on its own resources. Financially, however, it is dependent on state and municipality subsidies, like most other civil action organizations in a Scandinavian welfare state context. Today, the temperance movement is relatively weak compared to its heyday.

Most municipalities employ a prevention worker whose title is 'temperance secretary', and whose task it is to do prevention work in the locality. Nowadays, the temperance secretaries have in most localities become a part of the staff of the municipalities' health or youth work bureaus.

Alcohol-related civil action movements other than the temperance movement are few in Finland. Client-organizations, for instance, A-guilds for the clients of A-clinics, form a link and sometimes also an avenue for promoting the interests of these people.

In a Scandinavian welfare state context, a community action project like the Lahti project is an interesting attempt to encourage civil action around alcohol issues. Civil mobilization is, after all, a very central element of the community action. Also interestingly, there are plenty of examples on various state and municipal organizations which are applying practices that closely resemble or even consciously imitate the spontaneity of an ideal-type civil organization.

7. CONCLUSION: COMMUNITY ACTION AS PROBLEM CONSTRUCTION

The suggested model of the field of problem-construction raises the question whether community action should be seen first and foremost as problem-construction or also as problem-management. There may be nothing alcohol-specific in the answer, but it is worthwhile considering the possibility that alcohol-related issues may require a specific effort on the problem construction side, compared to some other more dramatic or more broadly distributed problems. The idea of symbolic crises, suggested by Neuman (1990) is useful here. Such crises touch immediately only a small number of people, but gain remarkable media coverage. Examples of these issues are environmental issues, drugs and poverty. They require visible public attention and definitional activities to become social problems. Presently, in many European countries alcohol is certainly not a 'symbolic crisis'.

Local media, local politics and administration and local civil action may rank differently in different countries when considering where to focus the efforts of problem construction. Still, the role of media is often supposed to grow in importance, and constructing a social problem without the influence of media is likely to be impossible in most cases.

With alcohol issues one difficulty facing a community action project is that alcohol problems certainly have in most countries no novelty as a social problem. Therefore, the task of community activists is a constant remaking of the problem. This requires tedious work in agenda-setting and problem construction.

4 Alcohol and the Imperative of Health in Mass Society: Images of Alcohol Policy among the Local Elites

Pekka Sulkunen

L07 Akseli(M):98 to me it's clear that availability increases the problem, there's no doubt, but what's not so clear is whether availability should be restricted . . . after all we're living in a free democracy, so to what extent can people be patronized? Personally I've always felt that grown up people can look after themselves, but when we have problems with people who cannot look after themselves then of course it's down to society to take over, and of course we all have to pay for it, for all the billions that diseases caused by alcohol use are costing.

1. THE PUBLIC HEALTH PREDICAMENT

A starting point for the Lahti research is that social problems are conceptual constructions. Any sociological intervention, in fact any reasonable sociological theory, must assume that some kind of communicability is the foundation of the social order, whatever its nature and whatever its degree of consensus.

Alcohol as a social problem is a particularly interesting case: the social history of 'the alcohol question' does not always reflect the prevalence or seriousness of alcohol problems in the reality of people's own everyday experience (see Chapter 2). Rather, alcohol, like drugs, is *perceived* as a cause of worry, often in ways that are quite unrelated to the extent of the problems they create. In the Nordic case the two even compete, drugs being the 'good enemy' as alcohol is much more difficult to combat because of economic and cultural interests related to its use (Christie and Bruun 1985).

Perceptions of alcohol as a social problem articulate general conceptions of society, especially the state and the individual self. Early temperance movements were vanguards of modernity in many ways: they represented rationality, controlled social order and the Protestant ethic. In the new consumer society the position of alcohol has become reversed: it represents 'modernity' in the sense of individuals' competence and responsibility to judge what is good for them, it stands for high standards of living, cosmopolitanism and ritualistic inventiveness as a means of social integration (Sulkunen 1983). In the modern welfare state the rationale for controlling alcohol use is no longer based on the rationalistic moral values of sobriety and frugality but on 'the public good' of reducing pain and cost to society (Edwards *et al.* 1994). Even so it is felt to be in contradiction with the values of individual sovereignty and responsibility.

This contradiction underlies what has been called the public health predicament of contemporary advanced societies (Sulkunen 1996). We are more aware than ever before that individuals' problems cause a burden to others and the society as a whole: as suffering and as costs. In all Western countries the health service is in a deepening fiscal crisis. In Deborah Lupton's words, health is no longer an individual problem that can recover from diseases with the help of medical technology. It has become a public imperative that must be actively promoted by many kinds of non-medical measures. Local community action projects such as the one we conducted in Lahti are one important form of the 'new public health movement' (Lupton 1995, 58).

We have more expert knowledge than ever before about the causes of problems, about the possibilities of treating them and about potential measures of prevention. Yet we are also more reluctant to accept any measures that might be interpreted as deflections from individual consumers' sovereignty, and all such attempts can be accused of being propelled by particular interests in the guise of the public good. In fact, one might argue that the whole notion of 'society' and with that, the notion of the public good, has become blurred. What is the society in whose interests one should accept that one can be deprived of the right to sell, buy or consume anything at any time? What is the public good for which sacrifices of freedom to choose and control oneself should be made, and how is each individual expected to benefit from it?

These are the questions that impose themselves in any reflections, public or private, on alcohol as a social problem today. It should be noted that as they are formulated above they do not refer specifically to alcohol at all. The new public health rhetoric itself is a discourse of moral neutralization: it does not take a moral stand in terms of lifestyles, consumption or alcohol use directly but talks of these only as factors influencing the health and general wellbeing of the population. It transforms moral and power issues into neutral expert discourse.

Yet in spite of vast expert knowledge on the causes and consequences of alcoholism, the construction of alcohol as a social problem is today only partly based on it. Equally important are general conceptions of the individual, the society and especially the state. In mass society, where great political ideologies no longer organise these conceptions, people are both confused and ambivalent about different possibilities. Alcohol policy is not embedded in distinct social doctrines, and therefore fairly abstract analytical tools are needed to understand the hidden or fuzzy texture of alcohol policy argumentation from this general perspective.

2. POSITIONS AND VALUES

When people construct social problems conceptually they do not do this in a vacuum, as if they were not themselves part of the world of which they speak. The construction of social problems is a process of verbal negotiation in which participants have ideas of the social world as a structure in which they place themselves. Talking about alcohol they also develop conceptions of themselves as individuals and as citizens, and whatever they say, they say from *a position* in their world. For example, when discussing alcohol policy they may look at it from the point of view of 'the public good' (if they believe in it), from a point of view of a parent, or of a consumer, and their opinions on, say, alcohol taxes will vary accordingly. These kinds of relationships between the structures of the world and the positions from which these structures are talked about are called

enunciative projections (Sulkunen and Törrönen, forthcoming/
b). When talking about alcohol policy people not only construct images of the world but also images of themselves by pro-
jecting themselves on to the actors in the world. Sometimes
they see themselves as those who have power to influence other
peoples' behaviour, at other times as those who are so influenced, or sometimes in both positions simultaneously.

Secondly, the construction of social problems is a process of
constructing *values*. In traditional norm-theoretical approaches,
values are understood as given and only applied to concrete
behaviours like alcohol use (Parsons and Shils 1951, 72; see also
Sulkunen and Törrönen, forthcoming/a). The problem with
norm-theoretical value concepts is that they assume that the
meaning attached to, say, drinking, is constant, known and independent of 'values' whose only function is to regulate understandings of acceptability (Pittman 1967; Bales 1946). In our view
the definitions of drinking itself are value-laden relationships between alcohol, society and the self. They are multidimensional
and not only matters of acceptability. The multidimensionality
of values can be grasped by the concept of modality (Sulkunen
and Törrönen, forthcoming/a). Acceptability is only one case of
so-called deontic modalities (permission: someone is not obliged
to do not-A), and can be a very important element in some patterns of argumentation, but there are others, as we shall see.

For example, the common Finnish images of alcohol use as
transgression of the boundaries of normal everyday life can be
understood as valuable in terms of the ability or power that alcohol gives to break norms. On the other hand, images of integrated or civilised social drinking are usually related to the values
of competence (knowing how to drink).[1] Correspondingly,
understandings of the functions and contradictions of preventive alcohol policy are related to value-laden conceptions of the
role of the state and its relations to individuals.

The theory of enunciative projections and modal values is the
basis of what we call reflexive intervention into the construction
of alcohol as a social problem. We not only interviewed the
Lahti influentials, we also made interpretations of what they had
told us and invited them to a feedback session to discuss our
'results' (Appendix). The analysis in this chapter is mainly based
on typescripts of the recorded feedback sessions.

Positions and values are important objects for reflexive

intervention, because they are elements of the participants' identities and understandings of themselves, at least in their relationship to alcohol use, but very likely also more generally as individuals and citizens. In this case, however, we did not even expect to meet homogeneous microcultures of the kind one might meet in working-class pubs (Sulkunen *et al.* 1985) or middle-class cafés (Sulkunen 1992): instead we expected to identify types of arguments about alcohol policy and see if and in what way our intervention would be received.

3. CONTROL AND TRANSGRESSION

Although argumentation patterns about alcohol policy can be looked at as reflections of how people understand the relationships between society and the self, it is not irrelevant what kind of 'intepretative repertoires' (Potter and Wetherell 1987) are available for the symbolic functions of alcohol itself. It is a well-documented fact (see, for example, Sulkunen 1993 for a summary) that in Finnish culture very strong connotations of transgression are associated with drinking. Alcohol is a drug and its use is embedded in rituals that mark a strong borderline between normal social life and life beyond its conventions. Many of these rituals imply the idea of control: the doorman in restaurants, restricted opening hours of off-licences, age limits, precise measurements of the dose, etc. And vice versa, alcohol control measures are usually interpreted as reinforcing the transgressive meaning of drinking (Partanen 1991, 217–35).

Such 'border controls' between the sober world and the world of intoxication are not necessarily seen as something negative. Reaching for the 'forbidden fruit' is not only a sin but also a sign of heroism. Heroic drinking, as Juha Partanen (1991, 236–50) has called it, implies and requires the rituals of transgression that the various forms of alcohol control represent. In fact, it was one hypothesis of the intervention study of the Lahti influentials (Appendix, Introduction) that one could expect to find a rather clearcut relationship between conceptions of alcohol as an object of consumption and conceptions of alcohol as a problem and an object of control. Those who would see drinking in terms of transgressing the norms of everyday life might be expected to define alcoholism in terms of lost self-control and accept external controls more willingly than those for whom alcoholic beverages are mostly an integrated part of normal life. The latter would, we thought, be more inclined to see alcoholism as a medical rather than as a social problem and consequently to see secondary and tertiary rather than primary prevention as the preferred remedy.

The interview protocol was designed to explore this expectation: the first part of the interview consisted of extracts from well-known international films, presenting both transgressive and non-transgressive drinking scenes. The second part consisted of educational material, including a video programme called *The Alcohol Roulette* produced by the Addiction Research Foundation in Toronto. This video defends the so-called total consumption theory, or availability theory, according to which alcohol problems can be prevented by limiting the availability, and thus the overall consumption of alcohol.

The idea of transgressive drinking was familiar to almost all those we interviewed but there was great variation in how they related it to their own behaviour. Some quite straightforwardly recognised themselves in the most transgressive film scenes; others recognised the pattern but took distance from it, saying that it belongs to the past or that it is typical not of 'us' but of others, such as young people, the working class, people in the country, and so on. A few persons had difficulty in understanding the pattern at all: for them alcohol use was not a transfiguration of the normal social world, and they thought that people who act like those in the film are either alcoholics or deviant in some other way (Sulkunen 1993).

A major conclusion on alchol policy argumentation appeared early in the course of our interviews. There was very little consistency in what people said. First, arguments were unstable within groups and even in different individuals' minds. Secondly, alcohol policy views were not in any systematic way related to understandings about alcohol or about alohol problems. Our initial hypothesis, that transgressive images of alcohol use would be related to conceptions of alcohol as a social rather than a medical or psychological problem, and that such conceptions would permit people to accept stronger external controls, did not hold true. Those who identified their own behaviour with the transgressive image of drinking were not more willing than others to accept public control measures to prevent alcohol problems. On the other hand, the interviewees who understood the need for primary prevention, especially preventive alcohol taxation, were not those who would associate transgressive connotations with their own alcohol use.

4. THREE VIEWS ON ALCOHOL POLICY

Obviously there was something wrong in our initial conceptualizations, and it soon began to appear that the fault lay in our understanding of control, which was too simple.

Early on we could identify rather easily two approaches to alcohol policy: the welfare state approach and neoliberalism. First, the ARF video already introduced the total consumption theory, which we have analysed as a 'modernist welfare state' philosophy in alcohol policy. The idea was understood and even accepted by some groups. The modern welfare state approach denies any moral superiority of the state over individuals, and therefore public intervention into private consumption needs specific justifications. Alcoholism is a disease, and should be treated as any disease. However, efforts aimed at its prevention are legitimate, not because of the pain it causes to the diseased individual but because of the suffering it causes to others, either directly in the family, on the roads or in the workplace, or indirectly as societal costs.

The responsibility of the state to take care of alcoholics is justified on three grounds. First, alcoholism is a disease and therefore not wholly dependent on the individual's free will:

> *L04 Lauri(M):894* it's a contradiction, because you would think that alcoholism is your own fault, and if somebody gets a heart condition or something in the kidneys, well that's not of your own making. But people discriminate against alcoholism say, is it right that enormous amounts of money is spent on that when it is your own fault. But then it is . . . it is a disease and it is not up to your own will it's up to chemical reactions or physiology, so I mean it is right that this problem is taken care of by society.

Secondly, even if alcoholism is partly incurable and also a moral weakness, it nevertheless causes suffering to others, and this may be reduced by investing public money in treatment:

L04 Leena (F):868 is it any good that alcoholics have been for so long treated in this country, and it's expensive too . . . but when you think of it if there is no money put into this, you'll see how there will be trouble indirectly, other people will have to suffer, maybe indirect benefits will follow [from treatment] even if the sick person did not recover. . . .

Thirdly, alcoholism as such is a cost burden to the health care system, and should therefore be prevented or otherwise controlled:

L02 Jussi (M):384 there was this TV programme, they talked about how much a liver transplant costs, that's 500 000, half-a-million, I don't know how many of these are done . . . in this town but when the bill comes to the city, to society, well that's an expensive liver if it's put to the same use as the old one.

The welfare state approach faces a dilemma. Public intervention into private consumer behaviour is believed to be inefficient and often dysfunctional, even if justified from the public health perspective. In our groups, price policy was felt to be the most acceptable one, on grounds of both efficacy and justice. Taxing alcohol was considered to be just because through taxes heavy drinkers cover part of the cost burden they cause to society, much like in the case of environmental problems.

The second pattern of argumentation was the neoliberal or libertarian idea that everybody should be responsible for him- or herself and that others should not be bothered with external controls such as heavy taxation or limited availability. It, too, contests the idea that the state – or for that matter anyone or any institution – might have moral superiority over individuals. The two groups of journalists (Groups 1 and 3) and one group of cultural personalities (Group 4) who represented this view, believed alcoholism to be an individual disease in the sense that it is hereditary, a disposition of the personality, but most of all a disease of the will and therefore a moral responsibility. The bottom of the problem is not signalled by loss of health or of social ties but by the loss of free will. The most serious alcoholic is the one who is not able to decide whether or not he or she wants to drink. From the social point of view, self-induced health problems are not relevant:

L01 Harri (M): 623 I think cirrhosis is not even a problem, just like lung cancer is not a problem. . . .

The thrust of this argument was that public measures re-
stricting the availability of alcohol negatively affect individuals'
competence to drink sensibly, and are therefore harmful to
society. This is a version of the 'forbidden fruit' argument but
has this new line: it is not that interdictions attract transgression but rather that they are an obstacle to individuals' own
competence to enjoy and control their alcohol use, and therefore they obstruct the civilization process which otherwise is
going on in society. In all these groups the idea of moderniz-
ing drinking patterns was very strongly emphasized.

In a later group (Group 5) we found a third approach, also
libertarian in its antipathy towards public alcohol control, but
distinct from the other two in one respect. Whereas both the
welfare state approach and the libertarian approach share the
view that nobody should or can have moral responsibility for
other people's behaviour, this other version of liberalism is
based on the idea that ordinary people are not mature enough
to handle alcohol without moral supervision. The objection to
state control was not that it is not needed; instead, it should be
returned to the (patriarchal) family. The 'socialist' model, where
the state has taken up the moral functions of the family, leads
to moral decay.

This understanding of the role of public powers in treating and preventing alcohol problems was individualistic on the
grounds that everybody should pay his or her own way rather
than depend on others. Thus, the objections to treating alcoholism – defined as addiction and disease – in public hospitals
was quite straightforward:

L05 PS(M):347 What should be done to alcoholics?

L05 Hannu (M):348 The same as to the Government: send
them to a logging camp (laughter).

L05 Mauri(M): 352 . . . the logging camp idea sounds good,
as I said before loitering is the mother of all alcoholics, when
people have something meaningful to do and they have other
businesses than just thinking about how to spend their day
they'll leave all other stuff aside, yes the logging camp is quite
a practical idea to put it roughly.

However, people defending this approach did not deny the moral superiority that the state might have over citizens:

L05 Hannu (M) you should think about the culture and about the kind of people. Finnish people have become used to obey and observe a strong central government under Swedish rule, then under Russia they picked up Russian habits like drinking. Finnish people don't seem to have the manners and even if you should give them responsibility you can't and then of course think about young people . . . if you let them decide like about smoking that's abandoning them.

Even the classical individualists were in favour of liberalizing wine sales moderately ('special counters in qualified grocery stores'), but then they underlined the importance of authority in the family:

L05 Reijo (M):376 I'm one of those who'd like to defend wine departments in general grocery stores. We've forgotten in Finland, it became a fashion to belittle the role of the family in the alcohol question as well, it was some kind of socialist East German model that children were taken out of the cradle straight to kindergartens. I wish we'd get back to the old safe society where the home had responsibilities. Somehow I like to be old-fashioned in this that the right ways in alcohol-related matters come from the family . . . in principle I'm against norms and strict control by society and that's why I said that wine policy should be liberalized.

The suspicion felt towards the state was not so much based on conceptions of universal sovereignty of individuals; it was rather a criticism of the idea that the modern welfare state could take over functions that in classical bourgeois society have been invested in the family.

5. DEFENDING THE PUBLIC GOOD

One of the groups where the total consumption theory was at least partly accepted consisted of municipal administrators and experts in local health and social affairs (Group 2).

The enunciative position (Sulkunen and Törrönen, forthcoming/b) adopted in this group towards society was constructed

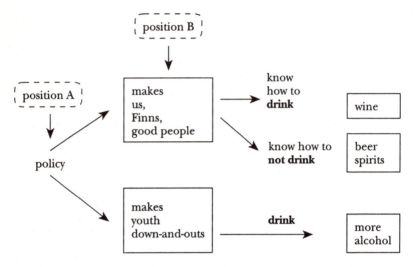

Figure 4.1   Causal structure of argumentation on alcohol policy

on the projection of 'us' as influential and socially responsible members of society. In the feedback session an analysis was presented to participants based on Fig. 4.1. When causal effects of alcohol policy measures are looked at from the point of view of consumers, they are often divided into two kinds. Effects on 'us' influence our competence to enjoy drinking and to control ourselves. 'We' are therefore seen to be modalized persons, equipped with competence (the modal capacity of knowing how to drink), while policy effects on 'others' may be direct so that 'they' simply react, for example drink themselves to an early death, if availability is improved (Sulkunen 1992). However, this group was looking at alcohol policy from the point of view of policy makers, instead of consumers or citizens:

> *LFBK02 PS:* this group places itself here [Fig. 4.1 position A] and not here [Fig. 4.1 position B], it's like the point of view of the policymakers on the matter here in this group, and this is different from many of the other groups in our study.

The analysis was accepted but reflectively, and with a good-humoured sense of irony:

> *LFBK02 Petri(M):* well, are we not in quite an important post in society (laughter).

LFBK02 Leo(M): or at least we should be able to give advice to others as to how they should go about it so that . . .

LFBK02 Petri(M): you're right, it's really a calling for us to take up that role, isn't it?

LFBK02 Anne(F): that's right.

In this group, too, the welfare state model of alcohol policy oriented to the control of total consumption was met with reservations. Too much control and care will reduce individuals' sense of self-responsibility and could lead to a laxity in keeping one's way of life within reasonable limits. But the reservation was still in line with the projection of 'us' as powerful representatives of the society at large:

LFBK02 Petri(M): aren't we talking here precisely about the problem of the consequences of alcohol effects, I mean if this bloke just dies then OK that's his problem, but when it causes problems to society, when society has taken on the responsibility to attend to all his needs, putting him into intensive care and using all the knowledge and technology we have, doing everything to keep him alive, even though this bloke himself gives sod all to living in this world, just couldn't care less, then you could ask whether we're actually giving sufficient opportunity to making these choices.

In another group (Group 4) the ARF video was an effective intervention and changed the participants' point of view from the one of a consumer to the one of defending the public good. In the first interview session most of them unquestionably supported the neoliberal view, arguing that in 'Continental Europe', where alcohol trade is free, there are fewer problems because controls do not obstruct consumers' competence in enjoying the pleasures of drinking. In this group the ARF video was exceptionally shown only in the feedback session.

LFBK04 Minna(F): it's quite interesting that this availability theory at least as far as I know has not been discussed in public to the same extent as we've talked about liberalization, at least I haven't heard anything, that if this is the result that these problems increase that the boil gets bigger and wider that was used to describe this [the skewed statistical distribution of alcohol consumption – PS] I think that's pretty shocking.

LFBK04 PS(M): how in general do you feel, how awk-
ward is this problem if you think that alcohol causes costs in
society and causes suffering and in a sense we all agree that
society must carry some responsibility, but on the other hand
this conflicts with the freedom of individuals, how do you
see this?

LFBK04 Minna(F): well on this basis I must say one is inclined to take the position that if it really gets out of control
to that extent, but I mean if we think of French habits, that's
been presented like they say that they've got lots of alcoholics
but it's still not everything's free there, the picture that's presented to us is too rosy, we haven't been given all the facts,
I don't know who wants to give this sort of picture.

Minna looks at policy information from the point of view of
a suspicious citizen, and later adds, in response to the interviewer's remark that availability control may contradict individual freedom:

LFBK04 Minna(F): well yes in a sense it does but if you
think of health whether in terms of health in society or physical health in individuals, then if its necessary from that point
of view then I would say that if you're unable to look after
yourself then society should step in and set things straight.

Other members of this group agreed, but great ambivalence
continued on individuals' own responsibility and right to demand care, especially in cases where smoking has damaged one's
health. Again we can see that support for control policy is easy
as long as it can be interpreted to be selectively directed at
'them' (smokers, those who cannot take care of themselves),
or when it is looked at from the point of view of 'the public
good'.

6. CULTURAL INTERMEDIARIES[2]

Some neoliberals reacted to the ARF video by denying its validity. In a group of journalists one participant formulated this
criticism as follows:

LFBK03 Helena(N):1004 the latter at least was a mess, it confused availability and in general drinking and the consequences of drinking, it was all mixed up, it wasn't just availability theory, it mixed it all up, is booze available, is booze used, then it just stated that where people drink more booze there's more alcohol, I mean that's clear, but as far as I can see that had nothing to do with if it's readily available, then it's used more, there was no proof of that. . . .

LFBK03 Maria(N):1009 the experience we have is that restrictions, they do not solve the problem anyway.

LFBK03 Susanna(N):1010 it makes it into a forbidden fruit, and we all know how tempting that can be.

LFBK03 Susanna(N):1016 everything, like to me this cartoon thing was absolutely awful like from above to below, let auntie explain this to everyone.

LFBK03 Eeva(N):1017 like to a child.

LFBK03 Helena(N):1018 but it was for Americans and they don't understand anything.

This is an example of the general ambivalence towards expert knowledge that is typical of contemporary risk society (Beck 1992; Sulkunen 1996). We are dependent on research for rational action and opinions, yet all knowledge is suspect of representing and promoting particular interests or ideologies. Here the participants accepted the positive correlation between total consumption and the prevalence of heavy drinking, demonstrated by researchers in the video. However, they refused to believe in the effects of availability on consumption because of its political consequences.

What is even more interesting, they did this by contrasting personal first-hand experience with the researchers' testimony, and the latter failed to convince them. They did not in fact even grant expert status to this claim ('there was no proof of that'). Although themselves specialists in information, they evaluated the video from a veridictory position (this is how it seems *vs* this is how it is) rather than from an epistemological one (this is what is believed *vs* this is what the truth is). The resulting contradiction is an illusion or – in their words – confusion, rather than an erroneous assumption that can be evaluated on the

basis of the participants' own expert competence. The veridictory stance places them on the same footing with everybody who
has experience of things, not in the position of someone whose
knowledge is superior to that of the audience. They are constructing a contract of confidence rather than building up legitimacy for their own authority (Sulkunen and Törrönen/b).

For ordinary citizens such a position would be quite expected.
However, for this group it reflects their understanding of their
role in society as journalists and explains why the position
from which they look at alcohol policy is that of an individual
consumer:

> *LFBK03 JT(M):* you also had this, like this other group
> of journalists that you started to think about things [from
> the point of view of policy objects] and you were annoyed
> that there's someone from above forcefully manipulating . . .
> in general you felt uncomfortable about sanctions, that they
> were unnecessary, restricting availability or other forms of
> control, in a sense what you were saying was that in the long
> run we should get rid of them, do you agree with this?

> *LFBK03 Susanna(F):* well yes I do.

> *LFBK03 Eeva(F):* absolutely yes.

This enunciative position first seemed odd to us, because the
participants in this group were journalists, not ordinary citizens,
and they were invited to the study in this very capacity. In mass
society theory it is often argued that journalists tend to see themselves as independent professionals who see themselves as informed gatekeepers rather than as advocates (Janowicz 1975).
Their legitimacy is based on their identity as representatives of
the public good instead of particular interests or points of view.

In the feedback discussion with our journalist groups it turned
out that their conception of themselves as professionals did not
correspond to the image of informed gatekeepers or representatives of the public good:

> *LFBK03 Eeva(F):* when you said that the purpose of this
> study was to talk with opinion-formers I must say I wondered
> who am I to be an opinion-former, I mean I'm just an ordin-
> ary reporter, I don't identify with any system and I certainly
> don't feel I have any real influence in the local community
> or in society.

LFBK03 Sami(M): journalists don't make the decisions.

LFBK03 Eeva(F): not a single revolution has ever started from a paper.

They see themselves as cultural intermediaries, to use Feather-stone's (1991) term, but with an emphasis on their audience's freedom of choice rather than on their own special competence as sources of information, ideas or values. In a sense, their understanding of themselves as journalists closely resembles their relationship to alcohol policy. They identify themselves not with 'power' but with those who are subjected to it. For them the idea that they should be sources of norms or of objective information as 'educators' is completely alien, because they themselves would not like to be 'educated':

LFBK03 Sami(M): the very word education, I mean the word itself says that the educator is not going to hand out all the information there is but he has a certain object, he's trying to turn it like a ship, but we as journalists we're like the ideological ideal, we distribute information and we're not educators, to me there's a clear difference, to me what we can do via the press to influence people is to disseminate information, if we give to people all the information that we can give them, then people can freely choose on that basis what they want to do, but if we start to educate them then we're no longer journalists.

LFBK03 PS(M): so what you're saying is that, you could rephrase that by saying that your only role is one of an inter-mediary and that's the most important thing.

LFBK03 Sami(M): that's the most important job.

LFBK03 Helena(F): recognizing that we always make choices and that those choices make a difference.

The journalist's job is rendered valuable by opposing it with the role of educators in terms of the modalities of obligation. Educators are 'deontic subjects' and the behaviour and thoughts of their audience are the object of their activity. In contrast to this, journalists are helpers to their audience, who are the real subjects making choices on the basis of the ability given to them by access to unconstrained and non-selective information (Pietilä 1995, 48).

In a similar fashion the other group of journalists reacted very negatively to an American educational video on alcohol and traffic that was shown to them in the first interview session:

LFBK01 PS(M):161 could I suggest my own interpretation here . . . you said that this video seemed infantile to you, it was associated with a children's programme which in a sense is annoying to adults, being force-fed this sort of children's programme, adults can cope better with shock therapies, regard them as more interesting, realistic, on the other hand I thought whether there could be a difference here, that this American version, in a sense it suggests or offers norms rather than just information and education, like look how it enters your blood- stream and like this is not how to behave, it sort of gives you behavioural rules and as such it's an infantile approach, someone said here that we all know this that it's not necessary . . . to explain to people . . . but on the other hand . . . when this sort of emotional shock education is provided it still leaves the viewer . . . the freedom of choice that he's not told what he ought to do, he does what he does but this shows him what it can all lead to.

LFBK01 Pete(M):163 yes I can accept that idea in the sense that if this sort of forced stuff is fed to us unconsciously then. . . .

LFBK01 Harri(M):164 yes I can subscribe to that as well.

LFBK01 Pete(M):165 I might like immediately get this reaction if someone tries to force something to me, in the shock film I can make up my own mind as far as that's concerned, but to me any situation where everyone agrees, I want to find something where I could disagree, it really annoys me. . . . I'll always start to dig up for something on the other side of the coin.

It is as important for themselves as it is to their image of their audience to be able to act as subjects. Rationality is an unquestioned value but only in so far as it is modalized as (inner) competence and ability (not obstructed by outsiders' use of power) to make choices and not as obligation (imposed by others) to make the 'right' choice.

7. MORAL AUTHORITY

The group (Group 5) where the classical liberalist understanding of the role of the state was most uniformly represented consisted of five influential local businessmen, from 49 to 62 years of age, in their grey suits, talking in a moderate matter-of-fact style. In the feedback session their 'conservatism' was stressed first in the context of their understandings of the relationship between alcohol and work:

> *LFBK05 PS(M) 3:* the impression I had was that the point of view was fairly traditional . . . the one thing that particularly struck me was that even the old Weberian Protestant ethic was fairly typical, should one say a fairly reserved attitude to all forms of pleasure in general, a very strong orientation to work, so that in almost every respect work came first and everything else followed.

> *LFBK05 Jouko(M) 4:* (to his pal): hello conservative!

> *LFBK05 PS(M) 5:* although they talked a lot about this [alcohol] in the context of working life, it still didn't provide any sort of relaxation as a counterbalance to work, even after the day's work you had to earn it by going for a long run or something else, a very reserved, perhaps even puritanical attitude to everything.

> *LFBK05 Reijo(M) 28:* yes the old saying that if you work hard you have to play hard, that didn't really come out here.

The researchers explained what they meant by classical liberalism underlying the differences between this group's understandings and the modern welfare state ideology or the neoliberal position. In contrast to the other two arguments, in this group the need for moral authority was stressed by some participants, but questioning the right of the state to replace the family in excercising it. The group congratulated the researchers for this interpretation, saying that the purpose of the original interview had left them perplexed but now it had become clear.

Conservatism was for this group almost a matter of pride, not something they would rather have secluded from sight. But it was not an ideological engagement either. They stood aside, talking about 'the Finns' as if they were not Finns themselves,

and their own uniformity in the interview was thought to be a
'coincidence', not a conscious and reflected matter of principle:

> *LFBK05 Reijo(M):12* the observations you had here, these
> that pointed to puritanism ... I don't know how you can gen-
> eralize this but the group we had here. . . .

> *LFBK05 Jouko(M):13* it happened to be really conservative
> ... I mean all of these blokes, they're all different of course,
> but it just happened that their thoughts happened to be
> along similar lines here.

8. POLITICAL IDEOLOGY VERSUS INDIVIDUAL CHOICE

One of the key themes in mass society theory has been that political doctrines become inconsistent and commitment to them
becomes weak. In our groups this was reflected in a lack of
correspondence between political engagement and ideas about
control policy: people took positions within and between the
three schemes we outlined – the modern welfare state, neoliberalism and classical liberalism – either arbitrarily or in the
context of their specific roles in society, as functionaries, journalists, employers, etc. This flexibility was striking in a group of
politicians (Group 6) whom we interviewed in a late phase of
our field-work.[3] All three schemes were apparent within the
group, but not integrated to the respective political orientations
represented by the participants.

The researchers noted this:

> *L06 PS(M):20* ... this was interesting and in a sense a rather
> difficult group to analyse in that it was put together in the
> democratic diplomatic Finnish way, both sexes and all age
> groups and all well not all political persuasions but quite a
> good balance in any case and so the end result is quite a wide
> spectrum of opinions, I can't say that this group was of this
> or that opinion, but all sorts of opinions were represented. . . .

The opinions on alcohol policy were mapped on to a space defined by two axes: one opposing moral authority and individual
responsibility, the other opposing the burden to society and
individuals' private problems caused by alcohol. The map looked
like Figure 4.2. In their reactions the politicians approved their

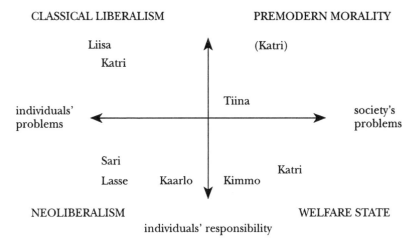

Figure 4.2 Alcohol policy views in Group 6 (Members of the City Council)

Liisa 38, Conservative, attorney
Katri 42, Christian Party, nurse
Lasse 63, Left Federation, retired construction painter, entrepreneur
Tiina 60, Green Party, teacher
Kimmo 23, Social Democrat, student
Sari 25, Conservative, student
Kaarlo 55, Social Democrat, journalist, local bank manager, entrepreneur

placements on the map but immediately explained their positions by reference to their personal rather than ideological backgrounds. It turned out that Lasse, a representative of the Left Federation (Communist), had a long experience as an entrepreneur 'on the other side of the barricade', and he also had the 'highest taxed income' among the City Council Members, which explains his anti-paternalistic attitude. Katri referred to her job as a nurse, which has shown her that

> *LFBK06 Katri(F):* ... yes alcohol really is a public-health problem, it's a big public health problem, perhaps it's my professional background why I speak about these things in this manner.

Probed on the ideological position of the Christian Party, she was unwilling to accept the idea that her alcohol policy views were related to moral condemnation of drinking, which would

represent a stand in the figure that is called 'premodern morality'. The party line, she insisted, was based on the view that
healthy lifestyles are the basis of their critical attitude to liberalizing alcohol sales. She is not a drinker but does not object to
other people having fun if it remains within appropriate limits.

In a similar fashion Liisa, a Conservative attorney, explained
her position by reference to her professional experience:

> *LFBK06 Liisa(F):* well a lot of it's this that because I see
> a lot of these things on the job, crime cases . . . alcohol is
> involved and not just in adolescents' cases, I mean for them
> it's involved in most of their cases in one way or another, and
> then I have a lot of family law cases, again alcohol figures in
> one way or another, so I mean obviously this is reflected in
> the comments I have been making here.

> *LFBK06 PS(M):* yes well but I was just thinking that this
> could also be related to this sort of traditional bourgeois ideo-
> logy this kind of classical liberalism.

> *LFBK06 Liisa(F):* mm yes of course yes there's plenty to
> chew over here (laughter) . . . it won't all go down in one bite.

The participants agreed that ideological debates have not
recently been very important in their political activities. 'It is
just these fiscal problems of the city, we've got no time for thinking about anything else, of course it would be good to talk and
think but that's not what we do these days' (Liisa).

Kaarlo (55), a Social Democrat, affirms that in his party the
ideological idealization of the 1970s is now over and has produced a hangover. The ongoing dismantling of the welfare state
is one of its effects. Party rule is no longer strong:

> *L06 Kaarlo(M):* I would say that this whole mentality of
> pulling down the welfare state . . . that we've now reached
> some sort of hangover stage that we're slowly beginning to
> give in and no longer sticking so firmly to these [principles]
> . . . then there's this aspect of the costs which is affecting
> things in the sense that we're forced to reform now . . . I've
> been at every party conference since 1981 and it seems to
> me that none of the decisions of earlier conferences count
> for anything, nothing of the old is sacred, we're taking a
> very short-term view on things, as long as we can cope for

the next year or so then everything's alright, we can forget our earlier principles.

Sari (25), a Conservative student, is first quite shocked about her own liberalism ('Am I now then completely without morality?') but then reflects on her position as part of a general reaction to welfare state paternalism, evokes arguments about its homo-genising effects especially in educational policy but then also recognises the drawback of neoliberal policy that it may lead to selective inequalities between school districts.

It is nothing new that politicians' stands in alcohol-related issues are free of party discipline. In Finland it is customary that when Parliament debates alcohol legislation, individual mem-bers can vote according to their conscience rather than having to adhere to their group's majority decision. Such political free-dom is usually thought necessary because parliamentarians' and their constituents' moral attitude to alcohol as such may vary and regional variations are often important.

Here we are not, however, discussing only moral attitudes to-wards alcohol as such: what is at issue is a wider question about values related to society, the state and the self that vary accord-ing to the point of view from which the politicians look at the matter. The difference in the interviewer's location on the map of arguments is not a difference in the norm-theoretical sense of values: acceptance or not of drinking as such. As mentioned above, even Katri, representative of the conservative Christian party that has a puritanistic ideological background and a tra-dition as 'the anti-alcohol party of Finland', emphasizes her approval of other people's drinking. The division between those who oppose alcohol control and those who are ready to accept it depends, first, on the position from which the person looks at these relationships, and second, how he or she understands the value of moral obligation from above as against the com-petence (of self-control) from below.

9. CONCLUSION: ENDOTACTIC VERSUS EXOTACTIC VALUE SYSTEMS

That alcohol is not on the political agenda proper does not mean that people are indifferent towards the problem. They are often confused about the way the problem should be understood and treated but they engage in discussions about it eagerly, even with some passion. They understand the public health predicament – the need to keep social health costs within bearable limits through preventive policy, which, however, tends to contradict individual responsibility and freedom of choice. Among the Lahti influentials the universalistic preventive approach that focuses on total consumption and general availability was accepted with difficulty, and mostly by those who could identify themselves as administrators or specialists with professional responsibilities to defend the public good.

But even so, the positions taken in the issue were largely arbitrary and depended on contingent factors such as professional background and to some extent age. Political ideologies were almost completely unrelated to opinions about alcohol policy.

Such contingency and arbitrariness in political issues is a key theme in the mass society theory. When commitment to political ideologies dissipates people become atomised and isolated in their individuality, falling prey to non-rational forces, emotional agitation and manipulation by the powerful through the mass media (Kornhauser 1959; Mills 1959).

Indeed public debates on alcohol issues in Finnish society, reflected in our discussions with the Lahti influentials, bear signs of the mass society syndrome. Liberalization of the alcohol control system, under the pretext of the requirements placed by our recent membership of the European Union, serves particular interests of the alcohol industries. It is supported by the major press and has not been seriously challenged by organised groups or social movements. The liberal tide in alcohol policy, even at the face of the accentuating crisis in alcohol-related health costs, could well be seen as a consequence of the end of politics in mass society.

In our interviews the mass society syndrome was reflected not only in the ideological contingency of views on alcohol policy. Also the enunciative position taken by the people who themselves are influentials, often with personal responsibility in municipal affairs, tended strongly to be that of private consumers subordinated to power and control rather than that of the powerful controllers or representatives of the public good. Even those who accepted society's preventive measures in alcohol policy often reverted to the distinction between 'us', who are competent drinkers, and 'them' who are incompetent to take care and responsibility for themselves (see also Sulkunen 1992). Control measures were seen to be acceptable and effective only if they are directed to the latter.

However, our interviews with the Lahti influentials also provides a corrective to the mass society view. First, the journalists, among whom were our most liberal interviewees, were far from the mass society model of media manipulation; if anything they were openly hostile to the idea that the media should or could influence their audience's opinions or attitudes in any other way than serving them as distributors of objective and pluralistic information. They considered themselves as cultural intermediaries, with an emphasis on providing their readers and hearers a possibility of choice, rather than on themselves as being sources of knowledge and even less of norms and values.

Secondly, in the analysis of liberalist views on alcohol policy the distinction between classical liberalism and neoliberalism is essential. The classical liberals stressed moral authority over individuals, and in this they were in fact more opposed to neoliberalist views than to the welfare state arguments, even though their practical conclusions were more in line with the former than with the latter. They stressed individuals' duty or obligation to society, whereas the welfare state and neoliberal arguments emphasised individuals' own responsibility, will and competence that were seen to be in contradiction with society's interference in alcohol consumption through restrictive controls.

Willing and competence are endotactic modalities whereas obligation is an exotactic modality (Sulkunen and Törrönen, forthcoming/a). By endotactic modalities we mean modal qualifications that derive from the subject: it is the subject who wills and knows how to drink and control her or his drinking. Obligation or duty are exotactic modalities in the sense that they are imposed on the subject from the outside.

A precise understanding of the current liberalistic thinking that is opposed to the state's role in controlling people's behaviour in the name of the public good should pay close attention to this distinction. In the traditional mass society literature (post)modern people are often seen to become excessively directed from the outside. C. Wright Mills' fear of the 'cheerful robots', or David Riesman's analysis of the 'other-directed character' striving to conformity with others in order to gain their acceptance, reflect a concern about people falling prey to manipulation or to a diffuse anxiety, in conditions where traditions have lost their regulating force and commitment to collectively maintained value systems fails. Such views seem less than convincing as an interpretation of the non-political but libertarian understandings of the individual as willing, competent and responsible self. The individual self is the endotactic centre of social life that sees any obligation from above or conformity to others as a violation of adult citizens' sovereignty and freedom. As our interviewees said about American society, the model country of individualism in popular stereotypes, tongue in cheek and fully understanding the irony:

L03 Helena(F): the whole culture is one where they have foolproof directions for everything, they've got instructions for like how to open a bottle, I mean the whole culture is so different that you can't . . .

L03 Eeva(F): it's more like a mass culture.

It is in the light of this endotactic value system that the imperative of health was seen as regards alcohol. Even those who understood drinking as a transgressive ritual thought that it was acceptable and desired in so far as it was the will of the individual and within the competence of his or her self-control. Any conformity to outside rules and regulations was seen as obstruction of these modal qualities.

NOTES

1   This kind of dichotomy was used in the analysis of our interview data and also in the feedback sessions. The theoretical inadequacies of this dichotomy are indisputable (Partanen 1991, 199–250) but for the sake of simplicity they had to be ignored in this context.

2   This section is based on Minna Pietilä's Master's thesis in sociology: ' "We set out as crusaders and realized that it is impossible" – Journalists' opinions on alcohol policy and on their professional roles in interview talk' (Pietilä 1995).

3   The following analysis is published with the permission of the persons involved.

APPENDIX TO CHAPTER 4: THE RESEARCH AND
INTERVENTION METHODS
Jukka Törrönen and Pekka Sulkunen

1. Introduction

What provided the basis for the relationship between the researchers and the voices in the field in the sociological intervention discussed above? And how did this relationship shift and
develop during the course of the research? These sorts of questions have attracted much attention in all types of action and
audience research (see Elden and Chisholm 1993; Greenwood
et al. 1993).

In a project that uses an experimental design and that aims to
produce generalizable conclusions about the effects of different policy options, the researcher's role *vis-à-vis* the field comes
close to that of a thief: he is smuggling the knowledge he has
gathered out in the field into the academic world, possibly giving it up for purposes of political decision-making. At the same
time the subject of the study is objectified, treated as a controll-
able mass (Foucault 1988; see Lupton 1995, 48–76). The guer-
rilla adopts exactly the opposite strategy: he identifies with the
interests of the community that is being researched and makes
use of his knowledge and skills to mobilize resistance at the
local level. His aim is to turn the local community into a competent subject capable of acting independently in the shadow
of more powerful forces (cf. the organic intellectual, Gramsci
1971; see Tester 1994, pp. 21–4). Further, the researcher may
also adopt the role of agent: criss-cross the field more or less at
leisure, as if in a foreign land. In this instance he will be working closely with the local people to effect the changes that the
project sponsor wants to see (Sulkunen 1991).

All these researcher roles and research designs have their
societal vocations and missions. In this project, however, we did
not take on any of these roles but that of critics. We wanted to
have a sociological intervention that calls into question the said
objectives as well as the conventional patterns of action that
both the field and the 'project' (science) adopts for itself and
imposes on others. This sort of sociological intervention comes
close to agent research. A good agent usually begins work by
analysing the field using the means of intervention. Two types

of theory are needed in this exercise: on the one hand a background theory of what this society is about in the first place, and secondly a theory of how people's statements should be analysed and interpreted (Sulkunen 1992).

Another thing that the agent and critic share is that they both regard their object of study as mobile, starting from the assumption that the voices in the field precede the researcher's gaze (Touraine 1981). However, a sociological intervention differs from agent activity in that it will not try to silence the voices in the field, to force them back into line, to put them on a pedestal; rather, the purpose is to pick them up and give them a good shake. The objective, ultimately, is to reinforce the voices in the field by providing them with the tools they need for self-reflection. This was what we wanted to do by coming back with the results within two or three weeks of the group interviews: at the feedback sessions we analysed the social identity of our opinion-formers and their position in the social structure, examined the consistency of and contradictions in their thinking, looked at alternative ways of perceiving alcohol policy and the field of social problems. The opinion-formers, for their part, confirmed those of our interpretations that they felt were right, showed where we had gone wrong, and drew attention to the places where we had stopped short in our analysis.

This kind of sociological intervention transcends the ancient dualisms we have between object and subject, theory and practice, action and structure, and so on (cf. Jordan and Yeomans 1995). It continues the tradition of dialectical, emancipatory research – with the difference that the target of emancipation comprises not only the subjects of the study but also the researchers (which explains the description of our approach as reflexive intervention).

2. Starting-Points, Main Themes and Identification of the Interviewees

What we set out to do in our study was to explore the views of local opinion-formers of alcohol as a social problem. The focus was on the problem of legitimacy: in what way and on what grounds did our opinion-formers consider it possible for them to address alcohol as a social problem from their own perspective of opinion-formers who wielded significant power in society?

Our baseline assumption was that their attitudes would depend on three factors: how they define alcohol, how they understand the social structure and how they see the relationship between public power and civil society (Sulkunen 1992).

The need for information was focused under three main themes. One concerned the ways of alcohol consumption. In Finland, patterns of alcohol use have traditionally been transgressive (Falk and Sulkunen 1983; Simpura 1993). The same still applies today, but with the continuing modernization of society people are increasingly looking upon alcohol as an everyday source of social pleasure.

The second main theme concerned views on alcohol problems. Traditionally, conceptions of alcohol have been closely interwoven with notions of cultural class differences. In Finland, views of the public prevention and treatment of alcohol problems have also shown an interesting ambivalence: on the one hand concepts of the state in modern society include the idea that all citizens are equal; on the other hand, alcohol problems are thought to be culturally and socially divided: alcohol problems do not concern adults and competent individuals, but young people and lower classes (Sulkunen 1994, Törrönen 1995).

In the case of the third main theme, that of alcohol policy, we were interested to find out how far people who regard themselves as local opinion-formers are capable of examining and willing to examine social problems from a general societal perspective rather than simply as individual citizens (cf. Holmila 1981).

In the identification of the opinion-formers we used what is known as the reputation method (Haranne 1976, 4). We started by asking the secretary of the Lahti alcohol education office to indicate two opinion-formers in town. We went to see these people and asked them in turn to say who they thought were opinion-formers in Lahti in business, in politics (and administration), in the mass media and in culture. We then went on to see the people who were mentioned at the top of each list.[1] We received new lists of names. This process continued until we reached saturation point, i.e. no new names were appearing on the lists any more. Thus the local opinion-formers identified their own closed elite network on the basis of reputations, very much in the same way as in the snowball method. The size of this network proved to be quite small, as indeed has been found in many similar studies of local power elites (see e.g. Hunter 1953): in a city with a population of 100 000, it comprised no more than some 30 people.

At the second stage we asked the top names on our lists to compile groups of six to eight people for group interviews. The groups were to include people who were active in the same area (e.g. business), who were influential, and who all know each other. Eventually we ended up with seven groups.

3. The Group Interviews[2]

The group interviews and the feedback sessions were held at the local hotel and catering college. They started in the afternoon, around 5 p.m. The group interviews lasted between three and four hours; the duration of the feedback sessions varied from 90 minutes to three hours.

The first theme covered in the group interviews concerned drinking habits. To stimulate discussion we started the interviews by showing drinking scenes from films.[3] Their purpose was both to inspire wide-ranging debate on different types of drinking habits and to facilitate the discussion by creating reference points for the exchange of opinions. As for the video scenes, they were included to make sure that each group talked about the same themes, i.e. to ensure inter-group comparability.

The idea of using video clips as a basis for conversation came from the tradition of audience and reception research that is currently very popular in cultural studies (for more on this, see Moores 1993). Our own solution to the contested issue between the semiotic approach and reception research as to whether the ultimate source of meaning is the text (video clip) or reader (viewer) is very simple. The text provides the framework and offers guidelines for the reader's signification; whereas the reader uses the interpretation repertoires he has assimilated as a resource in interpreting the texts (cf. Gilbert & Mulkay 1984). Hence a new text is created. The interpretations that the opinion-formers presented of the video clips can indeed be regarded as independent cultural products. In them they not only represent their relationship to the video clips but also construct for themselves different positions and angles on reality as they compare the clips with the real world.

There were six clips describing drinking habits and drinking situations. The first and the second scene were from the film *L'Invitation* by Claude Goretta. They show how a person called Rémy Placet arranges a party for her colleagues; it all starts pleasantly enough but in the end people are getting very drunk and the young woman gets carried away and arranges a strip-tease. The third scene was edited from the film *Un Homme et Une Femme*, by Claude Lelouche. Two single parents and their children are eating out in a restaurant. A relationship develops between the man and the woman. Alcohol has a secondary role in the scene, but as a fully natural and integral part of the meal. The fourth scene was from the film *Girl Friends* by Claudia Weill. The scene describes a group of women getting drunk and making intimate confessions among themselves. The fifth scene was in a more mythical landscape. In it a half-dressed woman, upset by a shooting incident, asks John Wayne for a whisky (*Rio Lobo* by Howard Hawks). The setting in the sixth scene was closer to reality again: a group of men who are going hunting are singing and drinking their heads off in the car (*The Deer Hunter* by Michael Cimino). This latter scene clearly articulates the transgressive type of drinking that is seen in Finnish films (the mythical triangle, see Falk and Sulkunen 1983; Sulkunen 1993). A man joins other men to leave society (control) behind and to step into nature (freedom), but in the end arrives in loneliness (existential anxiety). The role of woman on this trip is twofold: she appears either as a source of control or as an object of desire.

After each scene the opinion-formers were asked the following reception questions: (1) What happened in this episode? (2) Does this episode correspond to your own experience of alcohol use? (3) Would you have presented something differently in the episode? (4) Can you identify yourself with any of the characters? and (5) What will happen next?

There then followed a conversation on the question of how the use of alcohol at the local level resembles or differs from the scene shown in the video clips, on how the participants' own drinking habits relate to the examples shown, and on whether they think that different population groups have different drinking habits. They were also asked to tell a short story of a situation in which alcohol was consumed and in which they had been themselves involved; and to describe a society where alcohol is not used at all.

By way of an introduction to the discussion on the second main theme, i.e. views on alcohol problems, we compared alcohol problems with other local problems (unemployment, crime, environmental problems). The opinion-formers then talked about situations in which drinking is acceptable as well as situations where it is less so. Then, they were shown two clips: one scene of compulsive drinking (*Under the Volcano* by John Huston) and another describing self-destructive drinking (*La Provinciale* by Claude Goretta). The same reception questions were presented as above. These episodes also served as an introduction to the following conversation on alcohol abuse. In this section the opinion-formers were also asked to define the terms 'drunkard', 'heavy drinker' and 'alcoholic' and to consider the reasons for, prevention and treatment of alcoholism.

The third main theme of alcohol policy was introduced through educational videos (AAA's educational film *Traffic Safety and Alcohol* and ARF's educational film *Alcohol Roulette*). After the reception conversations we presented the following questions: (1) In what way should alcohol be made available for sale?; Can you give reasons for your opinion? (2) What kind of alcohol policy would you prefer to see (with a list of alcohol-policy measures shown to the participants)? (3) What kind of effects could alcohol policy have? (4) What are the reasons for alcohol-policy measures? (5) Compare alcohol and drugs: should the government and the local authorities take the same attitude towards them? (6) Who should be responsible for prevention and treatment? (7) At what level and how should alcohol problems be prevented: international, national, or the local level, or not at all? (8) Who are the most competent experts and prevention workers? (9) Is alcohol a special case; how should other public-health problems be dealt with?

Finally, to round off the meeting on a lighter note, we showed a clip from a French health education video *One Glass OK, Third Glass Welcome the Troubles*. The meeting ended with tea.

4. Data Analysis, Interpretation and Feedback

The group interviews were video- and tape-recorded; the video-recording was for the sole purpose of helping the transcriber identify who was speaking.[4] Once the transcription was completed, the material was prepared for analysis using a software package called WPindex, specifically designed for the analysis of qualitative material (Sulkunen & Kekäläinen 1992). The material was first divided into segments more or less corresponding to the turns of talk in the group discussions. These segments were then coded into theme categories. Once the material had been systematically coded, two operations followed. First, we picked out from the material relevant themes and combinations of themes for closer analysis. Secondly, we calculated frequencies for the occurrence of different coded themes as well as their relationships, taking the segments as our observation units. We call this contingency analysis (Sulkunen 1992, 167–9). This gives the researcher a clear picture as to which themes have been frequently discussed in the material (unconditional frequencies). But most importantly, contingency analysis gives us clues as to which themes are connected to each other in the interviewees' speech (conditional frequencies: for instance, we can identify the themes that have been raised in segments where both the quantity of alcohol use ($AA01) and the opposite sex ($AS03) have been discussed). For instance, when we calculated which themes the opinion-formers had talked about when they were dealing with alcohol problems, we found that types of drink were very much to the fore. This clue took us straight back to the material. It turned out that our opinion-formers did not talk about different ways of alcohol use by using the word 'alcohol', but rather such words as 'beer', 'wine', 'booze', and so on . So the result was quite banal. However, it did make clear how contingency analysis can be used for presenting questions to the material. When, in the group of male journalists, we looked at the themes that they raised in connection with the issue of alcohol policy, we found that self-control and its opposite, external control, were very prominent. This was an important clue on the road from observation to analysis and interpretation.

In the analysis proper we leaned on the so-called speech/ text interpretation theory (Sulkunen 1992). This theory proved to be an important tool of our sociological intervention. First, it helped us to analyse the way in which the opinion-formers constructed reality: what kind of categories, reasons, needs, obligations, desires, abilities and skills they projected on to reality. Secondly, the theory helped us to analyse the kind of position that opinion-formers take on reality: do they look at things from the point of view of the individual citizen, influential actor in society, or consumer in search of pleasure (see Sulkunen and Törrönen a and b)?

The transcription of the tapes, the preparation of the material and the actual analysis were all done within a very short space of time. We wanted to get back to our groups with the results within two to three weeks so that the issues discussed were still fresh in our memory.

The feedback stage was of course very much the climax of our sociological intervention. In the presentation of our results we followed the structure of the interview. In the case of the use of alcohol, the feedback revolved around the position of our opinion-formers *vis-à-vis* the mythical triangle of Finnish masculine drinking habits: Did they identify the triangle? Did they identify themselves with it? Did they take distance from it? Did they take an ironic attitude? Did they associate it with the past, with their youth? As regards the issue of alcohol problems, we focused on two points: whose was the alcohol problem according to our opinion-formers and who did they think has the responsibility for the treatment of alcohol problems? Finally, as regards the issue of alcohol policy, the feedback concentrated on the conversation around the availability theory (theory of total consumption).

5. Some Remarks on the Group Dynamics of the Feedback Sessions

The reception of the sociological intervention varied quite considerably between the different groups. The atmosphere in Group 1 (male journalists) was one of mutual confidence and openness. The journalists were amused to see how complex they were in their speech when it was unedited; they asked lots of questions; and they considered it a real discovery to hear our explanation as to how the solidarity of the male group on their mythical trip to inebriation is empty underneath the surface and leads eventually, at the end of the evening, to a cosmic experience of loneliness. Harri remembered immediately how some while ago on a crossing he had indeed staggered along the corridors of the ship all on his own. And Pete admitted to several times experiencing existential anxiety on the last legs of his trips to drunkenness.

The dialogue with the group of civil servants (Group 2) remained more distant. There was also some obvious internal friction within this group. According to Anne, the only woman in the group, ours was an emphatically masculine perspective: we completely silenced the voice of her and other women. She challenged many of our interpretations by saying that that is perhaps how men see things, but women don't; and at the end of the session she insisted that a group of female civil servants be called together to talk about the same themes.[5] There were also other tensions. These had to do above all with the interpretation of the concepts of 'risk society' and 'real life'. Reacting to our interpretation that the group members felt they were living in a risk society which stresses the meaning of choices and the artificiality of life, Vilho said that 'life has always involved taking risks. In the old days . . . there was no one there who forced you to go bear hunting. But even so they all did'; and Otto followed: 'yes and earlier there were nothing but risks; now at least we have a choice (laughter)'. There was also some resistance to the description of life as artificial: Petri stressed that 'I must say I can't really swallow that argument, that we don't have the option of a real, genuine life'; and Anne concurred: 'I'm pleased you said that because I was thinking that I can't accept that either'. However, these tensions did not entirely knock the bottom out of our intervention but rather highlighted useful points from which to pick up the dialogue. The tensions also made it clear how a sociological intervention addresses multiple levels: (1) how things can be perceived in general, (2) the opinion-formers' group culture and way of life, and (3) their self-identification.

The dialogue with the third group (journalists) was far more relaxed and laid-back. In this group, too, there was a gender imbalance, this time in favour of women. Not that this bothered Sami, the only man in the group; quite on the contrary, he clearly enjoyed being accepted by the women and being regarded as a sensitive man. In general the journalists seemed to enjoy for once being on the other side of the microphone, under the spotlight. They clearly enjoyed making their critical assessments of how we had interpreted their speech, contextualizing our interpretations openly to their own perspective of individualist liberalism. The level of mutual confidence between the researchers and the journalists was so high that we could take our intervention to the limit: we could safely be quite provocative in questioning their views and in offering them alternative conceptualizations without any risk of causing a conflict. When we said that they actually had no firm position on alcohol problems and alcohol policy at all, they took this as a compliment: but of course that is what is expected of journalists: they mustn't have any fixed views on anything, as Helena summarized. Later it turned out that taking a position would mean moralizing, regarding some way of life as better than another, which in turn would be in conflict with their journalist-identity, the function of 'neutral' mediation of information, and would lead to a Fascist attitude, to manipulation of the readership.

The fourth group of cultural opinion-formers consisted of wise old artists and cultural administrators. Again there was a strong sense of mutual confidence in our dialogue, but it was nevertheless far more formal than in the previous group. The sociological intervention, on the other hand, was clearly successful. In the case of one group member, Minna, it actually led to some sort of catharsis, inspiring a completely different view on both the transgressive male drinking culture and alcohol policy. She was surprised to find, firstly, that even in more cultivated circles people drank so heavily: 'I must say I was quite surprised because I knew these men [in the group], and finding that they could describe this as if it were their own experience'. Secondly, Minna's earlier views were completely shattered by the video *Alcohol Roulette* in which scientists described the availability theory and considered its social implications (in this group the video was shown exceptionally in connection with the feedback session). Before the video Minna had been of the opinion that alcohol should be made more readily available; but afterwards she began to doubt that position and in the end decided she was in favour of a restrictive alcohol policy after all. As regards the role of the intervention, Minna commented that it did made her think about the justification of her own positions.

The group dynamics with opinion-formers representing business life (Group 5) was very distinctive. These people sat in their chairs, looking very firm and dignified, listening to what we had to say about them. Having themselves presented long monologues in the group interviews, speaking as if their overhearers (Goffman 1981) consisted of their 200 employees, they now expected the researchers to do the same. They did not enter into a dialogue with us but simply confirmed in short comments the validity of our interpretations. As such they were very pleased with what they heard and also surprised to see us produce such a coherent and accurate description on the basis of what seemed to be a rather meandering discussion around more or less unconnected film clips.

In the case of politicians (Group 6) our sociological intervention assumed features of 'ideology therapy'. The politicians appeared to be quite lost in terms of how society should be built and how different value premises should be weighed within society. The breakdown of ideologies (party positions), the drying up of social movements, the individualization of opinions was all too clearly to be seen in their speech. The ongoing recession seemed very much to restrict their freedom of movement in political decision-making. That is why in the feedback session they were eager to know where exactly they stood with their views, how it was possible to give complete interpretations to social issues, what kind of options are available for future action. This was, in other words, fertile ground indeed for an intervention, and the feedback session turned out to be very intensive. The conversation flowed freely in an electric atmosphere.

But things don't always go as you hope they would. Only one single person came to the feedback session for the second group of cultural opinion-formers (Group 7). Perhaps, after the long winter, the brilliant sunshine outdoors was too much.

NOTES

1   We wish to thank Kari Haavisto for his invaluable help in drawing up the lists and in setting up the contacts.
2   The group interviews can be described as semi-structured (for more on group interviews as a research method, see Morgan (ed.) 1993, Morgan 1998).
3   THE FILMS SHOWN
    Scenes describing drinking habits
    (1) Scenes 1 and 2: *L'Invitation.* 1973. Director: Claude Goretta. Cast: Michel Robin, Jean-Luc Bideau, Jean Champion, Pierre Collet, Corinne Coderey, Rosine Rochette, Jacques Rispal, Neige Dolski, Cécile Vassort,

François Simon, Lucie Avenay, William Jacques, Roger Jendely, Gilbert Costa.

(2) Scene 3: *Un Homme et Une Femme.* 1966. Director: Claude Lelouche. Cast: Anouk Aimée, Jean-Louis Trintignant.

(3) Scene 4: *Girl Friends.* 1978. Director: Claudia Weill. Cast: Melanie Mayron, Anita Skinner.

(4) Scene 5: *Rio Lobo.* 1970. Director: Howard Hawks. Cast: John Wayne, Jorge Rivero, Jennifer O'Neill.

(5) Scene 6: *The Deer Hunter.* 1978. Director: Michael Cimino. Cast: Robert de Niro, John Gazale, John Savage, Christopher Walken, George Dzundza, Chuck Aspegren.

Scenes describing problem-drinking

(1) Scene 7: *La Provinciale.* 1980. Director: Claude Goretta. Cast: Nathalie Baye, Angela Winkler, Bruno Ganz, Dominique Paturel.

(2) Scene 8: *Under the Volcano.* 1984. Director: John Huston. Cast: Albert Finney, Jacqueline Bisset, Anthony Andrews.

Videos on alcohol education and policy

(1) Scene 9: *Traffic Safety and Alcohol,* AAA, USA 1978, for senior adults.

(2) Scene 10: *Alcohol Roulette,* ARF, Toronto 1983, for adults and senior adults.

Light relief

Un verre ça va, trois verres . . . bonjour les dégats!. CFES, France 1984.

4   We wish to thank Leena Jaatinen who did the transcriptions very quickly and competently.

5   We decided not to assemble a separate group of leading female civil servants. However, the two groups of cultural opinion-formers did include a number of women representing cultural administration.

Part II
Reflexive Intervention

5 The Educational Activities
Marja Holmila

1. INTRODUCTION

Alcohol education is among the most widely used tools in the primary prevention of alcohol-related problems. It is assumed that providing people with information about alcohol and about the risks related with drinking will contribute to the formation of attitudes that are unfavourable toward drinking, which in turn will contribute to changes in drinking behaviour. Much hope has been invested in education, and in many countries such efforts use up more public funds than any other preventive methods. A general conclusion that can be drawn from previous reviews is that alcohol education educates but education alone rarely influences behaviour. However, there is evidence to support a contributory effect. Where attempts to educate that employ either media or small group settings have been supplemented with other influences, or have supplemented environmental strategies, more evidence of efficacy has been found. Education strategies, in order to have any chance of effectiveness, need to be entwined with other strategies, especially those which more directly impact on the drinker's environment. When evaluated in isolation the popular, and often well resourced interventions of school-based education and moderation mass media campaigns have not been found to be effective (Edwards et al., 1994, p.180).

One reason for the limited success of alcohol education is that it does not operate in a vacuum. Alcohol education competes against a great many messages that promote the use of alcohol. The primary source of pro-alcohol messages is social reality itself, the widespread and visible availability of alcoholic beverages, and the presence and acceptability of alcohol in a variety of everyday situations and contexts. The influence of experience on people's conceptions of health-related issues tends to be more powerful than that of information provision.

Wise counsel given by alcohol educators is often discredited by personal experiences of social norms and behaviours (Montonen 1995a).

In spite of the often depressing research results on the effectiveness of alcohol education, it would, however, have seemed impossible to carry out a community project without various forms of communication. Simply informing the public about the intended and ongoing activities can be seen as education, but other types and more targeted information were also used.

One can find in the literature a host of recommendations aimed at improving the efficacy of alcohol education (see Montonen 1995a). According to Montonen, two central themes – 'comprehensiveness' and 'responsivity' can be discerned. Both reflect an acknowledgement that the success of alcohol education depends more on the target group's pre-existing interests and motivations, and the social and cultural environment rather than on the designs of educational interventions as such. Educational interventions are unlikely to make much difference unless the messages have some personal relevance to the recipients, and unless the recommended actions are feasible within the context of the recipients' everyday lives and receive support from their social environment.

'Comprehensiveness' means, in brief, that educational campaigns and programmes need to be supported by interpersonal interaction, for instance in the form of counselling or group activities, or to be incorporated in wider community-level prevention initiatives aimed at changing social and environmental factors. 'Responsivity' means that educational interventions need to start from the experiences, needs and interests of their audiences, and convince the audiences that the information, advice and suggestions that are presented will make a positive contribution to their lives (Montonen 1995a).

The educational component of Lahti Project was a product of several activists, and was not planned coherently in advance. Major ideas were often discussed in groups of activists and between the activists and the researchers, but the final output was a combination of preset goals and ideas, chance and individual initiative. This chapter will describe briefly the educational component of the project (see Table 5.1). Evaluation of its impact is discussed in Chapter 10.

Table 5.1   The educational activities in the Lahti project

Type	Local participants	Aims	Methods
Major happenings (Liquor Weeks, 'On the Wagon' Weeks)	Voluntary organizations, professionals and institutions	Wide visibility, unspecified audience	Use of a multitude of forms, contents and channels
Targeted happenings ('Is everything OK?', Drink-driving, Safety on the Lakes)	Specific local organizations and institutions	Wide visibility, specified audience	Use of printed material, and professional teaching
Produced materials	Project participants	Supporting the other forms of project activity articles	Leaflets, videos and posters
Media advocacy	All the local media channels	Information on the project, activating the media professionals	Personal contacts and mutual assistance

2. MAJOR HAPPENINGS

Liquor Weeks

The chief organizers of the Liquor Weeks were the local library and the national alcohol education unit. This educational event differed from the other events in the respect of research involvement – the idea came from a researcher (Marjatta Montonen) and the Weeks had been tested earlier in another town before organizing them in Lahti. The core of the Liquor Weeks was a selection of information materials placed at the public's disposal in the public library either as giveaways (booklets and magazines) or as items that could be borrowed for a week or two (books and videos). The exhibition covered a broad array of alcohol-related topics, ranging from product information to health information, drinking problems, treatment, and self-control of drinking. The material varied from glossy wine magazines to the *Big Book of Alcoholics Anonymous.*

The Liquor Weeks were an attempt to follow the idea of responsivity. The alcohol-related interests and information needs among any given population are usually not known unless researched, but there is good reason to assume that they are varied. Accordingly, one of the key ideas of the Weeks was to offer something to everyone. There exists a wealth of alcohol information materials produced by statutory agencies, voluntary organizations and commercial publishers; the exhibition displayed what was available, in the hope that members of the public might be able to find those that best matched their interests and perceived needs for information. Those members of the audience who have an active interest in drug and health-related issues tend to find the informational content familiar, superficial and too general. For this reason the exhibition varied not only in 'breadth' but also in 'depth': while booklets, magazines and videos offered more general and easily approachable content, the books were meant to offer deeper information to those who wanted to concentrate on them.

One of the organizers' ideas was that information needs to be centrally located so the public has easy access to it. In Finland the public library is a place where a majority of local people are likely to stumble across alcohol information in the ordinary course of their daily lives. The Finns are among the world's most avid library users. According to the statistics for 1993, 55 per cent of the inhabitants of Lahti were registered as borrowers, and if those who use libraries for listening to music, reading newspapers or just browsing are included, it has been estimated that 60 per cent of the population in Finland are library users.

It was thought that an exhibition set up in the library would play down the moralism often associated with alcohol issues – a possible barrier to information seeking. The Weeks were extended to cover also non-problematic aspects of alcohol use. By focusing simultaneously on both risks and pleasures related to drinking the Weeks attempted to show that the risks are located on the same continuum of drinking habits as the pleasures, and are to some degree present in every alcohol consumer's life. The idea of showing 'both sides of the coin' was emphasized as the leading principle of the whole event when the Weeks were presented to the media, and through them to the public. Efforts were made to inform the local and regional media about the event, and to incite journalists to cover the Liquor Weeks and related issues.

The opening ceremony was a high-profile event, including a speech by an assistant mayor, music performances and refreshments. Alcohol-free beer provided by a local brewery was served to the public throughout the opening day; students from the hotel and restaurant school took care of the practical arrangements.

The library assembled a collection of alcohol-related literature and several thematic exhibitions were set up in the library by the librarians and the national alcohol education unit. These exhibitions provided information on the effects of drinking on health, on treatment services, on history of alcohol education and history of the local temperance movement, on calorie content of different drinks and on heavy drinking. Four thematic catalogues were produced on the alcohol- and drug-related literature available in the city's libraries. Several public events were arranged in the lecture hall including concerts, poetry readings and lectures. During the Weeks around 50 000 visits were registered in the library. Approximately 34 300 copies of booklets and magazines, and approximately 20 000 anti-drink-driving information cards were distributed. The number of books and videos borrowed from the exhibition was about 320. A brochure listing all the alcohol and drug related treatment and support services in Lahti was picked up by 2500 persons.

Feedback from the public was overwhelmingly positive. Even if there was a lot to see besides the core materials, three out of four commentators on the exhibition mentioned the booklets and magazines as the most interesting component of the programme. The selection was praised for being many-sided, interesting and available free of charge.

The Liquor Weeks were also visited by teachers and employees of health or social services. For these professionals working with alcohol and drug education and prevention, the exhibition provided a rare opportunity to see on one occasion the variety of materials that are available and to select some for later use. In that sense this happening provided a two-step flow of information in the community.

'On the Wagon' Weeks

These happenings were aimed at activating local organizations and reaching out to the general public. The theme for the weeks was adopted from a Finnish tradition of campaigning in a collective and competitive manner for a sober month each year. For instance, many individuals keep each February alcohol-free and this is a legitimate reason for refusing a drink.

Organizing the Weeks involved many people in Lahti. More than 30 representatives from different organizations or institutes came to the planning meeting. Among the voluntary organizations were sport clubs, Lions Ladies, an AIDS centre, the church, youth organizations, the amateur theatre Timotei, a temperance organization, the women's home economics club Marttas, and a Christian association running a centre for the homeless. The professionals or institutes that had previously been engaged in the Lahti project were also involved, including the hotel and restaurant school, the department of health, the youth workers, the police, the local brewery and Alko's local store.

The Weeks were advertised visibly by posters downtown, in the local newspapers and on the radio. An advertisement appeared in the main papers and a paid announcement was read over the radio. A press conference was also arranged. The organizations spread the information to their members, too. The youth clubs made 4000 badges with the Week's symbol and sold them.

The main activity of the Weeks took place in the central shopping mall. Tables were set up for a bazaar in a space hired from the shopkeepers. For two weeks, there were ongoing activities in the bazaar. Each of the organizations had their programme presented, and in addition to that, some message related to the theme of the week. The themes ranged from the women's club's theme 'Alcohol and Calories' to the theme 'Have a Sober Day' chosen by the centre for the homeless.

One could buy some products in the bazaar, or pick up free material on alcohol and its dangers. The posters had pictures and texts, and a video featured alcohol education material. Most important, however, were the persons assigned to the tables. Many discussions took place between them and the passers-by. The youth workers especially and the young men representing the sport clubs inspired many young people to stop for a chat. The middle-aged and older people, on the other hand, formed a continuous queue for the free blood-pressure measurement which was provided by the two nursing students hired as assistants for the weeks.

The street theatre group 'Källi' had two performances. They dressed up for a fashion show, entitled 'Different stages of drinking', and walked around the shopping mall with white noses attached to their faces. A small conflict arose when they formed an honour guard in front of the liquor store, and clapped their hands for each customer leaving the shop. Someone complained, and they were told to leave.

On a few days, free non-alcohol drinks were served at the bazaar. The drinks were provided by the local brewery and the Alko's outlet. The servers were students at the hotel and restaurant school. This service was a major attraction, which enticed people to stop and have a look at the bazaar.

Even if the bazaar was the focal point of the activities, the weeks were not limited to that. There were smaller exhibitions in the libraries and the unemployed persons' activity centre. Lectures were arranged one evening for parents and at the actvity centre for the unemployed. The A-clinic held an open house for a day. The youth houses arranged a carnival. Two firms selling cars had a weekend happening promoting sobriety on the road. The local brewery made coasters promoting non-alcoholic beer and lower limits for risky drinking, and these were given to customers in the city's restaurants.

The impersonal contacts of the shopping mall exhibition were supplemented by some face-to-face contacts. An announcement was published in the local newspaper that during two days, 25- to 55-year-old men and women could have their blood tests taken and analysed for GGT gamma-glutamyl-transferase, free of charge, in the central health-care centre. Feedback on the test results was given by telephone. A total of 156 persons (101 men and 55 women) had their blood sample analysed, and

30 of them had an advanced GGT level. During the telephone conversation, about half of them reported heavy alcohol use. In addition, some of those whose blood sample was normal were heavy drinkers. The nurse giving the feedback characterized her contacts with the people as ideal for intervention – relaxed, good-humoured and practical. 'On the Wagon' Weeks had encouraged people to think about their drinking, and the individual act of having your blood tested offered people a forum for doing something about it.

The Weeks also engaged many young people in essay writing and painting. Teachers in colleges and vocational schools were contacted by letter asking them and their pupils to take part in an essay competition on five given topics. Awards would be given for the three best essays. The reviewing team consisted of a newspaper editor, a teacher and two youth workers. There were 100 essays submitted to this competition. Another competition was arranged for designing the poster for the weeks. A panel consisting of local artists selected the winner.

The city council was asked to take part in the Weeks by abstaining from serving alcoholic drinks during its receptions. The proposal was warmly welcomed but the formulation was softened into 'strives to abstain from serving alcoholic drinks'.

The Weeks gained a very high visibility in the city. As many as 92 per cent of the respondents in a survey conducted immediately after the Weeks said they remembered having seen or heard something about the Weeks, and 60 per cent said the same half a year later (see Chapter 10).

3. TARGETED HAPPENINGS

'Is Everything OK?'

The third and last major happening during the project was the one arranged by the local coordinator and the students in the Lahti nursing school. It took place in the spring of 1995. Planning, carrying out and reporting on it was a diploma project for the students of one class; the class worked in close cooperation with the wider project, and the project also gave the Weeks some financial support.

The happening concentrated on educating adolescents and

their parents. The action took place in several locations. In five schools the nursing students set up an educational happening with exhibitions, games and competitions on specific themes. The themes were alcohol and sexual feelings, alcohol and family, first-aid, mixing alcohol and drugs and facts about alcohol. A bus circulated around the city distributing information. Well-known local personalities gave speeches on the topic 'Alcohol and Feelings' on the city market square. A drawing competition was arranged in the primary schools.

Besides its target group, the young people in Lahti, the project also increased the level of knowledge among the nursing students, who had to learn about alcohol and how to respond to the problems created by drinking.

Drinking and Driving

The education regarding drinking and driving had three outlets: the driving schools, voluntary driving and boating associations and car dealerships. In cooperation with these three parties, educational events were organized and/or educational material was distributed.

The driving schools provided some education on alcohol and drugs. During the project an additional leaflet was given to each pupil, and in order to emphasize the importance of staying sober while driving, each pupil was given a bottle of non-alcohol beer as a gift from the local beer company.

Bigger campaigns were arranged together with the voluntary driving association whose street volunteers distributed educational material. They could be easily identified by the anti-drinking sticker attached on their car window. The biggest car dealerships took part in the 'On the Wagon' Weeks by having an anti-drink-driving day on their premises.

4. PRODUCED MATERIALS

The Lahti project did not concentrate on producing new educational material. Often different happenings or meetings were supported by delivering existing materials. Three separate leaflets were produced during the project. One of them was targeted to adolescents and their parents, one to the parents of nursery schoolchildren, and one to heavy drinkers (see Appendix 2). In addition, the local participants produced several posters, two videos and many articles and reports.

The leaflet *You Feel Better When You are Sober*, for the young and their parents was locally produced and funded. It contained information on the habits of the young in Lahti. It also gave factual information on alcohol and drugs, and discussed the parents' role and possibilities for them to influence their children's behaviour. The leaflet was delivered to all the schools of the area.

The results of the feedback questionnaire attached to the leaflet and given to the adolescents and through them to their parents show first of all that it is not easy to reach the parents through their children: in many cases, the children would not bring educational material home from school. On the other hand, the results that were achieved indicated that the parents appreciate various kinds of information and support in the task of educating their children about alcohol and drugs. They need to know how adolescents generally drink, how alcohol affects young people, and they need support in handling conflicts with their youngsters. The adolescents also find it interesting to read what they should expect from their parents and how the parents are supposed to act in regard to their children's drinking. Alcohol's biological impact is also unclear to many and interests them.

5. MEDIA ADVOCACY

The use of mass media to advance a social or public policy initiative has been called media advocacy (Wallack 1990). One of the ideas in the project was to try and form a link with the local media professionals, increase their interest in alcohol issues and activate them into taking up the preventive point of view in the local media. The media were approached in order to achieve coverage on preventive issues. Local press conferences were regularly arranged in connection with the events of the project. Special care was taken to ensure that all the research results obtained in the project were fed to the media. A number of individual journalists and radio editors became key persons in the process. Many journalists were also engaged in the study on the local key persons' alcohol policy opinions described in Chapter 4 and the study acted as an intervention in their alcohol policy thinking.

During the first two years, the researchers produced many descriptions on drinking habits and the harm related to drinking. The media found this material useful. It was also interested in the major happenings that took place in the locality, and published news articles based on them. The editors very seldom, however, undertook any preventive writing on their own initiative. On the whole, the media's role in preventive efforts in the locality could perhaps be characterized as sympathetic but fairly passive. It was willing to publish either ready material or news on local action, but did not take an active stand in favour of prevention.

The reason for this is, perhaps, to be found in the way the professionals in the media define their task and their professional identity. On the basis of group discussions among journalists during the intervention study, it was possble to draw the conclusion that the journalists usually define themselves as mediators of 'pure knowledge' (Pietilä 1995). This is the professional ideal that brings with it an attitude of critical resistance toward any outside influence on their work. Results of social research were willingly published when the researcher could be quoted as the source of the information. Reports on local events were equally valid material, but they had to have the quality of 'news' – which often means that either a great number of ordinary people or some individuals with power are involved, or that the event has an interesting point of view.

The local journalists' professional ethos of being the mediators of pure knowledge is a clear contradiction of the local media's close contacts and dependence on local business (Pietilä 1995). In a preventive project, the local media could of course be used as a publisher of paid advertisements. The Lahti project paid for some advertising of the biggest happenings both in the local press and the radio, and in this connection, the preventive message was in the same category of media material as advertisements. Toward the end of the project, the contact with the media became more and more instrumental. The project bought space for advertising some events or to publish educational material, as in the case of the information on guidelines for controlling one's heavy drinking.

6. THE CONTENT OF THE EDUCATION

Most of the messages sent to the audience during the project were rather general. They aimed at increasing people's awareness of alcohol problems, of making them think about their own drinking and the drinking of those in their environment. The concrete topics were often formulated in a process together with the local participants. The project had very few pre-set ideas of how one should talk to the audience. However, a general agreement stressed the importance of a public health point of view, and the dominance of alcohol over other drugs in the Finnish culture. In that way, the focus of the education was kept in the general population rather than targeted special groups, and discussion concerning drugs other than alcohol was not given very much space.

As an exception to the general rule, special attention was given to two types of information. First of all, teaching people how to measure the amount of alcohol they consume was given special attention. Besides repeating the message that one unit of alcohol is equivalent to 12 centilitres(cl) of table wine or a restaurant portion of vodka (4 cl), the number of units in different types of commonly purchased drinks was also repeated in various contexts. The idea was to help the individual follow how much he/she was drinking. The other repeated message was the lower limit of risky drinking, both during a single occasion and during a week. The limits were given both for women (5 units per occasion and 16 units in a week) and for men (7 units per occasion and 24 units in a week). The message was published several times and through different channels, in leaflets, articles, posters and speeches. It was also a part of the health-care intervention of heavy drinkers.

7. SUMMARY

The educational processes in the Lahti project did not follow any clear pre-set plan. They developed as the process went on, and the actors behind this process were numerous. The local coordinator was particularly active, and the national unit for alcohol education was actively involved, too. The local organizations, institutions and individuals were free to carry out their ideas. The researchers had a particularly strong input in organizing the Liquor Weeks and producing the leaflet for heavy drinkers. In the other events and products the researchers had mainly the role of a discussant and a commentator. All plans were always discussed in joint meetings between the activists and some of the researchers.

Alcohol and drug education in Lahti has not been from 'those who know' to 'those who don't'. The emphasis was in bringing forward the equality of those sending the message and those receiving it. A lot of the educational activities took the form of face-to-face contacts. First of all, preparing the events meant cooperation with various individuals. The event itself often took place in a market-type surrounding, ensuring a free flow of people and information. When printed text or picture material was used, it was always in the context of wider action. Materials containing factual knowledge or aimed at increased awareness had the role of technical support for other activities.

An overall characterization of the diversified education during the project could perhaps be that the educational activities aimed at empowerment, mutual communication and increased awareness rather than at teaching people. The emphasis was in promoting the equality of all parties. However, attempts to increase people's knowledge on some facts was also included. The process was not pre-planned but developed as it went on, and education was always linked with the forms of action in the community. The lack of a clear plan of information may be seen as a weakness as well as a strength, and it was caused by chance and lack of resources rather than being a contemplated strategy.

6 Brief Intervention in Primary Health Care
Pekka Sillanaukee

1. INTRODUCTION

Alcohol-related consequences and harms are concentrated among heavy drinkers and drinking constitutes a health risk for these persons. Heavy drinking frequently leads to alcohol dependency and to a multitude of other medical, psychological and social problems. On the basis of the AUDIT questionnaire the proportion of heavy drinkers in Lahti were 18 for men and 4 per cent for women (see Table 11.7). Drinking has been considered to be the cause of a significant amount of long-term health problems when the consumption exceeds 18.5 litres in a year among men and 12.5 litres among women. Heavy drinking during one session is also risky: especially when alcohol consumption causes 1 per ml blood alcohol content during a single drinking session, the risk for acute health problems is highly elevated (Sillanaukee *et al.* 1992).

Health care plays an important role in preventing and treating alcohol-related problems. The risk-reduction initiatives in primary health care can support the national and local population based policies in reducing the harms caused by alcohol consumption (Edwards *et al.* 1994; Anderson 1991; *European Alcohol Action Plan* 1994). Already in 1980 a WHO expert committee stressed the need for efficient methods in detection of persons with harmful alcohol consumption before health and social consequencies become pronounced. Treatment in the early phase may arrest the disease process before a more serious and destructive phase of illness is reached. The committee called for the development of strategies that could be applied in primary health care settings with a minimum of time and resources. These efforts were designed to link a new generation of screening technologies to low-cost early intervention strategies (Babor *et al.* 1986).

Brief intervention can be described as any therapeutic or preventive activity of a short duration undertaken by a health care professional. In contrast to the conventional alcoholism treatment, brief intervention is commonly performed by personnel who have not specialized in addiction treatment, it usually takes place in a primary or specialized health care setting instead of an addiction treatment setting, and the treatment goal is usually moderate drinking, not abstinence.

The studies published during the last ten years have shown the method to be powerful as well as cost-effective in reducing alcohol problems. A recent review was based on 32 controlled studies in 14 countries enrolling 6000 problem drinkers (Bien *et al.* 1993). The study discovered that the course of harmful alcohol use can be effectively altered by well-designed intervention strategies which are feasible within relatively brief contacts such as primary health care settings and employee assistance programmes.

Although the duration or frequency of brief intervention may vary, it generally ranges from one to five sessions, which last no longer than one hour. Minimal intervention refers to the shortest or least intensive activity that has a therapeutic or preventive effect (Babor 1992). Studies have aimed at finding the optimal visiting frequency and duration. For example, in a study in which the intervention had a positive effect in comparison to the control group, no difference was found between a major and minor intervention (Nilssen 1991).

A high proportion of health care patients have an underlying alcohol problem which often is not identified by a doctor. A Finnish study in a university hospital found that 27 per cent of the male patients and 11 per cent of the female patients were heavy drinkers. The physicians identified less than half of them (Seppä and Mäkelä 1993). Similarly, several other studies have indicated that physicians in various health care settings often do not recognize (Murphy 1980; Kamerow *et al.* 1986; Reid *et al.* 1986 and Coulehan *et al.* 1987) or treat alcohol abuse (Murphy 1980; Wallace *et al.* 1987).

Reasons for the failure of identification and treatment can be found both in the doctors, patients and the existing diagnostic instruments (Cornel and van Zutphen 1989). Health care professionals may lack knowledge about health risks linked to alcohol abuse, and have limited skills in screening and giving brief intervention. They can have stereotyped ideas of alcohol abusers and negative attitudes about the prognosis. The patients again may fear being labelled as alcoholics and thus hide their drinking. Examples of lacking diagnostic tools are laboratory tests which are inadequate for screening and structured questionnaires which do not fit into routine work in primary health care. Also, giving a patient an alcohol-related clinical status is not usually useful at the early stages of drinking. These are all barriers for brief intervention. Consequently, a certain amount of resistance among the health care professionals may have to be overcome and attitudes need to change before early intervention programmes can effectively be started within the health care service.

The primary health care centres have a lot of potential in carrying out the intervention programmes. Primary health care centres are usually the first place for any patient to seek medical help. Almost all people visit a primary health care centre at least once a year, and heavy drinkers are likely to do so more often than others. Different clinical findings and symptoms like tremors, black-outs, astritis, headaches, diarrhoea, depression, anxiety, high blood pressure, being overweight, frequent short periods of sick leaves and visits to the emergency department without specific symptoms are common among alcohol abusers, but may be caused by other factors as well. Correct information of the patient's alcohol use increases the quality of the treatment in general.

Little is known about which types of patients would benefit most from brief intervention. Most of the studies made so far have been with men. Studies which also include women indicate the women do not necessarily benefit beyond that from screening alone or that the effects of brief intervention may have gender differences (Anderson and Scott 1992; Babor and Grant 1992). Women may also require their own type of intervention. It is also important to focus on the timing of the brief intervention in the patient's drinking career for finding out as early a phase as possible which is still cost-effective. Motivational issues are probably also important. For example, one recent study by Healther *et al.* (1995) showed that motivational interviewing was more effective than skill-based counselling when the patients had a low initial motivation to change.

2. THE GOALS AND THE PROCESS

A primary intervention study was carried out in the primary health care centres of Lahti. The aims were: to increase knowledge of alcohol-related health problems among the health care professionals; to study the prevalence of heavy drinkers in primary health care; and to get experiences of carrying out brief intervention as a part of the routine clinical setting.

A multi-professional working group was formed to carry out the intervention. The chairman of the working group was the researcher, and the local health care administrator acted as the secretary. The other members were doctors and nurses from the health care centres, and some officials from the health care administration. The working group consulted experts in the alcohol field.

The working group discussed the plan designed by the researcher, and as a result of that discussion, the process described in Figure 6.1 was agreed upon. The project was planned to take three years, and its target group was all the 18–60-years-old patients visiting the health care centres for any reason. Their alcohol consumption was screened by using a general health questionnaire including two questions regarding alcohol consumption (quantity and frequency of drinking), and the CAGE-instrument (see Ewing 1984). The questionnaires were given to the patients when they arrived at the clinic, and they filled them in before entering the general practitioner's room. The doctor consulted them normally, but also went through the alcohol questions in the health questionnaire. If the patient could be classified as a heavy drinker either on the basis of the self-reported alcohol consumption (more than 190 g of pure alcohol per week for women, and more than 280 g per week for men) or on the basis of the CAGE-instrument (plus two or more for women, and plus three or more for men) and this result was confirmed by the doctor, the patient was invited to participate in the project. If he or she was not willing to participate, the reason for that was asked. Patients with severe psychiatric diagnosis, severe somatic disease like cancer, documented history of alcoholism or those waiting for a major surgery were excluded from the study.

Patients who were detected as heavy drinkers, and who were willing to come again, went first to a laboratory for testing of

112

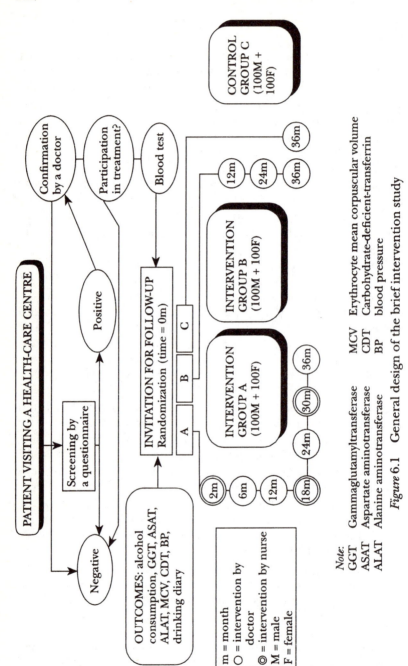

Figure 6.1   General design of the brief intervention study

Note:

GGT   Gammaglutamyltransferase   MCV   Erythrocyte mean corpuscular volume
ASAT   Aspartate aminotransferase   CDT   Carbohydrate-deficient-transferrin
ALAT   Alanine aminotransferase   BP   blood pressure

m = month
○ = intervention by doctor
◎ = intervention by nurse
M = male
F = female

alcohol markers selected for the study (GGT, ASAT, ALAT, MCV and CDT; for meaning of abbreviations, see Notes to Figure 6.1). Blood pressure was measured in order to further motivate the patient to take part in the project. Heavy drinkers were invited to come again to see the general practitioner within two weeks from the first visit. At the beginning of the visit they were randomly assigned to three different groups. The aim was to compare two interventions with differing intensity. Group A received more frequent intervention (four times during the first year and then twice per year). Group B was also given brief intervention, but only once a year. If a patient did not arrive to an intervention session, he or she was reinvited twice by a letter. The control group C was only encouraged to reduce their alcohol consumption and they were informed about their laboratory results. The patients in group C were not told that they would be invited to come again for endpoint evaluation after three years.

During the period of almost four years 41 general practitioners and 15 nurses were involved in the project. The study was started in one primary health care centre, and later three other primary health care centres joined in, covering all the health care centres in the city. Also the occupational health care centre of the municipality joined in. In the end the total patient population of the city of Lahti was covered.

3. EDUCATING THE GENERAL PRACTITIONERS AND THE NURSES

Before starting the intervention process, all of the practitioners and nurses took part in counselling. The counselling lasted two days and was led by the researcher. It was based on group work and joint discussions as well as lectures. Alcohol as a health problem, prevention strategies, the role of health care and brief intervention were covered during the first day. The actual working plans were discussed in more detail on the second day. In addition to these two education sessions, yearly project development days and two project group meetings were organized for benchmarking, and for changing ideas and experiences.

The counselling dealt with the following issues:

- identifying heavy drinkers
- giving information about the harmful effects of alcohol
- providing motivation for a change
- giving intervention to the motivated heavy drinkers
- setting personal goals
- giving advice on how to reach the set goals
- monitoring alcohol consumption during the later visits and setting new goals if needed

There is no rule for how best to find out about a patient's alcohol use. Patients are not always willing to discuss their drinking. Moreover, symptoms caused by heavy drinking can vary considerably. One typical indication is that as the harms start to accumulate, the person pays several visits to the doctor without any apparent reason. A start can be made by asking lightly does the patient use alcohol, has he been a teetotaller all his life, or has he stopped drinking alcohol lately. It is wise to ask about the drinking over a period that is long enough to be relevant. From that answer the number of standard portions per week can be calculated. It is also worth finding out about drinking habits: is the drinking done for the purpose of becoming intoxicated and/or does it lead to binge drinking? This gives additional information about the likelihood of the patient having acute alcohol problems, alcohol tolerance and the risk of developing alcohol dependency. When the amount of alcohol consumed at one time leads to a blood alcohol level exceeding 0.1 per cent (for men 7 standard units and for women 5 units), the probability of having different kinds of accidents is significantly increased.

Structured questionnaires can illuminate the case histories and help in recognizing heavy drinking, such structured questionnaires as CAGE (Mayfield *et al.* 1974), MmMAST (Pokorny *et al.* 1972) and AUDIT (Saunders *et al.* 1993). In Lahti, CAGE was used because it contains only four questions and thus could be added to the health questionnaire used in the project. Laboratory markers give independent information about alcohol consumption and they are useful not only in the detection but also in the follow-up both for monitoring the effectiveness of the treatment and for supporting the individual's motivation.

The most accurate diagnosis of heavy drinking can be formed by combining various indicators – the etiology of various illnesses, the information gained in case histories, health examinations, and, if necessary, questionnaire and laboratory marker data.

Information about the detrimental effects of alcohol use and advice in how to change one's drinking habits must be given in an unemotional and non-judgemental manner. The patient must become aware that he or she is in a high-risk group and that he or she alone is responsible for any change. It has been found that the most efficient intervention programmes are the ones that have offered advice with empathy without moralizing. The patients are supported and encouraged to have confidence in their own ability to change their drinking habits. The goal is to decrease the daily and weekly alcohol consumption in a way that takes into consideration the patient's individual situation. In certain cases (binge drinking, violence, medication, sickness, and so on) the patient is advised to abstain from alcohol completely. Otherwise, the aim is controlled drinking, with the individual agreeing to a personal goal: for example, consuming 15 drinks in a week instead of the previous 30.

A *Guidebook for Controlled Drinking* (Appendix 2) was published for the project and it was given to the patients as a part of the brief intervention treatment. The 12-page guidebook contains information about the harmful effects of alcohol use, guidelines for measuring one's own drinking, limits for risky drinking, advice in how to reduce drinking and how to cope in various social situations without drinking. It also contains a drinking diary. One of its benefits was in making sure that the information given to the patient by different members of the clinic staff was consistent.

4. EXPERIENCES FROM THE PROJECT

At the time of writing this book (autumn 1995) the intervention in the Lahti health care centres is continuing. The results of the effectiveness of such brief intervention are not yet available, as all the patients will not have gone through the process, and all the data has not yet been analysed. It is, however, possible to describe the experiences of how to manage brief intervention as part of the routine primary health care work.

The prevalence of heavy drinking varied between 13 and 21

per cent among males and 6 and 10 per cent among females in the primary health care centres, and respectively between 18 and 19 per cent and 6 and 7 per cent in the occupational health care centre (results from two pilot studies with the sample of 5009). When up to every fifth male and every tenth female can be considered to be a heavy drinker, and the average visiting frequency in the primary health care is 2.4 times a year, it is natural and important to use primary health care centres as a place for health education and brief intervention.

Results from the project strongly supported the observation that people tend to underestimate their alcohol consumption. Persons whom the study identified as heavy drinkers and whom the general practitioners identified as such, estimated their typical weekly drinking in the questionnaire only as 10 units for men and six for women. When during the same visit the doctor asked again about alcohol use, about a third of both women and men gave higher values than originally, but still their estimates remained low. Therefore, the possibility of heavy drinking cannot be excluded even if a patient's own report of his or her drinking sounds moderate. It seemed to be more the rule than the exception that the actual alcohol consumption was greater than the self-reported amount.

Most of the patients selected for the study had a positive CAGE test and this was the most frequent reason for the doctor to start questioning the patient about his or her alcohol etiology. It seems to be useful to use structured questionnaires like CAGE at least in the training phase of a brief intervention because it is a relatively easy and sensitive method for finding the right target group. When the general practioners or nurse's skills including the 'clinical eye' for detecting heavy drinkers improve, it is possible to stop using the structured questionnaires or to use them only in specific situations.

Laboratory markers gave additional help in the detection of heavy drinking. During the detection time, 76 per cent of the male and 74 per cent of the female heavy drinking patients had at least one of the laboratory markers above the normal range. One reason for the high figure was that there were five different markers. A disadvantage of using a combination of markers is that the specificity remains usually low. On the other hand, many of those markers are ordered frequently in any case, and the combination use (Sillanaukee *et al.* 1992) was proved to have a high sensitivity also in the present study. One way to have a good recognition rate is to use structured questionnaires or the doctor's estimate to pre-select possible alcohol abusers from the total patient group and to use laboratory markers for confirmation of suspicion of alcohol abuse. A pilot study in the occupational health care centre showed that when using CAGE as a detection tool, only 12 per cent of men and 20 per cent of women were false positives. Another limitation in structured questionnaires is that the cut-off values may vary according to the country, culture, gender or age.

When a patient was recognized to be a heavy drinker and asked to join the study, the reaction was usually positive. In the occupational health care centre about half of the heavy drinking patients were willing to reduce their drinking and to participate in the project. In the whole study 92 per cent of the patients who were willing to take part in the intervention came to the first consultation. The main reason for refusing to participate is that the person does not feel himself or herself to be a heavy drinker or that the status of heavy drinker in the occupational health centre might cause problems at work. The general feeling among the doctors and the nurses has been that the patients' attitude regarding the detection of heavy drinking and suggestion for brief intervention treatment was more postive than was estimated when the project started.

The treatment groups A and B and the control group C consisted of 414 heavy drinking persons, of whom a little less than one-third were women. The given intervention differed in intensity between the groups A (147 patients) and B (139 patients) and the control group consisted of 128 persons. After a year, 67 per cent of the patients (192 persons) attending the first consultation in the intervention groups A and B were still taking part in the project.

The consultation time in brief intervention varied between five and 20 minutes among the general practitioners and between 10 and 40 minutes among the nurses. During the first intervention session the doctor clarified the heavy drinking limits and, together with the patient, tried to find a personal target drinking level. The doctors reported that it is important to talk about any possible health risks or economic problems related to the patient's drinking. The general opinion was that it is important to find at least one concrete benefit in reducing the level of alcohol use. It is also important to avoid inflicting guilt, and to talk about the patients' future rather than their history. The doctors had also noticed that one has to be motivated in making the intervention, as the patients are sensitive in noticing if the doctor does not take the brief intervention seriously.

During the further visit it is important to evaluate what has happened to the patient's drinking since the last visit. Elevated laboratory markers can motivate the patient for further reduction of drinking. If the patient has been able to reduce the drinking, he or she is further motivated to continue the same line when asked about the benefits he or she has recognized, and congratulated for good development in the laboratory values, reduction of weight and so on. If the patient has not been able to reach the goal, it is important to check if the goal was realistic and to define a new goal and a strategy.

As an example, changes in a 44-year-old man's CDT values reflected the patients' drinking status during the first 18 months. During the detection time his self-reported alcohol consumption was only 8 units a week, but he had four positive answers in the CAGE questionnaire. Of the laboratory values ALAT was slightly elevated and CDT was strongly above reference values, confirming the suspicion of heavy drinking. During the first two months his self-reported alcohol consumption was still eight units a week, but CDT was reduced significantly (from 49 to 8 units per litre [U/l]) being now in the normal area. The patient reported to have had a heavier drinking period (10 units a week) before the third intervention session and that was confirmed with a significant elevation of CDT. After that the patient reported drinking more moderately (6 units a weeks) and the laboratory values supported this.

Experiences received in the project so far indicate that brief intervention requires experience and skills. It should be given in an individual way to each patient, finding out which reasons, goals and tools are most effective in each case. The message to a patient should be as generative and optimistic as possible, and it should also have a high motivational impact. It is also acceptable that even a well-performed intervention sometimes does not give good results. But sometimes the mere fact of pointing out the high level of drinking works as a stimulant for reduction of alcohol use. These differences can be explained by the variance in the patients' situation and willingness to reduce their drinking. If a person does not feel that he or she is a heavy drinker, or he or she does not understand and believe in the association of drinking and health problems, it is not sensible to give the brief intervention. However, if the patient's drinking is paid attention to one way or another every time he or she visits the health care centre, it is likely that the heavy drinker will move from the pre-understanding phase to an understanding phase, and thus be more willing to take part in the actual intervention.

The doctors and nurses told that the following opinions had been expressed by the patients they had seen:

- Many patients were confused in the beginning and asked: what is this going to give to me? In the treatment group A request for frequent visits could be a surprise and in the control group C only one visit without any further treatment could be a disappointment.
- Some felt ashamed to be recognized as a heavy drinker.
- The patients felt irritable or anxious if the goals had been unrealistic or if they had not been reached. This was common among those who had several health problems and those who had a more serious drinking problem.
- The intervention created feelings of fear that alcohol had already damaged the body.
- Those who had reduced their drinking felt thankful and relieved.
- The majority of the patients showed a positive and motivated attitude.

The doctors and nurses had following experiences of their own work:

- One could lose contact with the patient because there was not always enough time to check the health questionnaire properly.
- The treatment personnel felt uncertain about their skills in giving the brief intervention, especially in the beginning. Would the patient be able to define some goals for him/ herself, or was one just going to talk about the problems?
- One felt frustrated if the treatment did not work. This was more often the case with the more dependent patients.
- Not all heavily drinking patients did want to participate in the programme.

- The treatment personnel felt helpless with the multiproblem-patients, who have such complex situations that it is easy to understand why they drink. Cooperation with different professional helpers would be important.
- It is difficult to estimate the patient's real drinking level. If the laboratory tests give normal values, it is more difficult to convince the patient that he or she drinks too much.
- The nurses felt that their message is not always as authoritative as the doctor's advice.
- The project had increased the general practitioners' and the nurses' ability to detect the heavy drinkers.
- New, unexpected cases of heavy drinkers were found, especially among the young and the females.
- The treatment personnel felt they acquired new skills in health education and counselling and their ability to detect heavy alcohol use increased.
- The general quality of treatment has increased as it now also includes alcohol-related issues.
- There were feelings of success when the patient had found a way to reduce his or her drinking and had reached the set goal.
- The general practitioners' motivation for brief intervention increased during the project.

When the project started, the nurses' attitudes in giving health education and in carrying out brief intervention was much more positive than the doctors' attitudes. The strongest resistance for taking up the project came from the doctors. The reason behind this may be that it is not easy to engage in health counselling with the required empathy and encouragement if one still feels suspicious about the success of the treatment or has insufficient skills to perform motivational brief intervention. Another reason for the resistance among the doctors was that the project meant starting a new working routine in the fully loaded job without any additional payment for doing so. A third reason is that at the time the project was started, there was a reduction in the health services and its resources in the municipality.

During the course of the project, the general practitioners' attitudes became more positive when their own knowledge and skills increased. This underlies the importance not only of the education before the project but also of the continuous development of the work as experiences amount (Pringle and Laverty 1993). The same applies to the nurses, even if they had a more health-education-oriented attitude already at the beginning of the project.

One general finding of the project was that it is important to describe the brief intervention clearly in each clinical centre separately, and think carefully about the subcomponents of the intervention in joint discussions with the different professional groups of each centre. The patient flow should be estimated and the cost-effectiveness of the treatment monitored during the process. In doing this, it should be kept in mind that there is no one universal way of conducting brief intervention. It should not be regarded as a homogeneous entity but as a family of interventions varying in length, structure, target group, goals of the intervention, the responsible personnel and the impact of communication, including intervention philosophy (see Healther *et al.* 1995).

Due to the research setting, a strict protocol was followed in repeating the intervention to all those in the intervention group. In a non-research setting it is probably important to carry out one brief intervention session for each patient, and to continue the intervention only when the patient feels a need for it, or the general practitioner or the nurse finds it for some reason essential. The number of visits and their frequency can thus be adjusted to the patients' individual needs.

Even if various clinical trials show that brief intervention in health care can reduce alcohol consumption and harms related to drinking, there are lots of questions which each clinical centre has to find an answer for, before the full potential of the intervention can be reached. Many of these questions are practical. Some of the questions raised in Lahti dealt with keeping up the personnel's motivation, of finding effective detection methods for the early phase of alcohol problems, which suit the routine practice of the health care centre, creating a good first intervention session, creating sufficient medical records for evaluating progress and being able to assess the treatment goal during each later visit. Maintaining the patient's motivation is one challenge, as is defining criteria for sending the patient into more specialized treatment if needed. There are problems of work-site organization: there is a need to find the right kinds of working relationships between the general practitioners and the nurses. A decision also needs to be made when it is better to treat the patient yourself and when to direct him or her to another local doctor or nurse who is more specialized in health education and brief intervention.

Alcohol use is a major health problem and frequently associated with other risk factors. It is often hidden under the medical disease or other problems, and it is difficult and expensive to treat in a later phase. For that reason it is important to continue developing brief intervention to make it a routine part of primary health care. The major milestones are mastering the process itself and overcoming the educational and economic barriers.

7 Responsible Service and Drinking Environments

Marja Holmila and Kari Haavisto

Availability of alcohol is one of the most important factors influencing drinking habits and, consequently, alcohol-related harms. In the world of international marketing and trade agreements, localities are losing what little influence they have had in where and at what price these beverages are sold. The experience of trying to create action on regulation of availability in Lahti shows that particularly relevant for communities in this respect are the face-to-face contacts between the sellers and the buyers, and the issues linked with the community's ability to control people's destructive behaviour.

1. THE MARKET FOR ALCOHOLIC BEVERAGES IN LAHTI

There are three types of venues where alcohol can be bought in Lahti. The State Alcohol Monopoly has three shops where strong liquor and all kinds of wine can be bought. Medium beer (maximum of 4.6 per cent volume of alcohol) is sold in food stores and most cafés. Fully licensed restaurants serve all kinds of alcoholic beverages.

The availability of alcohol has increased rapidly in Lahti. The number of restaurants grew from 36 in 1982 to 54 in 1994. The number of places serving medium beer has grown even faster during the past 12 years: from 62 to 125. About one-third of all alcohol consumed in the city is purchased in restaurants and in bars selling medium beer; two-thirds is bought from the shops (Mäkelä 1994, pp. 7–9).

Already before the new alcohol law, some changes were made in Alko's outlets in Lahti. The monopoly opened a new self-service shop in October 1992 with extended hours. The shop is open until 8 p.m. on Fridays and 4 p.m. on Saturdays. The extra hours are important in the competition for the sale of medium beer, and in response to the public's requests for easier availability of alcoholic beverages. The extra hours proved important for the new Alko store: in March 1993 it sold one-third of its Friday sales after 6 p.m., and the business was most brisk during the hour before closing (Alko's records).

One-fifth of the inhabitants of Lahti never shop at Alko, and one-half go there less than once a month. Only 5 per cent visit the monopoly shop at least once a week. Men buy alcohol from Alko more often than women. During the first four months, the extended hours in the new shop had attracted mostly those under 25 years of age and those drinking frequently (Holmila 1993).

Medium beer has been sold in Finnish grocery stores since 1969. In Lahti 14 per cent of women and one-third of men generally buy medium beer from a grocery store at least once a week. On the other hand, 45 per cent of the women said they never purchase medium beer in a grocery store or supermarket (Holmila 1993). It is likely that in many households the men buy the beer and the women buy the food.

Law forbids the sale of beer to persons under the age of 18. However, young people in Lahti find it easy to get beer. Every fifth 14-year-old boy and every tenth girl in the same age group said they had bought medium beer in a shop (Haavisto 1993, p. 7). The enforcement of the regulation concerning the minimum legal age is thus not very efficient.

Bars and cafés serving medium beer range from lunch places and highway service stations to barren rooms visited by the marginalized and the poor. Many of the bars are more accessible than the restaurants to those with little money.

The leadership of the bar catering to marginalized people lies in the experienced hands of the hostess. Her role is a combination of care and control resembling that of a parent. Occasional conflicts are solved with the unquestioned moral authority of the hostess. It is in the interest of the customers to help maintain order. Some of them are petty criminals and any additional visits by the police are not desired. Many find it important that the bar can maintain its reputation and continue to be open.

The owner here is extremely friendly. She's like a second mother. We call her 'Iron Mother'. If she sees that you are in bad shape, she brings you something to eat and tries to help. Doesn't try to make anyone drink. Shows the door out easily. Saves and protects (A customer in a Lahti medium beer bar; see Holmila *et al.* 1989, p. 24).

One hostess defined her role in the following way:

This is a home for these people. A kind of social welfare office. People can be contacted here, and we also keep in touch. Just today we wrote joint postcards to some customers who had to go to prison. I consider myself to be a kind of nurse. Everybody is welcome here (op. cit., p. 24).

Not all of the 95 places selling medium beer in the city belong to this category of bars. Medium beer is served in a wide range of cafés and bars. During the economic recession from 1992 to 1994, many empty business sites attracted the interest of entrepreneurs wanting to start small medium-beer bars. The number of these outlets grew from 100 to 125. The owners of more established businesses thought many of them did not maintain the best standards (discussion in a meeting with the restaurant industry 27 January 1993 in Lahti).

Fully licensed restaurants have a special role in promoting the controlled use of alcohol. This role is on one hand caused by the harms that are typical to these locales. Public drinking causes public violence and disturbance. On the other hand, the special role can be seen to be caused by the positive potentials of these locales for changing drinking habits and drinking norms. Also the fact that young people are the most frequent visitors in restaurants is important in itself. Public drinking contributes disproportionately to certain types of acute alcohol-related problems, such as violent behaviour and drunken driving. Also, changes in drinking patterns often begin in public drinking locales. Although such changes in drinking patterns have often created new forms of consumption and increased the problems, public establishments could also be where trends toward moderation may be set in motion (see Single [forthcoming], p. 3).

Young adults in Lahti are the most frequent visitors to restaurants. Nearly one-third of the 18- to 24-year-olds, one-tenth of 35- to 50-year-olds and only 3 per cent of those older than 50 visit a restaurant at least once a week (Holmila 1993). The inhabitants of Lahti, and Finns in general, seldom go out to restaurants to eat. The main purpose is to meet other people, to drink and maybe dance or listen to music.

A questionnaire was distributed on a Friday night to the patrons of three restaurants in downtown Lahti. One of the questions asked was, had the respondent drunk any alcohol before coming to this restaurant?

Two-thirds of the respondents had had something to drink, usually at someone's home. The average 'starter' for women was 2.8 and for men 4.8 units of alcohol. The rationale of this habit is often economy – it is cheaper to drink at home than in a restaurant. Therefore, several of the customers must have been rather drunk already when entering the restaurant. Limits for the legal drinking age were not well observed. Half of the females and 72 per cent of the males in the study said they had been served alcohol in a restaurant before the age of 18 (Holmila and Haavisto 1994, pp. 212–15).

2. VIOLENCE AND DISORDER

The police in Lahti are often involved in solving cases of public violence, which regularly are alcohol-related. For instance, in 1993, the police dealt with 395 assaults, out of which 277 were alcohol-related (Mäkelä 1994, p. 15). The local discussion and action around alcohol problems had for a long time had public violence as one of its focuses. The personal interest shown by the police chief inspector in preventing the public violence was one of the main reasons for this issue becoming an area of research and project activity.

Various studies have shown a clear connection between violence and alcohol use: a great part of violence is triggered by intoxication. It has been observed that even a temporary reduction in the overall level of drinking leads to a decline of violence cases (Pernanen 1991, p. 30; Österberg 1991, p. 112). Thus a sweeping change in drinking habits is likely to bring about a decrease in alcohol-related violence, too. It is, however, important to find other methods of reducing violent behaviour. A promising strategy to complement other approaches to prevention is the manipulation of drinking environments to influence the rate at which drinkers consume alcohol.

Alcohol-related domestic violence against children, women

and old people is common too (Report of a Committee on Violence, 1991). Domestic violence is more difficult to prevent since outsiders often don't even know about it, and the police do not have the right to interfere unless asked. In the case of public violence, it is at least in theory possible to interfere directly.

As a part of the Lahti project, the police collected data on all the cases of violence that came to their knowledge from January to June 1993. A short questionnaire was filled out on each case. This data has the same limitation as all police records; it includes only a small portion of domestic violence cases. The police examined 147 cases of violence during the study period.

In the majority of cases (71 per cent) the perpetrator was a man who had consumed alcohol. A woman who had been drinking was the perpetrator in every tenth case. Alcohol played an important role also among the victims: 64 per cent of victims were under the influence of alcohol. The violence took place most often on the streets (42 per cent), in somebody's home (26 per cent) or in a restaurant or other licensed premises (22 per cent). More than half of the violent persons were under the age of 30, and the violence often took place between persons in the same age group (Holmila and Haavisto 1994, pp. 4–5).

There were only a few cases where the violent incidence in a restaurant did not involve persons who had been drinking. This seems natural, as people almost always consume alcohol in restaurants. The questionnaire data from the three restaurants in downtown Lahti also showed that alcohol-related disorders, aggression and violence were common experiences.

The patrons had commonly witnessed various incidences of disorder or violence during the last year. Sixty-six per cent of men and 43 per cent of women had noticed fights or scuffles in the restaurants they had visited. Quarrelling or disagreements had been still more commonly observed. Many respondents had themselves been objects of mild forms of violence. About one-half of the respondents said they had been pushed or shoved. Every fourth man and 13 per cent of women had been threatened. Five per cent had been victims of attacks causing a bruise or a cut. Many had been controlled by the restaurant personnel. For instance, 18 per cent of the men had been refused entry to a restaurant, and 13 per cent had been told they would not be served any more (Holmila and Haavisto 1994, pp. 213–15).

In the same study, the majority of the patrons considered excessive drinking to be the most important reason for violence or disturbances in the restaurants. More than half of them also said that the restaurant personnel should restrict the customers' use of alcohol (Holmila and Haavisto 1994, pp. 215–16). The patrons clearly connected disturbances with drunkenness and expected the restaurant personnel to act as controllers of people's drinking.

The law states: 'A drunken person may not be admitted in the licensed premises. A customer who disturbs the peace or whose drunkenness is clearly noticeable has to be removed from the premises' (Onniki and Ranta (eds) 1995, p. 1734). The customers, however, usually come to restaurants in order to become more or less drunk. The restaurant personnel has to live with these two contradictory expectations. Usually the personnel interfere only when the customer has had enough to drink and must go home, not earlier. The servers' interpretations of the concept 'drunk' varies (Puskala and Miettinen 1995, p. 8).

> If he/she can stand up, I recommend a glass of water and a short break. If the person is too drunk, she/he must go. They can be very drunk, but still they know how to behave and understand what is said to them.

> We serve those who still can take some. If not, we take them out. Next one comes in.

> Doesn't everyone come to a restaurant for the purpose of getting drunk?

> Especially the younger customers are like that. There has been a change in the drinking habits in Finland, and the rhythm is awful: ten drinks an hour.

Regular customers are often treated differently because the servers know how they react when drunk. The bouncer's responsibility is to keep order. The number of bouncers has been reduced, however, and many restaurants no longer hire them. Some restaurants have them during the weekends but not during the week.

3. THE CONTROVERSIAL RESPONSIBILITY

Influencing the supply of alcohol seems an integral part of any community intervention. Drinking habits are not formed solely by patterns of demand – marketing and availability are extremely important factors. When the Lahti project started, we had no specified idea as to how one should deal with the issues of supply in the community context. Local communities do not have so many means of influencing the sales or production of alcohol. It was, however, thought to be important to make an effort to create some process in this respect.

The process was started by arranging some meetings with the local restaurant industry, the local beer company and the local branch of the state alcohol monopoly. Preparations for the new administration of licensing surveillance as well as the process of formulating the new alcohol law (see Chapter 2) were issues of current interest, increasing the industry's willingness to take part in these discussions. The meetings were preceded by several face-to-face meetings with the relevant persons where the Lahti project was introduced to them. At the same time data on purchasing habits, violence in public places and the restaurants were collected. It may be that the ongoing data collection and the possible publicity following it was one of the incentives for the industry to take part in the first round of discussions. The first meeting took place in January 1993, and the second in April 1993.

The first meeting focused on restaurants. Both the server personnel and the managers/owners were represented. The police and researchers presented their reports, which are described in the previous pages. The managers stressed the fact that the number of restaurants has grown too fast, causing the quality of the locales to deteriorate. Entrepreneurs can start again with a new licence after bankruptcy. The servers' representative said that the increased competition has led to a reduction in the numbers of people working in the restaurants. When, at its worst, there are 600 patrons and four waiters, how can one pay any attention to possible drunkenness or to prevent disorder? The restaurants have also increasingly shifted to self-service and employing bartenders. She also said that many waiters and waitresses are afraid of being susceptible to unpredictable violence. The situation is especially risky if there is no bouncer, and if one is working alone. The threshold of calling the police can be high; some owners have told their employees not to call the police but to handle the conflicts themselves. There is a risk of losing one's respectability, and consequently, one's licence, if the police are called too often (notes on the meeting on 27 January 1993).

The second meeting involved civil servants and members of the municipal council as well as representatives from the alcohol and restaurant industry. It was arranged with the city's drug policy group. Presentations included research reports from the project group and talks by the business sector. The title of the meeting was 'Local drug and alcohol policy – does it exist?' The distance between industry representatives and those involved in health promotion was wider than in the first meeting. The industry representatives gave straightforward talks in favour of freedom of competition, open pricing of alcohol beverages and free advertising, concentrating mainly on economic issues. The emphasis was to stress the benefits of free business also for the customer. Members of the municipal council cited individual observations of alcohol-related harms, but generally took no clear line on issues of alcohol supply. The meeting seemed to lack a clear focus.

One of the rationales for the fact that top officials in the city generally gave their full support for the Lahti project was that the city could save a lot of resources if some of the alcohol-related problems could be prevented. In the issues relating to responsible service of alcohol, they however had to consider the other side of the question, too. The alcohol industry and restaurants are a substantial part of the city's economy. In addition, interference with any sector of business life would place them in a negative light in the opinions of many politicians. The deputy mayor gave the opening talk at the Liquor Weeks in March 1993. He mentioned that the alcohol industry and the restaurant services are an important part of the economy and the goal of a prevention project is not to attack them, even if the city has an interest in prevention of social and health-related costs.

The city government has a limited capacity for influencing the supply of alcohol in certain settings. The city council gives a statement when someone wants to open a new restaurant in the area. The municipality also gives temporary licensing rights for festivals or special occasions. During the course of the project the municipality dealt with one interesting case. A church-owned apartment in a suburb was sold to a man who wanted to open a striptease bar. The municipality council was divided on this issue, and the chairman's vote was a decisive yes. The chairman said later that he had had some afterthoughts on the issue. Should he have voted against the licence after all? However, the bar was in the end not opened because the local inhabitants made a collective plea against it.

The project coordinator made an attempt to bring forward the server liability issue as a topic of public discussion. She wrote an article, 'An accident in a restaurant', in a local newspaper. The article told a true story about a young man who had been served alcohol in a local bar until he was very intoxicated. After leaving the restaurant he fell down on the restaurant staircase, hitting his head so badly that he died. This article was intended to create discussion on server responsibility, but the reaction was slightly different from what was hoped for. The editor of the second local newspaper referred to the article in his column. He claimed that the idea of someone being responsible for a drunken person's staggering is plain silly. He asked, 'What is the difference if a man dies when hitting his head on the corner of the restaurant table or if he falls off the pier in his summer cottage and drowns?' The height of folly in his opinion is that some people have sued tobacco companies for having caused lung cancer. He then hoped that these features of 'the old patronizing society' would disappear when Finland joined the European Union.

The project group also attempted to create action on issues of supply by engaging in discussions with the representatives of the consumers' association. The national office showed considerable interest, but the local representative did not; and these contacts led to no action.

The local beer company took part in some of the educational events promoting their non-alcohol beer. The company printed coasters containing an educational message, and offered non-alcoholic beer during the biggest educational events. The cooperation was finished when the non-alcoholic beer was taken off the market: it was not financially succesful.

4. SERVER TRAINING

Server training was the area where some progress was made. From the very beginning the project had various contacts with the Lahti restaurant school. The principal showed interest in co-operating. The pupils worked as servers of non-alcoholic drinks on many of the occasions arranged by the project – for instance during the Liquor Weeks and the 'On the Wagon Weeks'. Four of the pupils carried out data collection and wrote seminar papers on topics related to the project. The school facilities were used for many meetings during the project.

The principal of the restaurant school believed that the alcohol policy system in Finland was going to change, the monopoly system would be dismantled and the restaurants would be more autonomous. They would have to learn to purchase their products without using Alko as a mediator and therefore would have to know the products and the market better. The responsibility of serving alcohol was previously, to a great extent, carried out by the Alko monopoly, whose strict surveillance and detailed regulations created a feeling of security and clarity of norms among the restaurant personnel. In the future, the restaurant owners would have to take the initiative (discussion with the principal, 30 September 1993).

In some discussions it was said that the most difficult part in the training of the restaurant personnel may be in giving them adequate psychological skills. The waiters should be able to handle difficult customers and relieve the tension in a potentially aggressive individual. One restaurant owner called his bar 'a psychiatrist's office'. The patrons' unpredictability is accentuated by many factors: intoxication, mixing pills and alcohol, people coming to public drinking places when they feel particularly lonely or stressed, the stress of being in crowded rooms with other drunk persons, the erotic atmosphere in dancing restaurants, the highly emotional scenes, for instance, between ex-spouses and ex-lovers. It is not surprising that the skills required by a good barman or barmaid are several.

The restaurant personnel are supposed to have three different roles. First, they are in the restaurant to serve the customers and to fulfil their wishes. Second, they are meant to sell products and services for profit. In addition, they also have the role of a supervisor – they aim at preventing disorder and accidents and they intervene when conflicts occur.

The job contains many contradictions, but the different goals can be combined through the joint efforts of everyone involved. Recognizing drunkenness as well as an abusive drinking style, and knowing how to refuse the service of alcohol in these cases are important skills of the responsible server. Prevention of drinking and driving has often been one of the important goals of server training. Drinking styles can be directed also by manipulating the selection of drinks or their prices. Marketing and decoration influence the image of the place and how people behave (Mosher 1983; Smythe *et al.*, 1995; Simpson *et al.*, 1986; Stockwell *et al.* 1993).

Planning server training in Lahti involved teachers in the Lahti restaurant school (Fellmanni Institute), members of the project group and a restaurant owner. The training course consisted of two afternoons with lectures and a written homework assignment. The course was advertised in the local restaurants and newspapers. It was free of charge. The first afternoon there were 160 persons, half working in the restaurants and half were pupils in the restaurant school. The homework assignment was completed by 120 persons, who also attended the second afternoon two weeks later. All these 120 persons were given a certificate for the course (Haavisto 1995).

The first day was titled, 'Changing Field of Service'. The talks dealt with the coming changes in the legislation and their impact on the restaurant business and the organization of surveillance. The speakers included representatives from the authorities and the restaurant business. The local police talked about their experiences patrolling local restaurants and other activities in maintaining order.

At the end of the day the participants were given three articles to read, and a list of questions relating to these articles. The articles described the disturbances of order in the local restaurants (Holmila and Haavisto 1994), changes in Finnish drinking habits (Simpura 1993) and young people's drinking (Ahlström 1994). The participants were asked to answer one question on the basis of each of these articles. The fourth question was: 'What are the special challenges in restaurant work today?'

The second day was titled, 'People in the Restaurant'. A psychologist talked about the environmental factors influencing people's behaviour and the possibilities of regulating this with the messages and gestures available to the personnel. A customer, a server and a restaurant owner each gave a talk.

In their answers to the question on current challenges for restaurant personnel the course participants expressed both positive and negative experiences.

The work load and responsibility is growing when Alko's surveillance is finished.

Cuts in the numbers of the staff causes problems in surveillance: one has to sell even if one's soul suffers.

One doesn't need any special skills – all you have to know is what medium beer looks like.

The real challenge for the servers' work was expressed as follows:

To educate the customers in the middle of the mundane service work so that they will be in a good mood and not get pissed out of their heads and lose their memory, start quarrelling and then suffer awful hangovers.

To encourage people to use self-control and to make them accept the foreigners and not immediately start quarrelling just because they don't understand each others' language.

The participants in the course were generally satisfied with the training. More time for discussion was requested. The course was felt to be a success also among the organizers. A second training session took place in Lahti in the autumn of 1995.

5. SUMMARY

When the project started, we had no specified idea as how to deal with the issues of supply in the community. As a result of contacts with the local police, the problem of violence and disorder particularly in public places became central. All other types of questions relating to selling or producing alcoholic beverages proved to be difficult to carry out, as no local actors took interest in them, and there was strong resistance from the local business sector for any such measures. The city authorities were not willing to get involved in any such battles concerning an economic situation where revenues were badly needed. In addition to the local police, the restaurant personnel expressed interest in developing better ways of handling the difficult situations they were constantly facing in their work. As a result of the project, both these professional groups were supported in their work of maintaining public order and minimizing alcohol-related violence. The idea of server training is new in Finland, and having been successfully completed in Lahti has gained some interest as a model in other localities as well.

8 The Young and Alcohol
Marja Holmila and Kari Haavisto

1. SURROUNDED BY AMBIVALENCE

In any community, young people are the ones whose drinking arouses the most concern. Intervention in young people's lives is considered legitimate as they are not thought to have the same sovereignty as adults. The society has a moral right to interfere in their lives. Being young they are also believed to be more receptive than older persons who are already set in their ways, and being in schools and colleges they seem to be the easiest target group to reach.

Even if there is general agreement that selecting youngsters as the main target group of preventive efforts, the goals of preventive action are not consistent. Young boys and girls are faced with ambivalent messages and a lack of coherence concerning the appropriate ways of using alcohol.

For instance, even if adults are concerned about young people's drinking problems and express the need to 'do something about it', this concern does not always lead to logical policy recommendations. When asked in a telephone survey, 62 per cent of the respondents in Lahti said they supported liberalization of alcohol laws so that wine could be sold in supermarkets. When asked whether this would increase alcohol problems among the young, 64 per cent thought this would be the case. Only one-third of the respondents thought the problems would increase among the adults. Obviously, the adults' need to buy their wine easily is more important to them than the possible ill-effects on the young.

There are a lot of double messages for the young about the legitimacy of drinking. At the same time as educators warn children and teenagers about the harms caused by drinking, beer has been advertised in the cinema, TV and street posters. In January 1995 it became legal to advertise mild alcoholic drinks also on TV and in the newspapers. Even if the law forbids selling mild alcoholic drinks to those under 18 years of age and hard liquor to those under 20 years of age, teenagers face no

great obstacles in obtaining drinks (Haavisto 1993, p. 7). Someone will always buy it for them if they cannot do it themselves.
Many of those buying drinks for minors do not consider their
action illegal (Ahlström 1991, p. 186).

Young people and even small children have more experiences of adult drinking than is often assumed. It is difficult to
protect children from the impact of alcohol use, especially when
it takes place in their own homes. As many as 23 per cent of
the 18- to 24-year-olds answering the telephone survey in Lahti
said that one or several of their family members was drinking
too much. Negative experiences resulting from parents' drinking are not rare or limited to specific groups of youngsters.

2. PLAYING WITH THE BOTTLE: YOUNG PEOPLE'S DRINKING HABITS

Between the ages of 13 and 17 the adolescents' leisure focus
generally shifts from adult-organized activities to casual activities and finally to commercially organized leisure. These trans-
itions occur roughly at the ages when the main relationship
issues – sex, peers, parents – come into focus. The differential
effects of sex and social class can influence the general leisure
pattern to produce possible overlapping patterns. For instance,
the earlier physical and psychological maturity of girls under-
pins their relatively earlier transition toward a focus on peers
and casual leisure pursuits, and then toward more exclusive dat-
ing and commercial leisure provision. It may also reflect a more
rapid move to social sophistication, if not maturity (Hendry
1989, p. 248).

In this framework, the age between 14 and 15 is important.
It is roughly during those years when most youngsters move
away from organized leisure activities to 'hanging out', and
when peer relations take over the relationship dominance from
the parents.

A survey was conducted among adolescents (14-year-olds) in
Lahti (Haavisto 1993). A team of youth workers took the questionnaires into all of the school classes for this age-group and
collected them from the pupils. The response rate was 91 per
cent.

Half of the boys and somewhat less (41 per cent) of the girls

Table 8.1   Frequency of drinking, 14-year-olds in Lahti,
percentages

	Girls (517)	Boys (482)	All (999)
At least once a week	8	6	7
Two to three times a month	13	13	13
More seldom	38	31	35
Never	41	49	45

Table 8.2   Frequency of drunkenness, 14-year-olds in Lahti,
percentages

	Girls (516)	Boys (477)	All (993)
At least once a week	6	6	6
Two to three times a month	14	12	13
More seldom	29	27	28
Never	52	48	44

had not drunk any alcohol. Eight per cent of the girls and six
per cent of the boys drank at least once a week (Table 8.1). It
is likely that the girls 'equality' in this respect does not indicate a profound change in gender roles but is due to drinking
being considered a sign of maturity. Girls generally reach their
puberty earlier than boys.

Drinking is almost a synonym for drunkenness for the youngsters in Lahti (Table 8.2). The percentage of those who had
never been drunk was only slightly higher than those who had
never consumed any alcohol. The distribution of drunkenness
is similar to the distribution of drinking frequency. In other
words if a young person reports having consumed some alcohol, he/she also reports having experienced drunkenness. The
14-year-olds seem to drink mainly to get drunk or, alternatively,
do not register as 'drinking' the times they simply tasted some

alcohol. Similar results have been obtained in national surveys (Ahlström *et al.* 1994).

The most common drink for the boys was medium beer (33 per cent), and for the girls it was wine (39 per cent). Spirits were surprisingly popular, too. One-fourth of both the boys and the girls said their most common drink was hard liquor (Haavisto 1993, p. 7). The popularity of wine among the girls and spirits among both genders is strange also for the reason that these beverages are sold only in monopoly stores – where, according to the law, wine is available only for those 18 years of age or more and liquor is available only for those over 20 years old. The most common place for drinking was outside, in the parks, forests and the children's playgrounds in the evening after the younger ones have left.

The pupils had most commonly bought their drinks with the help of a friend, presumably an older friend. Sixty per cent said this was the most common way of getting drinks. Parents got the drinks for 6 per cent of the respondents and, in addition to that, 8 per cent said they took drinks from their homes, probably in secrecy. A stranger had bought the drinks for every tenth adolescent. In exchange for money, drinks are bought for those who are too young to be served in the liquor store.

Only 4 per cent of the 14-year-olds said they 'usually' bought their drinks themselves. However, when asked whether they had ever bought medium beer in the shops, 18 per cent of the boys and 11 per cent of the girls said they had done so (Haavisto 1993, p. 7).

In the essays that the schoolchildren wrote for the competition during the 'On the Wagon Weeks' under the heading 'When we drank' or 'In the summer cottage', descriptions of heavy drunkenness, accidents and passing out were the rule. The cultural patterns of boozing were well internalized and the course of events was often stereotypical – in spite of the young age of the writer.

ON A SCHOOL TRIP

We got on the boat, but it was terribly crowded, and I nearly lost my friend. We found our cabin and organized our things, then went out to look for someone to buy us beer from the shop. . . . After taking the beer to the cabin we went to look around.

An hour later we started drinking the beer in the cabin. We listened to music and played cards until we went to our friends' cabin. The atmosphere was great and everybody was just beginning to get drunk.

Much later Jari and I went to the disco. Having boosted our self-confidence by drinking the beer, we picked up two good-looking girls. We went to the cabin with the girls where I passed out almost immediately.

Jari woke me up in the morning in Stockholm. I tried to go downtown, but was not able to because I had an awful hangover. I went back to sleep.

In the evening on the way back to Finland we started drinking again. The evening and the night were spent approximately the same as on the way to Stockholm. In the bus on the way to Lahti I slept almost all the way (16-year-old boy).

Where the boy above recounts the events without giving them any meaning, a girl in her essay concentrates on analysing the feelings of drunkenness. In the latter half of her essay, she describes her feelings of remorse and guilt. Also this young writer is well acquainted with the Finnish combination of unrestricted 'drowning' into intoxication and deep guilt afterwards.

When I drink, I forget. I am not able to think, I forget my thoughts. When I don't think, I feel light, floating. I don't exist, I feel no pressures, no pain, no caresses. My body is numb, my feelings are artificial, distorted by alcohol. My real feelings are covered up, drowned in the intoxicating liquids. I cannot see them or touch them. Everything else is somewhere far away, voices and lights, and I can look at them only through a small peeping hole. Everything floats there slowly in a foggy chaos. I am in a hurry yet have endless time. I only know that I must hurry, live fast, because my wonderfully unconscious existence will soon be over. I dread the moment, but luckily forget to think about it. . . .

In the morning I wake up having slept too little. My mouth tastes bad. My stomach is like a plastic bag filled with air, full but empty. Only now I feel mentally tired, empty. I am sad and disappointed in myself. Again I have reached the existence of emptiness by intoxicating myself, by drinking myself empty. I wish I could empty myself by talking, writing or painting. But all that is impossible for me; I feel inadequate

and futile. Now I have again reached the sought-after existence for maybe a month, maybe a week, with the only method
I know: by drinking.

> (A girl, 16 to 18 years old; first prize in the essay
> competition during the 'On-the-Wagon Weeks')

3. TAKING CARE: THE STREET SERVICE MONO

The teenagers in Lahti drink mostly outdoors. The street service Mono (ski boot in Finnish) for the young in Lahti started
in its current organized form in the spring of 1991. The activity
started as special operations during the annual ski-jump competitions, which attracted lots of celebrating youngsters into
town. Nowadays the activity takes place weekly. The social youth
workers who were running Mono (for descriptions of Mono's
activities, see Haavisto 1995) became some of the most active
local participants in the Lahti project. The network around
Mono formed a basis for many of the activities in the project.

Mono's adults consist of 30 to 40 volunteers and the social
youth workers. The volunteers are trained for their tasks and
they are committed to take part in patrolling whenever it is
their turn, usually every third Friday.

Every Friday between 9 p.m. and 2 a.m. a group of adults
patrol the streets of the city and help the young people they
meet. During major festivities special operations are organized.
The main target group is the less than 18-year-old girls and boys
who are temporarily in crisis or in risk due to alcohol, drugs
or violence. Mono has a resting base, first-aid kits, alcometer,
radio telephones and a car that was bought with the money
obtained as donations. Those on call wear a large orange badge.
The workers divide themselves into three groups: one at the
resting base, one in the car and one or more walking. The resting base is cosy and tidy, and there is always one adult who
concentrates on caring for those brought there.

Mono's workers wake up those who have fallen asleep on
the streets, take them either to their homes or to the resting
base, stop violence (sometimes by calling the police), and help
those who need medical care either because of intoxication or
because of having been hurt. They also contact the parents,
and attempt to meet on the following Monday those youngsters

and their parents who had been in trouble or intoxicated on Friday.

A lot of the contacts in the streets are limited to friendly discussion. Some youngsters drop by the resting base for a chat and to use the toilet. The following figures describing Mono's activities during the period between autumn 1993 and spring 1994 give an idea of their weekly routine. On average Mono's workers contact 60 youngsters every Friday. Nine persons visit the resting base, three are woken up sleeping in the street, one injured is given first-aid, two are taken home and every other Friday one is taken to a hospital or an emergency polyclinic. The average age of the girls visiting the resting base is 14.8 years old and of the boys it is 15.7 years old. Usually the reason for visiting the resting base is heavy intoxication. Girls more often than boys are taken there, and boys more often than girls are given first-aid due to injuries from fights and accidents (Mäkelä 1994a, p. 8).

Kari Haavisto described some of the events on the night of Friday, 21 August 1994:

At 10 p.m.:
We walk on a muddy path on a steep hill. There are lots of empty bottles and Alko's plastic bags, but no young people. Down by the pedestrian road we see about 20 kids, one of them vomiting. We slide down the hill and go to talk to them. The whole group is from the neighbouring town, preparing themselves for the night's fights in this canyon.

At 11 p.m.:
The car has been called to the athletic field. There has been a fight and a young boy was kicked and injured. Two girls who say they have had nothing to drink are still there. The other one's father is coming to meet them at 12.30 a.m. We take the boy to the health centre, and the girls to the centre of town.

At 12 p.m.:
We walk around downtown, and wake up the kids sitting and sleeping on the pavements. One of them gets so scared he starts running away.

At 2 a.m.:
The volunteers and the evening's coordinator go through the

events of the evening. Everything is discussed so that each of us can go home feeling okay.

The Mono workers have considered their role: Are they making an intervention or are they just facilitating the youngsters' drinking? From one Friday to the next they meet the same Minna or Mika and take him or her safely indoors, wipe the vomit from the chin and make sure the child doesn't freeze in the frosty night, but do they do anything to stop him/her from drinking? The workers have decided that the parents are always telephoned and if this doesn't work (if the parents don't care or are drunk themselves), the young person is asked to come to a discussion the following week and escorted from home if she/he doesn't come. The workers do not keep their information secret, but contact professional helpers too. The most important links are with parents, first-aid clinics and the police. The main thing is not to be pals with the young, but to act as responsible adults and try to abort a drinking career (Kämäri 1993, p. 5).

Mono has also tried to make the community see what is going on in the streets and parks. They have repeatedly invited parents and local politicians for organized walks in the city during Friday nights. This has often been an eye-opening experience for them.

Mono's impact can be seen in the reduction in numbers of adolescents arrested for drunkenness which has happened hand in hand with Mono's contacts with the young people in the streets and in the office (Table 8.3).

4. ACTIVITIES WITH THE ADOLESCENTS

The Lahti project did not start from any planned overall strategy for youth education but used the grassroots approach in developing the methods. The idea was to create a lasting change in the community, to activate local energy and to use the local people's creativity rather than bring money from outside for a temporary input.

It is difficult to summarize the various activities among the youth in Lahti. A lot of the action was embedded in the everyday work of the local activists and was incorporated into what

Table 8.3   Number of adolescents arrested for drunkenness, 1990–94

	1990	1991	1992	1993	1994
under 15 years	9	3	4	4	8
under 18 years	192	178	144	115	128

Table 8.4   List of youth work activities in Lahti project

'Mono' street service

Distribution of educational material in the schools

Surveys on school children's drinking

The Crazy Girls

Local rock bands produced a CD to support 'Mono'

During the 'On-the-Wagon Weeks': exhibition in the Bazaar, theatre action group, essay competition in the schools, alcohol-free carnival

School class visits to the Library Week

A video on drunkenness

Theatre production, *The Wizard of Oz*

Involvement of the parents

Involvement of the parish confirmation schools

Development of education in the primary schools

Writing up the coordinated programme for drug and alcohol prevention in Lahti

was there already. The Lahti project only gave the extra support that was needed to carry out the work. Much of the input was small in itself, but the project networking gave it wider meaning. A list of activities is presented in Table 8.4.

The Theatre Production

Lahti has an amateur theatre for children and adolescents called Timotei. Lasse Kantola who was taking a degree in the field of youth work, wrote and directed a musical, *The Wizard of Oz*, for this theatre, based on the classic fairytale written by L. Frank Baum. The musical criticized commercial youth culture and drug use. The text was a combination of the original text and new texts and music. The work was already proceeding when the link with the Lahti project was made. The project supported the play financially by advertising it, paying for the costumes, which were made in the workshop staffed by unemployed youth, and by purchasing tickets to be given away at schools. Marjatta Montonen studied how the play was received among schoolchildren and wrote reports about the musical and its creation together with Lasse Kantola (Montonen 1994; Kantola and Montonen 1993).

The production turned out to be a series of interlinking forms of creative action for young people of different ages. The actors wrote analyses of their roles, gave them identity, dreams and problems, past and future. They also wrote about the experience of practising and acting in the play, and commented on the difficulty of alcohol and drug use as a topic. The audience was also activated. Teachers from three schools brought their classes to the theatre, and afterwards asked them to write about the experience and to draw pictures or make puppets of it. The texts were analysed in the report of the project (Kantola and Montonen 1993, pp. 41–52) and the drawings and puppets were exhibited in the library. The same pupils were later shown an educational video and asked to compare the two types of education (Kantola and Montonen 1993, pp. 53–63).

The play was performed eight times, and more than 1000 young people saw it. It received good reviews in the local papers, and was also included in the programme of the national festival for the children's amateur theatres.

Professional drug educators have often used drama as a tool, but in the whole field of alcohol and drug education drama is not a common form. The challenge is to be able to achieve good quality drama with small resources. Small-scale local productions for the young are not costly, but the problem is often the lack of dramatic skills. Youth projects using such methods have, however, taken place in various parts of Finland and in other countries, usually with good results (Montonen 1994, pp. 442–7).

The number of people who went to see the *The Wizard of Oz* as well as the critics' articles in the newspapers showed that the production in Lahti had succeeded well in making good theatre. The texts written by the school children who saw the play denoted among other things that the play had reached its audience and given them material for thinking.

Crazy Girls

Problem behaviour among girls had caused alarm among the youth workers in Lahti. Most of the youngsters helped by Mono, the street patrol, were girls under the age of 16. They used alcohol and pills or both and acted aggressively or self-destructively. The social youth workers and Lahti project decided to answer their call: Let's be crazy but let's do it without drugs.

The Crazy Girls project was started in the autumn of 1993. It was aimed at offering an active alternative to alcohol and drug use and to strengthen the young women's self-confidence, to develop their social skills and ability to cooperate in a group. The 13 girls were easily found on the streets of the town, and more were willing to join than could be taken. They had different backgrounds and experiences, but were all known to Mono. The youngest girl was 12 and the oldest was 15. Their experiences with alcohol and drugs were different, ranging from first drunkenness to heavy use.

The project gained a lot of publicity both locally and nationally. The idea was exciting and the experiences were encouraging. Lealiisa Kämäri, the social youth worker running the project, wrote and spoke well. The goal of the people in the project was to give positive messages and to point out possibilities and tasks rather than problems. The whole team was full of enthusiasm. Both Kämäri and a student doing her thesis wrote about the project (Kämäri and Pyykkö 1994; Kämäri 1993).

The first Crazy Girls group worked during the autumn undertaking challenging activities. Discussions and self-reflection took place on the side, but creative action and role-playing to work out thoughts and feelings were also used in an organized way. Four months included a lot of action: furnishing the meeting room, making prints, trinkets and hats, baking, painting, night-time nature excursions, riding, a self-defence course, visiting the theatre, climbing, dancing, concerts and singing. The most visible part of the activities was role-playing, which was documented in a photograph exhibition. Each girl spent two months planning her role. They were then made up and dressed as their favourite character ranging from Dead Virgin, Snow White and Joan of Arc to Scarlett O'Hara. A photography student took a picture of each one of them, and these were exhibited in a real art gallery. Several hundreds of people visited the exhibition. The local newspaper published pictures of the girls and their parents, who were proud of their daughters and what they had accomplished.

Commitment to sobriety during the project was the most important rule in the group. Failing to keep this promise once would lead to a warning and twice would mean having to leave the group. The severity of punishment was instigated by the girls themselves. One girl failed to keep the rule, and had to leave in the middle of the project.

The girls faced social pressure to drink and had to learn to resist. Alcohol was offered to them by their friends and pressure was put on them to drink at least 'when no one is looking'. One of the girls described the reactions like this: 'Friends think we are completely crazy because we don't drink, or they are afraid that we will change and will not be friends with them any more. Or maybe they are envious and would like to be one of the Crazies' (Kämäri 1993, p. 30).

The parents were also included in the project. The parents' group (the parents of eight girls) met every other week together with the family consultant and volunteer workers. Parents were given information on questions relating to the lives of girls in their daughters' age group. The most important goal for the group was to support the parents and give them an opportunity to share their experiences, to see that other people have similar problems and to free themselves from the anger and disappointment they felt for their children. Parents said the family atmosphere had become more positive during the project. The project was discussed on a national television show, where one of the 'Crazy' mothers talked beautifully about learning to reach out to her daughter again, and the camera showed the girl's face as she listened to her mother.

The work was made possible financially by voluntary workers who helped execute the project. The Lahti project supported the group with a small sum of money. The voluntary workers were given training and meetings with experts were organized.

After all the success and visibility there still were difficulties in continuing the Crazy Girls project. Funding was the first problem. The city of Lahti eventually gave the sum that was needed to continue it. The second group of Crazy Girls started in January 1995. This time the problems were different, and once again the youth workers learned the lesson they had learned many times before: nothing is ever self-evident with young people. The second group was dissolved rather quickly and did not reach its goals. The young require your total attention and 'Home Alone II' is never the same as 'Home Alone I'.

The Schools

The local schools were involved in the project, even if no attempts to develop new methods or contents of work were made. The schools were seen as one of the most important institutions in the community, touching the lives of a great number of the people living in Lahti. There was a shared feeling that schools should have a stronger link with homes and parents than is presently the case.

An educational leaflet was distributed to all pupils in the sixth and eighth grades for them to give to their parents. Thirty-eight per cent of those parents who should have received the leaflet replied to a follow-up questionnaire. They rated the leaflet generally as very informative.

Teachers were informed about the major events during the project. Many classes visited the Liquor Weeks in the library, and the essay competition on alcohol-related themes during the 'On-the-Wagon-Weeks' produced 100 essays. Younger children drew pictures during art classes. Social youth workers visited all the eighth grades when they collected data for the survey on young people's drinking, and gave a talk about alcohol and drug use in that context. During the last campaign, 'Is Everything Okay?' in the spring of 1995, the nursing students visited all the schools and organized information happenings there.

When parents, health-care workers and teachers discussed the topic, it was generally thought that one should start the education at a younger age than is currently taking place. Parents and teachers in two primary schools started a project together with the project coordinator Sirkka-Liisa Mäkelä for the development of early alcohol education.

The main difficulty in working with the schools is their minimal contact with the rest of the community. There is a large number of schools, teachers and pupils in any community. Schools also have a busy curriculum, and teachers have learned to avoid extra demands coming to them from the outside. Schools have also given up the integrated role they once had in the community. Where the village school once was the centre of all cultural and educational life and the teacher's informal authority was recognized by all, the modern school focuses on carrying out its curriculum and the teachers have no special role in the wider community. Parents' relations to the schools are rather distant, and discussion between teachers and parents tend to become strained and accusatory when alcohol issues are talked about. It is as if both groups secretly suspect that the other is neglecting their duties when children and young people misbehave (discussions during the parents' evening, 7 September 1994).

The Church

The local church was interested in developing the confirmation schools, which all 15-year-olds belonging to the church attend. Educational material was written, and discussions on drug issues were made a permanent part of the curriculum in the confirmation schools. Intensified contacts with the parents were developed. All the parents of those attending the confirmation school (about 1000 young people every year) were invited to a discussion evening during the winter. The ministers of the parish stressed the importance of values and moral courage. Parents need encouragement in their role as the controllers of their children's behaviour (discussion on the prevention of young people's alcohol and drug use, 1 June 1994). Together with the Lahti project they organized the open discussion evening 'Kännikinkerit' for parents and other educators and wrote down the 'ten commandments for parents to protect children from alcohol and drugs'.

5. WHAT SHOULD THE BIG ONES DO?

Within a prevention project, adolescents seemed automatically to form an important 'sub-community' within the community. Their drinking is visible, and everybody worries about the young. In the course of the project, the way of seeing the young people's drinking problems changed to some extent. They ceased to be an isolated group, and the attention of discussion focused more and more on the adults' role in transferring drinking habits from one generation to another.

Lack of clarity of norms concerning the acceptability of young people's drinking was brought forward in many discussions during the project. The professionals working with adolescents in Lahti brought forward the problem of reacting to the increasing presence of alcohol in the Young People's Community Centres during Friday evenings. The formal policy forbids drinking and intoxication on these premises. However, controlling this is difficult. Alcohol is smuggled in or it is drunk outside, 'around the corner'. At times the youth workers have mixed feelings about the right balance in being strict or permissive. They sometimes are worried that those who want to drink will go into town and spend their evenings on the streets if they are not let into the youth centres. They would thus be 'lost' from the good influence of the youth workers. A few years ago the youth workers even tried to allow sales of medium beer within the centres' premises. This experiment was terminated, though, as it proved to increase all kinds of difficulties (memos from meetings 8 December 1993 and 1 June 1994).

In a parents' meeting organized by the church the parents had a long debate about what would be the 'right' way of drinking for themselves. Should they drink and get drunk at home when the children are present or should they go out to a restaurant, and should they admit their habits or should they hide them? The right balance between controlling and permissive attitudes towards the youngsters' use of alcohol also seemed a problem. No agreement was reached.

The parents' and their teenagers' attitudes were looked at by sending a questionnaire to all the 14- and 16-year-olds and their parents in the schools of Lahti. Unfortunately, the response rate to this survey remained very low – only 38 per cent of the sample returned both the parents' and the adolescents' questionnaires. The results can, therefore, show only some basic tendencies, and they will be presented shortly.

When asked what would be a suitable age for the adolescents to start consuming alcohol, girls generally mentioned lower ages than boys. Parents' and adolescents' opinions on the suitable age for using alcohol were compared. The biggest differences were in the opinions of mothers and their 16-year-old daughters. There was nearly a two-year gap in what the 16-year-old girls thought to be the best time for starting drinking and what their mothers thought. The differences were smaller between parents and their 14-year-old daughters, and between parents and boys in both age groups. These results indicate that the situation is particularly conflict-loaded in the homes of 16-year-old girls, and especially between girls and their mothers.

When asked whether the parents discussed the harmful consequences of drinking with their children, both the parents and the child answered yes in the majority of the families. In about one-fifth of the families, however, the parents alone were of the opinion that the issues had been dealt with, but the youngster had not registered or could not remember such discussion.

The majority of the parents considered it unacceptable to buy alcoholic beverages for their teenagers' parties, but one-quarter could do so, depending on the circumstances. As many as 74 per cent of the 16-year-olds said that it is acceptable for the parents to buy alcohol for their teenagers. Here the adolescents were clearly less law-abiding than their parents.

However, the adolescents generally thought that they would be punished for intoxication. More than half of the 14-year-olds and one-third of the 16-year-olds believed they would be punished if they came home drunk. This belief was probably not based on experience, as only 29 per cent of the parents of the younger age group and 19 per cent of the older age group said they would punish their child in such a situation.

Discussions on parental attitudes and the best ways of influencing the adolescents' drinking were, whenever the participants of Lahti project were involved in them, intensive. However, lots of problems remained unresolved, especially those related to the parents' action as controllers or their position as role models. It was usually emphasized that parents should be more involved in alcohol education, for instance in cooperation with the teachers and other adults in schools.

6. COORDINATING THE ACTIVITIES

As several groups of professionals, many organizations and groups of volunteers work with children and the young in Lahti, the need for coordination became apparent during the course of the project. The drug policy group in Lahti prepared a joint program for alcohol and drug prevention among the young (Mäkelä and Teräväinen 1994). The programme itself is an important document, and the process of creating it may have been even more important. Representatives of all the sectors working with adolescents were invited to three subsequent meetings where the present work and the major challenges were dealt with. All participants prepared a written document about their work and ideas. One discussion evening was arranged for the parents. The written programme reports the experiences, thoughts and opinions expressed in these meetings. It is a living document of actual work and processes, not only a document of good intentions.

7. CONCLUSIONS

Young people in Lahti get acquainted with alcohol at a rather early age. They drink mostly in order to get drunk. The most immediate risks for them are caused by heavy intoxication: accidents, alcohol poisoning, violence. The street service Mono has made an attempt to protect the young from these consequences of drinking. Information about the alcohol content of different drinks and the effects of alcohol in a human body was given high priority in alcohol education during the Lahti project, with the aim of helping the individuals to avoid the acute harms related to intoxication.

It was observed that the children grow up in an environment characterized by ambivalent alcohol-related messages. Age limits for purchasing alcohol are generally supported. It would be difficult to find a decision-maker or a respectable citizen who would not be in favour of these measures. However, restrictive measures that would protect the young but would at the same time also limit the adults' liberties of purchasing alcohol are not accepted. Many adults cause great suffering for their children by their own drinking. The adults' inability to master alcohol is obvious to the young. The majority of adults use alcohol as a part of normal life, but their values and norms about it are still full of contradictions and strong emotions. The adults support educational measures for the young without being able to decide what are the norms and attitudes one should teach them.

The adults working with the children and the teenagers cannot escape the moral challenges connected to alcohol issues and concentrate on 'facts' alone. Many discussions during the project reflected the need to involve the parents in defining the norms of drinking. It was felt that without coherent messages shared by both the professional educators and the family, it is difficult to influence the young.

During the project, the focus shifted from looking at the young people as an isolated part of the community into looking at them in relation to the adults, in particularly in relation to their parents. The focus of the prevention of the adolescents' drinking turned from an abstract age-group into a sub-community formed by meaningful relationships of upbringing.

9 Family and Other Close Persons
Marja Holmila

1. THE PAINFUL CONTRADICTION

Family relations are for most people the most encompassing and enduring of their social ties. The family's relevance for the prevention and treatment of alcohol problems is well-known. For these reasons alone, families deserve a special focus in community action. In Lahti, however, the interest in family was based on the awareness of the widespread harm that heavy drinking causes to others. An attempt was thus made to look at ways of helping the family members in their stressful situation.

The painful relationship between the drinker and his or her loved ones seems to remain a difficult one to understand. It poses difficult moral questions, and brings us face to face with the dark side of human nature. The relationship has been conceptualized or named in various ways both in everyday thinking and in clinical research. In everyday life the phenomenon has to a great extent been surrounded by collective denial, silence and avoidance.

Alcohol-related injuries are often approached from a highly individualized point of view. Alcohol's impact on the individual's own health or mortality is given a high priority in public discussions about alcohol. The fact that drinking causes considerable, and often irreparable, harm to others is paid less attention. Yet the victims of others' drinking are numerous, and often they are the most vulnerable members of the community. The lives of children and the elderly can be extremely stressful because of family members who drink.

During the old temperance movement the sufferings of the family were one of the important arguments and incentives for fighting against alcohol use. Nowadays the logic is different: the significant others have a private problem, the remedy of which is therapy or some other type of individual counselling. This change reflects the changes in family structure and family ideology as much as changes in social response to alcohol problems.

The society seems to have a need to classify the intimate others of drinkers as having certain qualities. Their role in the wider community is seen in light of the fact that they have accepted or become victimized by the private role of being a drinker's significant other. This creates an ambivalence in their social image; the private role is encouraged by positive values of responsibility and caring, while the process of labelling signals negative assessments of personal defects.

The harmful effects of drinking are not only recorded by the professional helping agencies or the statistics. The ordinary citizens have a direct and a very substantial experience of these problems. It is important to mediate this link in order to make society at large aware of the misery that alcohol at its worst can cause.

While planning the Lahti project it was thought that a step forward from the trappings of victimization and labelling could, perhaps, be achieved if the problems experienced by the intimate others could be seen affecting the whole community, as they eventually do. If their experiences could be brought 'out of the shadows' without moralism or malicious curiosity, both the community and the individual family members could benefit. The guilt and shame weighing on the intimate others could be lessened and their abilities to control their own lives made easier.

The problems experienced by the intimate others are an important argument for preventive efforts in the drug and alcohol field, but it is not an easy task to find suitable forms of action in this context. People's private lives need to be kept private, and the society does not have a right to interfere unless asked to do so. The outsider always runs the risk of making things even worse. During the project, working methods in this field were developed in the community.

2. WHO ARE THE INTIMATE OTHERS?

A local telephone interview was carried out in Lahti with a sample of 702. It was based on the telephone directory and consisted of the population age of 18 or older. The age and gender quotas represented the distribution in the population. Those who refused to take part in the interview were substituted with new respondents. The respondents were asked, 'Are

Table 9.1   Percentage of those who reported having one
or more close people drinking 'too much'

| | Men | | Women | |
	Finland (489)	Lahti (346)	Finland (541)	Lahti (356)
At least one close person drinking	44	42	46	49
The drinker(s) is (are):				
family member(s)	5	5	7	13
relative(s)	18	14	24	26
friend(s)	23	20	23	14
colleague(s)	9	12	4	8

there persons close to you who in your opinion drink too
much?' and if yes, 'Are these persons your family members,
relatives, friends or colleagues?' The third question was, 'Has
the drinking of this person/these persons close to you affected
your own life?'

Almost half of all the respondents said that among those close
to them someone was drinking too much. There was only a small
difference between men and women in this respect, and the
socioeconomic status had very little impact on how common
this experience was. Data from the whole of Finland gave similar
results, showing that Lahti is not a special case.

The gender differences became apparent, however, when one
looked closer at the respondents' answers. More women than
men had a heavy drinker among their relatives or inside the
nuclear family. Men's close-by drinkers were more often colleagues at work or friends (Table 9.1).

To some extent the gender differences here can be explained
by men's heavier drinking. Because more men than women
drink heavily, having a heavy drinking spouse or a partner is
more likely for women than for men, and having a heavy drinking friend or a colleague is more likely for men than for women.
However, the gender difference in having a drinking relative
cannot be explained by the gender of the heavy drinker – a
male drinker should have approximately as many male and
female relatives (e.g. parents, children and siblings). It thus

Table 9.2   The effects of a close person's drinking,
respondents in Lahti

		Percentage of those whose lives had been affected by a close person's drinking
Women	(356)	30
Men	(346)	16
All	(702)	24
The drinker(s) is (are):		
family member(s)	(63)	64
relative(s)	(141)	41
friend(s)	(120)	28
colleague(s)	(67)	34

seems that women are more sensitive toward or aware of their
relatives' drinking problems than men.

The intimate others' drinking can be considered more of a
problem if it has affected one's own life in some way. Twice as
many women in Lahti (30 per cent) than men (16 per cent)
said that others' drinking had affected their own lives (Table
9.2). The result is compatible with the previous observation of
women's intimate others being more within the circle of family
and relatives, and men's among their friends and work colleagues. All in all, 24 per cent of the respondents said that their
lives had been affected by someone else's drinking.

The survey results show that while there are hardly any differences in how often a man or a woman reports having an intimate other drinking too much, there are clear gender-based
differences in whose alcohol problems are acknowledged and
to what extent this has affected the respondents' own lives. This
difference also influences men's and women's alcohol policy
opinions.

3. THE EXPERIENCES AND ACTIONS OF INTIMATE OTHERS

An in-depth interview was conducted with a group of people (25 women and 25 men) close to a problem drinker. The

respondents for these interviews were recruited with a news-paper advertisement headed: 'Does someone close to you drink too much?' The respondents were asked to telephone a given number so the time for the interview could be arranged. People could remain anonymous if they wished. This ad was published in three local newspapers in Lahti.

As a response to the ad, at first 19 women and three men came to be interviewed. Three female interviewees came from the family members' support group, where the same ad was also distributed. Due to the small number of men in the first data set, a second attempt to recruit men was carried out in connection with a telephone survey. When asked personally, several men were willing to come to the interview. This method led to equal numbers of men and women being interviewed.

Heavy drinking causes a multitude of serious problems for the intimate others (Table 9.3). More than half of those inter-viewed talked about economic problems, violence, continuous fear, quarrels and failing health due to the stress and deteriora-tion of family communication. Women generally mentioned more problems than men and they also talked a lot longer. The men's and women's accounts were closest when mentioning violence, failing health and deteriorated family communication. Women expressed fear more often than men.

The most common problems mentioned by all were eco-nomic. Alcohol is expensive, especially in restaurants, and drink-ing often causes other costs such as paying for other people's drinks, losing money by carelessness and taxi expenses. When the drinker's ability to work is reduced, the economic problems become severe.

> When mother died, father fell apart. One day I came home from school and all the furniture had been carried out to the yard. From then on I lived wherever I could (30-year-old son).

The descriptions of violence ranged from verbal threats to actual violence resulting in physical injuries or a death in the family. People talked about fistfights, strangling, knives and guns.

> He tied a string around my neck on a Saturday evening after he had drunk a bottle of spirits. A year later he tried to kill me again and then I called the police (43-year-old wife).

Table 9.3   Harms caused by a close person's drinking
(interviewees in Lahti)

Harm caused	Number of persons talking about the harm		
	Women	*Men*	*All*
Economic problems	21	12	33
Violence	18	14	32
Fear	22	10	32
Quarrels	19	9	28
Interviewee's or other family member's health	16	11	27
Deterioration of family communication	15	12	27
'Dr Jekyll and Mr Hyde'	19	8	27
Disorderly everyday life	16	8	25
Sexual problems	16	5	21
Drinker's obsessive jealousy	10	5	15
Distrust	16	2	18
All interviewees	25	25	50

Quarrels and lack of family communication were also often described. The worst quarrels happened often when the drinker was drunk and everybody lost their temper easily. In order to avoid quarrelling, people had learned to avoid each other, which again resulted in the deterioration of family communication.

The interviewees saw many of their health problems as consequences of the stress and fear they lived in. Some had physical injuries caused by the drinker's violence. Couples had sexual problems. Everyday life was often disorderly. There were no shared mealtimes or joint activities. Household duties or child care was neglected. Many drinkers seemed to demand services from the other family members without any reciprocity.

He telephones after midnight and tells me I must come and meet him with the car. When we get home, I must cook a meal for him (50-year-old wife).

The interviews of the intimate others contained a rich vocabulary of emotional words. These were retrieved from the text in the qualitative data analyses. The most common single feeling mentioned was fear. All in all 32 interviewees talked about fear, which could be attributed to several causes. It could be related to the drinker's violence or threats of violence. It could also be motivated by the awareness that lots of things can happen to the drinker, and she or he can cause accidents. The intimate others worried about road accidents, attacks of illness, suicide, medicine overdoses, fires, damages to the furniture or the house, stealing and public humiliation. The children were particularly frightened of the parents' quarrels. If the drinker is currently sober, the intimate other is afraid of the next drinking bout.

This kind of life is not worth living. One is afraid and nervous all the time (46-year-old wife).

Fear prevents the intimate others from protecting their rights. It also leads to sleepless nights, stress, continuous need to be on the alert and easily colours the person's whole attitude to life.

It is all my property, actually, I could sell everything and leave him, but I am sure I would be dead by then (43-year-old wife).

There is nothing I can do but be on guard or feel fear (76-year-old mother).

Other often-mentioned emotions were anger, hate, suffering, exhaustion, shame and guilt. All these negative feelings take their toll on the intimate others' self-confidence and mental health.

One of the strongest feelings is a certain kind of continuous bitterness of why this is happening to me. Sadness, too (47-year-old man, divorced).

Perhaps there is a sort of hate and contempt against the drinking and against my father. . . . Sometimes I get into a rage against alcohol. I want to go and break all the bottles. It is senseless anger, of course (23-year-old daughter).

Bitterness and anger and aggression. What right does she have to drink? I am her child and she has to be a mother to me, I don't have to be a mother to her. She will never understand it, I think (17-year-old daughter).

Nothing but awful sadness and pain (44-year-old wife).

At the same time as the intimate others feel anger and pain, they feel guilt and shame for their own misery. The interviewees expressed guilt for not being able to endure the situation any more, of the fact that other family members were suffering, of somehow causing the drinking, or having made wrong decisions in their lives, of having been angry at the drunken person, of supporting the drinker financially and of being poor company.

The drinker doesn't generally make it much easier for the intimate other to stop feeling guilty. It seems that alcoholics are very tempted to accuse others for their problems because that prevents them from facing the fact that they must stop drinking – the most difficult task for them.

One feels ashamed for having been so stupid as to have put oneself into such a situation (24-year-old widow).

The guilty one has to be someone else because he cannot look himself in the eye (43-year-old wife).

One could think that the guilt and shame felt by the intimate others would lead to impaired self-value and social isolation. To some extent this was the case. It is also important to notice that the need for isolation was not only caused by the shame, but by the fact that 'normal' sociability almost always includes drinking. It inevitably causes embarrassing situations for the intimate others of heavy drinkers who cannot control their drinking or their behaviour. One of the problems for the intimate others is to balance their own need for social acceptance with people outside the family and the drinker's wish for protection and secrecy. It is sometimes also in the drinker's interest to keep the problems inside the four walls of the home. Thus the drinkers are likely to inflict guilt on other family members if they reveal the family secrets to others.

Most of the emotions described in the data were negative. But there would not be all this pain if the intimate others had not loved their drinkers.

When he was going through his awful binges I hated him, but otherwise I had to say he was my best friend. He taught me quite a lot . . . I cried really bitterly when he died (28 year-old son).

I guess he was so dear to me because he really had no one else but me (67-year-old mother).

The interviewed persons had been engaged in various kinds of actions in order to cope with or change their lives. Research has attempted to form typologies of action, and it has been possible to distinguish differing orientations to the problem (Orford 1992, p. 1515; 1994, pp. 417–29). Most intimate others go through many phases, try different approaches and change their behaviour in the hope of being better able to influence the drinker's behaviour. It might be more correct to see different coping styles as phases in a process rather than basic action orientations. Wiseman (1991) talks about 'definitional careers' and Asher (1992) uses the term 'moral career' in analysing the experiences of wives of alcoholic husbands.

Avoiding the drinker's company and efforts to try and exclude him/her from one's own life were commonly mentioned by the interviewed persons in Lahti.

We discussed with the family counsellor that a drinking person needs help and support and I agree he does. But I am no longer going to be that support, I have had enough (46-year-old wife).

I have left the house many times. It depends, it is no good to stay when she attacks and screams and makes a great hullabaloo, it is better to leave than to stay and listen to it (43-year-old husband).

Leaving can also be a demonstration where the intimate other hopes to change the drinker's behaviour by frightening him or her with rejection.

Yes I was hoping, one is so silly as to believe that if I leave him he cannot manage and for that reason stops drinking. I had such silly ideas before I learned that an alcoholic never stops drinking for anybody else but for himself, never for other people (46-year-old widow).

Ignoring the drinker or excluding him or her is a more subdued form of avoidance. The intimate other may be in the same building with the drinker, but tries to forget his/her existence.

> I have learned to be in my own company. It is good because then we don't quarrel, I don't feel like nagging or anything. I am fed up, I have tried good words and bad words . . . and it has led to nothing, so now I just keep to myself. (46-year-old wife).

Almost all of the interviewed intimate others had tried or currently were trying to control the other's drinking, but often had had to learn that the drink is more powerful than their influence. Many of them had given up trying to prevent drinking, but continued trying to be around in order to prevent the worst consequences of drunkenness.

> Sometimes I and my brother poured out his liquor and put something else in the bottle (16-year-old daughter).

> I cannot leave home at all, I am afraid of what will happen when my sons and their father start fighting (57-year-old wife and mother).

Sometimes family members thought that by sharing the drinking situations with the intimate other they could reduce the harms.

> In the early days I sometimes went to the pub with him. I thought he would drink less if I was with him, but I couldn't keep it up. I would have become an alcoholic myself, and it did not help anything (46-year-old widow).

Interviews contained only a few descriptions of efforts to cover up the drinker's behaviour, and usually the intimate others had learned to stop doing so. Not talking about the problem to other people was sometimes caused by the fact that others did not want to hear or know about it.

> It was forbidden to discuss his drinking. People said he drank because he had had such a hard life. He was allowed to drink, it was fine (28-year-old son).

4. PRINTING OUT THE EXPERIENCE

The experiences of family members were also used in the media. For instance the third-prize-winner in an essay competition among schoolchildren described the experiences of a child in a family where the mother drinks, and this essay was hung out as a poster in the shopping mall exhibition during the 'On-the-Wagon' Weeks. An editorial in a local newspaper quoted large parts of it.

> The clock on the night table shows 3 a.m. It is dark, except for the dim light coming from under the door. They are still awake in the kitchen. I lie in the bed quietly and listen. Whispers, shouts, giggles, swearing and screams – it all comes to my ears as one big mess, soon exploding in my head. I am so tired. . . . I have a history test tomorrow, but how could I have studied when I cannot even sleep? Mother doesn't care, she hasn't cared for a long time. She is an alcoholic. . . .
>
> Weekends are the worst. I come home from school and every time, as far as I can remember, mother has been sitting in the kitchen with a bottle of wine in her hand and crying. There is no food because there is no money. My little sister Riikka and I are used to eating at school as much as possible, and Riikka spends the evenings with her friends. I cannot do that because I no longer have any friends. Who would want to visit us when mother is always drunk? Even the relatives have stopped calling; they don't want to interfere, I guess. But no one seems to realize how alone I am. I do the tidying, the laundry, I get Riikka from school, I do the dishes, go shopping and take care of mother on the side.
>
> Partying turns into fights. 'Bloody cow, to hell with you', can be heard from the kitchen. My heart beats in my throat, I curl up under the blanket so that I can't hear. I am scared. Suddenly the door opens and Riikka stands there crying. 'Can I come and sleep with you, I am scared', she says.
>
> Sometimes I feel I can no longer go on, I would like to finish this whole shit. Can a life like this give me anything? It would make no difference if I didn't exist. But what would happen to Riikka? She is so small, seven years old, and only started school. She is the only person who keeps me holding on to this life. Sometimes I decide we will run away together,

Riikka and I. We will go somewhere far away, away from this hell smelling of cigarettes and beer. We will go somewhere where we can start anew and plan our future. We will find a place where we are happy. And yet I am always thinking, 'not today, but maybe tomorrow'.

Fighting in the kitchen gets worse. Someone throws glass on the floor. Mother shouts and swears, 'You don't fucking touch me, you don't start hitting me'. . . . More screams and blows. Mother calls for help as loud as she can. I wake Riikka up and tell her to take the blanket and the teddy bear with her, we must go. Mother has told us to always go and ask for help from downstairs if something horrible happens, and call the police.

There we stand again, behind the door of the Virtanens. I don't even feel any shame anymore, this has happened so many times. Mrs Virtanen comes and opens the door, we don't have to say anything, she understands and lets us in. She says, 'Mother will be better tomorrow.' And I know she is lying.

Kati, 17 years old, March 1994.

5. GROUP CONSULTATIONS FOR FAMILY MEMBERS

In addition to conducting research among the intimate others, involving family members and other close persons of drinkers in group consultations and in youth work were the forms of action used in the Lahti project.

In a questionnaire among the population of Häme district, the region where Lahti is situated, people expressed a need to learn how to influence and help those who drink too much. When asked what kind of information on alcohol would be most useful to the respondents, there was more interest in learning how to help others than learning about the harmful effects of alcohol use or ways of treating alcoholism (Hämeen lääninhallitus 1990, p. 36). Nearly half of the respondents said they would like to learn how to take part in helping others control their drinking. The drug policy group in Lahti had also raised the idea of approaching the family members.

The idea for the sessions was for counselling, not for therapy nor for open discussions. The first sessions were organized in an adult education institute, the later ones in the primary health-care centre. The participants could come without any commitments and were free to take part in the discussions or remain silent. The sessions took place on two evenings with one week in between, and the participants were given homework. The consultant was experienced in running group sessions, had special training for drug counselling and a degree in psychology. The local coordinator for these sessions was a nurse, who had also previously worked in the drug field. Usually 15 to 30 persons took part in the sessions.

The participants in the counselling sessions did not recount their experiences or life stories, as is usually done in Al Anon groups. This was not forbidden, but the goal was to remain in the present, and to keep feelings slightly in the background. The goal was in finding a solution for the intimate other, and in activating the participants in developing action to solve their problems. No pre-set goals were pinpointed. The solution was searched step by step through exercises. The consultant gave an introduction to what is known about the problems the participants share and opened up the discussion. He made sure that everyone had a chance to talk and feel comfortable in the group. Only small, practical solutions were suggested, and the rest was left for the participants to work out. Some issues prompted discussions and differing opinions. The participants asked, for instance, what is meant by enabling. Does taking care of the bills and performing daily chores mean enabling? Some of the participants of the open counselling sessions met later in smaller groups without the counsellor.

The local organizer, a nurse, was an important link between the counselling sessions for the intimate others and other services available in the city. Through her the whole family could try and deal with its problems in whatever ways were considered best. She had the possibility of seeing the family members alone or together with the drinking member, she could help the drinker go to treatment in special alcoholism agencies and she formed links (naturally with the consent of the client) between different actors in the client's environment.

During 1993, three session with two evenings each were organized and 112 persons attended them (Mäkelä 1994, p. 19). During 1994, there were two sessions with 45 persons attending, and in 1995 two sessions and 29 persons. After the sessions, the groups have met again six to eleven times without the consultant. The counselling and the groups have now become a permanent element of the municipality's services.

6. THE POWER OF NAMING

The intimate others of drinkers have for quite a while been helped with self-help therapy and support. Al-Anon was founded to provide support for families in which one or more members have a drinking problem. The movement adopted the Twelve Steps used by Alcoholics Anonymous and used the disease concept of alcoholism as a way of explaining what was happening in these families. The terms 'co-alcoholic' and 'co-dependent' stem from this self-help movement. In addition to organizing the groups, the movement has also produced a considerable number of self-help books, undoubtedly addressing a basic need and providing help and support for their readers. The co-dependent movement has also succeeded in affording families of problem drinkers a more elevated status within treatment agencies than was previously the case. As a result, the demand for professional treatment for persons identifying themselves as intimate others of drinkers is likely to have increased. In spite of its beneficial impact in the lives of the drinkers' family members, the notion of co-dependency has been criticized for creating new negative traps for these people.

The intimate others of problem drinkers are in various ways deeply and cruelly hurt by the drinking person. At the same time they see that he/she is helpless in the face of addiction. The soul-splitting experience is hard for outsiders to accept or even believe. The cultural image of the drinker's family reflects this emotional dilemma. The overall reaction has been dual, halfhearted and contradictory. There is also a strong need to forget the whole problem and all its moral dimensions. After all, it does tend to take the edge off the happy celebrations of the majority. One way of forgetting the problem is to classify the intimate others of drinkers as deviant, and thus being somehow guilty of their own destiny. Naming the persons rather than the situation they are in, works as a powerful method of collective denial. This is where the labelling paradigm and lay notions of co-dependency have often become handy, especially in the case of wives of alcoholics, and not always without hostile undertones. As Paul Roman notes, the term 'codependency' comprises a broad, vague, but rich folk hypothesis. It contends that the intimates of alcoholics engage in behaviours that reinforce and embed deviant alcohol use. The folk theory also suggests that such behaviours represent psychopathology among these significant others (Roman 1993).

The term co-dependency refers to a postulated condition. The term has an interesting evolution as a concept from being a descriptive term to assuming the status of diagnosis. There is a large body of literature addressing various aspects of this concept. Depending on the writer, co-dependency is defined as either an illness, a cause of illness, a relationship addiction or a spiritual void. The condition is seen to affect particular individuals, all family members, communities, states and even whole nations (Hands and Dear 1994, p. 438). Recently several critical reviews on the discussion of the co-dependency concept have been published, all of them pointing out the lack of conceptual clarity (e.g. Appel 1991; Asher 1992, Krestan and Bepko 1991; Hands and Dear 1994).

Krestan and Bepko (1991) discuss the wider issues of close relationships and family patterns from which the co-dependency concept stems. According to these authors, the familiar language of co-dependency, while it represents an effort to name and articulate pain, has become a mythology in which the leading characters are defined as victims and as sick. They suggest an alternative language for describing such families: co-dependency needs to be redefined as over-responsibility, and over-responsibility needs to be understood as a positive impulse gone awry.

Recent clinical studies conclude that the approach to find disturbed personality traits, which characterize the spouses of alcoholics, have not succeeded, and there is increasing support for the view that spouses of alcoholics are essentially normal people trying to cope with impaired partners (Rychtarik 1990; McCrady and Hey 1982). The stress-victim perspective has been identified as providing the main alternative to the disturbed-personality view of spouses. Drinking produces a continuous stress for others in the family, and different kinds of negative impacts on their health and ability to control their lives (Orford 1984).

Besides making the lives of the intimate others more difficult, the co-dependency concept can be harmful also from the point of view of preventive measures. It emphasizes the individual and recommends treatment as a remedy. However, individual help can only alleviate the pain or support the individuals in coping with their problems but it cannot prevent them. Also, if the intimate others are understood as persons with deviant personalities, the 'ordinary people' can wash their hands and leave all responsibility to professional treatment agencies. Attempts to classify the problems of the intimate others as individual problems become illogical, however, when as many as 40 per cent say that someone close to them is drinking too much, as was the case in Lahti.

7. CONCLUSIONS

The problems of the intimate others of drinkers should also be an important argument for prevention of alcohol use in the communities. The costs of alcohol use for families are hard to measure in exact terms, but the data from Lahti as well as from many other studies show that living with a drinker causes considerable stress and the family members' own health is for that reason at risk. Children growing up in alcoholic families are perhaps most vulnerable (see Christensen 1994; Cork 1969; Orford 1984; Johnson and Rolf 1990, pp. 162–93).

At the same time, it is important to keep on investing in helping the individuals who are facing difficulties due to other people's drinking. The help itself can emphasize the preventive element: the goal is to help the intimate others find solutions in their everyday lives so they can better cope with their stress. Coping with stress, the threat of violence or other maltreatment is essential for bettering their quality of life. This again prevents the health risks they are facing. Along these lines, the support courses arranged for the intimate others in Lahti avoided the image of treatment and emphasized the cognitive, solution-oriented approach and open elements in the intervention.

Helping the intimate others is somewhere between prevention and treatment. The helping persons involved have to have an understanding of both. Alcoholism treatment, social work and health-care centres are all relevant. On the basis of the discussions and interviews in Lahti it seems important that the person meeting the intimate others of drinkers has experience and knowledge of alcohol and drug problems, not only of psychology, family dynamics or child development. The psychiatrists or primary health-care workers do not always have the ability to understand the reality of drinkers' intimate others, and can sometimes fail to help and even increase the guilt felt by the family member.

We can ask as Hamilton, Barber and Banwell (1994, p. 374) have asked: How can we capture the strength and energy, enthusiasm and interest that exists in communities for families and family-related concerns? How do we connect this with research-based knowledge? And how do we encourage and facilitate the potential role of families in the range of preventative interventions?

For a long time alcoholism treatment has used the family members as a resource for helping the alcoholics. There are also examples of the prevention of alcohol problems advocated by persons with firsthand experience: Mothers Against Drunken Drivers, the early temperance movement (e.g. Appel 1991), health promotion activists, writers and researchers. Having a family experience of alcohol problems seems to affect people's opinions of alcohol and its consequences: readiness to see alcohol problems as social problems is increased if the person has someone close to them drinking too much, and especially if his/her own life has been affected by someone else's drinking (Holmila 1994).

The problems caused by someone else's alcohol use are often made worse by the reactions from the wider community. The feelings of shame and guilt which the labelling notions increase, are strong impediments to a positive change. It is important to change the social attitudes and ideology toward these people in order to reduce their pain. Those affected by others' drinking are, on the other hand, an important resource for any community in preventing alcohol-related injuries. Their motivation and insight are important assets, and it is a shame that so much of them has in the past been wasted by labelling them sick or deviant.

Part III
Assessing the Utility of the Lahti Project

10 Process Evaluation
Marja Holmila

1. THE EVALUATIVE VIEWPOINT

Evaluation results depend on the criteria one uses to assess the successes or failures of the action. The apparently simple question 'How well did it work?' is in reality a very complex one. How to define what is to be considered an achievement or a change, who makes these definitions, what scientific methods are best in describing the examined phenomena?

The major lines of conflict in the evaluation literature are found particularly between those researchers who emphasize the relevance of process evaluation and those who concentrate more on effect research (Albrecht and Otto, eds, 1991, p. 404). The effect research tests the claimed relationship between specific measures (independent variables) and effects (dependent variables) excluding rival explanations. The proponents of effect research particularly adopted the methodological model of experiment as their ideal. Those researchers who paid less attention to the outcome of intervention but were more interested in its process adopted the paradigm of action research. According to action researchers, decisive quality criteria of evaluation were no longer validity and objectivity but communication, transparency and relevance (House 1980, pp. 249–57). This countercurrent led in the 1970s and 1980s to fixed fronts between the action research proponents and those with scientific experiment as their ideal.

In addition to the more basic difference between action research orientation and experimental studies, evaluators have the choice between quantitative and qualitative data. Qualitative evaluations are useful when programme goals are not stated clearly, and totally objective measurement is difficult. It is useful also when great care must be taken to understand the setting of the programme, when the goals are vague, or there is a contentious atmosphere, or rich programme content (Posavac and Carey 1992, p. 210). The importance of the evaluator in gathering the qualitative data personally is often stressed in the literature.

As a way out of the fixed frontiers between different types of evaluation the multimethod approach (Albrecht and Otto 1991, p. 404) was used in this study. The evaluation had both quantitative and qualitative outcome components, qualitative process evaluation, formative evaluation of working methods and an experimental follow-up of the health care intervention.

It has been noted that even if outcome questions are often the first questions posed to the evaluator, they should be the last ones answered (Pirie 1990, p. 206; Rutman 1980). In order to ask the right questions for the outcome evaluation, the project's character and place in the wider context needs to be understood. A crucial element in defining the relevant questions for the evaluation is to fully understand what type of action is being evaluated.

Patton talks about utilization-focused evaluations. These evaluations begin with identification and organization of specific, relevant decision-makers and information-users (not vague, passive audiences) who will use the information produced by the evaluation. The evaluator works with these persons to determine relevant questions, from which then flow the appropriate research methods and data analysis techniques (Patton 1980, p. 59).

The criteria for the success or failure of a project should be selected in close consultation between the evaluator and the stakeholders involved in the project (Posavac and Carey 1992, p. 28). The values, needs, implementation and goals of the stakeholders will affect the way evaluators can make sense of the usefulness of the project.

There are at least three different types of stakeholders for the Lahti project. First, there is the general public that might be interested in increasing their understanding of the community they live in. In that sense the study has the sociological task of describing and analyzing social life in the community. Second, active representatives of local communities need models and estimates of the usefulness of similar action. The process descriptions are particularly helpful for them in developing their own course of action. They also need some estimates of outcome. Third, health promotion professionals in the local, district and state level need to be able to assess the utility of local action in order to know if it is sensible to promote and support these projects. Outcome results, even rather simple ones, are particularly useful to all those responsible for budgeting.

2. THE PROGRAMME THEORY

Evaluation literature uses the strict term 'programme', which doesn't always correspond to the more or less sporadic and intuitive reality of the development projects. Pirie notes that often the first major contribution an evaluator makes to the project is extracting and documenting the plan (Pirie 1991, pp. 203–6). In defining the content of the programme, one should postulate its theory. A programme theory is based on the assumptions about the causes of problems and the best ways to solve them.

In Lahti the programme theory consisted of seeing drinking problems predominantly as social rather than individual problems. Drinking habits are determined by the culture and the social and economic environment. Different individuals, however, experience alcohol-related problems to a differing degree. Consequently prevention should simultaneously take place both on the social and the individual level. For instance, heavy users are an important group to pay attention to because they and their family members are the individuals suffering most of the harms caused by alcohol, but prevention policies need to try and influence the whole population.

The second assumption about causes of problems and about best ways to solve them was that alcohol use is influenced both by supply and demand; that is, by consumers' needs and by the interests of those who make money on either producing or marketing drinks. An effective prevention policy takes both of these aspects into account. Influencing the supply of alcohol on the local level is limited, but some issues of control and responsible service are best approached locally rather than nationally or internationally.

The activity in the project consisted of several small (or medium-sized) elements, but not totally without overall planning or general framework. The principle from *Gestalt* theory, which states that the total result is different from the sum of the elements, applies quite well. Many actions with seemingly invisible effects alone have together a large effect (Aaro, 1992,

p. 12). This can be explained by such factors as the invisible effects of single campaigns accumulating and leading to more substantial changes in behaviour over time, and health education campaigns influencing the general public indirectly through mass-media coverage of health topics.

The community representatives – the participants of the project – had differing roles and interests in the community. The city has its advocates for healthier lifestyles, and it has its health and social professionals, with their own values and interests. To counterbalance them, there was the influence of the local alcohol industry and restaurant business. The influential persons have their special role as leaders and spokesmen of the community culture and its informal power structures. The media professionals see themselves as mediators between the rank and file and those in power.

The working methods in Lahti were based on dialogue. This meant that neither of the often discussed polarities, grassroots or top-to-bottom approach, were taken as a starting point. The work in the project was aimed at being a constant, open and equal movement between the grassroots and the expert point of view. Voluntary grassroots organizations and welfare state professionals each have their role in the prevention efforts. The task of the researchers was to engage themselves in open discussion with different actors and to use the information gathered from the co-partners as a tool for sociological intervention. The project team tried to form links with whoever was available. In practice, the health, social and youth work professionals of the city were perhaps the most important resource for the project, because of their initial preparedness for prevention work.

3. THE PARTICIPANTS' EXPERIENCE AND RATINGS: PREVENTION IS FOOD, LOVE AND COMMON SENSE

The process of starting, carrying out and finishing the project was all well-documented, and the researchers were closely involved in all these stages. The main problem in using this data is the possibility of a subjective bias: the project provoked strong commitment among those involved. The researchers' personal involvement may have meant that at times we only saw what we wanted to see. This is not a new problem for community action projects and it has a lot in common with the methodological problems well known to anthropologists and those involved in intensive qualitative research.

In this context it is useful to turn to the local actors. It could be said that many of them, too, had a self-interest in seeing the project through rose-coloured glasses. This bias was to some extent reduced by the fact that it was possible to ask the opinions of a large group of people. The participants' questionnaire was sent to 84 persons. Some, although rather few, of these people had been engaged in several types of work, but most of them had taken part in one particular area of prevention work in the community. The number of returned questionnaires was 51.

The participants replying to the questionnaires were generally satisfied with their experience. This is not very surprising as it has often been noted that participants in any programme generally rate their experience as satisfactory. There are various explanations for the positive rating bias: cognitive consistency, self-selection, general response style of not wanting to appear critical or ungrateful (Pirie 1991, p. 204).

It is more interesting to look closer at the activists' ways of formulating their experience. They were asked how they would define the prevention of alcohol problems. The difficulty of this task was reflected in the given answers so that very often one defined what prevention is not, rather than being able to say what it actually is. Prevention was said not to be 'absolutist attitudes towards drinking', or 'merely stating restrictions and prohibitions'.

The participants' definitions for prevention can be classified in three groups: preventing harm, promoting controlled drinking, and 'brakes on'. The preventing harm approach stresses the importance of avoiding risks in drinking and reducing the consequences of intoxication or addiction, rather than reducing drinking as such. Promoting controlled drinking means stressing the importance of finding pleasurable, controlled styles of drinking and avoiding the dark side of alcohol use, which according to this line of thinking can be separated from the enjoyable use of alcohol. The 'brakes on' model aims at slowing down any further growth of alcohol use or abuse. Prevention should stop the harm from escalating.

Information and education were mentioned more often than any other form of prevention. A conspicuous fact is the number of statements stressing the importance of 'truthful' or 'right kind of' information. Sometimes the phrase 'right kind of' referred to presenting objective facts, sometimes to matter-of-factness. In some statements this was contrasted with giving orders and restrictions, in others it was contrasted with inefficient education using the wrong kind of methods.

Most opinions that the participants gave on prevention concentrated on talking about how to influence the use of alcohol, not how to control or regulate supply. Only four respondents mentioned the traditional alcohol-policy methods: price, availability and control. The reason for so few mentioning these methods can be threefold; either people do not generally believe in these measures, or they consider them inappropriate on the local level, or they find them no good as justification for their own role as community activists or professionals.

The definitions of prevention were, however, not only on the individual level, even if influencing the individual was given a high prominence. Community level was also mentioned, and given a rich meaning. Influencing community means, for example, changing the opinion climate so that a more open discussion on alcohol would become possible. It also means that the society is aware of the costs due to drinking, and tries to prevent them. Several participants stressed the importance of social welfare: preventing alcohol problems starts from preventing general social problems. Cooperation between different parts of the community was recommended. The links with other areas of life and with the basic features of community life were summarized in the definition of one of the youth workers: 'Prevention is food, love and common sense.' The community's task was also to act as a guide or a teacher in developing the characteristics of responsibility and self-control in the individuals.

On the basis of the answers given it seems that the project activists had no single definition or outlook as to what prevention means. The scale of given definitions was large and contained differing elements. The participants' opinions differed clearly in how 'anti-alcohol' they were, and how much they stressed individual responsibility.

When asked which kinds of things should have been given more attention in the project, 31 respondents answered. Half of the comments were about the content of the project, and half were about motivating the actors and getting them involved, that is, about the project organization and structure. Most of those commenting on the motivation and education of the participants were involved in the heavy drinkers' intervention in health care centres, and they had found the beginnning of the work somewhat difficult. The personnel was not motivated or adequately informed about their tasks before the onset of the intervention. The early phases were thought to have been too hectic, and the health-care personnel were not adequately involved in the planning. For many the start had meant a command from above, and this had caused reluctance.

Comments on the content of the action were various. Four people said that one should have focused on the children and the young even more, and another four stressed the importance of cooperation with parents and other educators. Three participants said that there had not been enough information about the project and its goals, especially at the beginning. Two respondents would have liked more specified goals and campaigns, and one respondent said the work should have been closer to the grassroots. Some participants were concerned about the future of alcoholism treatment and less concerned about prevention.

The participants were also asked what were the strongest and weakest sides of the project. The best features of the project were:

- its multidimensionality and wide involvement
- reducing the mysticism of alcohol
- opening up to the community
- cooperation between different approaches and organizations
- possibilities for real action, enthusiasm, not just a project on paper
- increasing the interest and knowledge among the professionals
- bringing the topic into the community, out of the offices
- research involvement

The weakest sides of the project were:

- lack of motivation and involvement at the beginning in some areas of work
- increased work load, limited time, wearing out

- efficiency could have been better; the focus of the project was too broad
- the attitudes and commitment of the actors varied
- not enough information on what was happening
- too short a time to achieve real changes
- too scientific

The replies seem to bring forward two contradictory elements: visibility and efficiency on the one hand, and grassroots intiative, openness and local involvement on the other. The dialogical, time-consuming approach has the merit of creativity and wide involvement, while it may at first be weaker in creating visible and efficient action, which is better achieved with a more formal approach.

4. SUMMARIZING THE PROCESS

Influentials

The intervention study aimed at analyzing the local key persons' ideas on alcohol as a social problem. The study was conducted in a manner which made it at the same time an intervention into the participants' thinking. The objects of this reflexive intervention were not only the key persons, but also the researchers.

The researchers also presented their results in a few meetings and press conferences, usually creating a lively debate. The intervention can be said to have created some processes of thinking and reflection in the locality, but to what extent, it is difficult to measure.

Brief Intervention in Primary Health Care

An experimental study was carried out in the primary health care centres of Lahti, starting from a few and spreading to cover the total patient population of Lahti. The aims were to increase knowledge of alcohol-related problems among health-care professionals, to study the prevalence of heavy drinkers in primary health care, and to get experiences of brief intervention as a part of the routine clinical setting.

The intervention was successful in covering the whole city: all of the health care centres were involved in the intervention. Maintaining the activities will be the main challenge for the future.

Setting Up Educational Events

The educational interventions during the project were based on the idea that the success of education depends more on the target groups' pre-existing interest and motivations, and their anchoring in the social and cultural environment rather than on the designs of the educational interventions as such.

The project arranged several major happenings in market-type surroundings; it spread out some printed materials, published posters in the public areas and put a lot of emphasis on media advocacy. Producing information and creating action were often connected to each other as elements of one and the same process.

Youth Work

The project contained a rich variety of activities for the city's young people. Many discussions during the project reflected the need to involve the parents in defining the norms of alcohol use. It was felt that without coherent messages shared by both the professional educators and the family, it is difficult to influence the young. As it is very common to consider the youth as the main focus of drug and alcohol prevention work, the realization that the young are not an isolated part of the community can be considered an important achievement of the process.

Families

The counselling sessions arranged for the intimate others in Lahti avoided the image of treatment, and emphasized the cognitive, solution-oriented approach and open elements in the intervention. These group sessions for family members proved to be very popular, and have become a permanent element of the municipality's services.

Sales Surveillance and the Responsible Serving of Alcohol

The preventive intervention in Lahti focused on two interlinking issues: 1) prevention of alcohol-related public violence and 2) promotion of responsible service of alcohol. Prevention of public violence focused on influencing the ongoing changes in the system of sales surveillance, as well as on creating public discussion by publishing local data on violence. Server training courses for people working in the field were arranged together with the local restaurant school in order to promote responsible service of alcohol. These courses succeeded very well, and will be continued by the local school in the future.

The project did not succeed very well in its efforts to engage the locally relevant parties in discussion and action over local limitations of alcohol supply or other types of local alcohol policy, other than surveillance of the outlets. There may be many reasons for this failure, but of the most important reason was probably the fact that the time was not right for this kind of action. The general alcohol policy climate in Finland was at the time very liberal, and further liberalization was to be expected when Finland joined the European Union.

Inspiring New Networks

A frequent comment from the persons involved in the Lahti project was that during this process they had made new contacts and started cooperation in networks they hadn't previously been in touch with. The project had created new types of local networks among the welfare professionals in particular, and to some but lesser degree between professionals and volunteers. The traditional way of working within the municipal structure is to follow the hierarchical procedures inside one's own administrative sector, and horizontal ties between, say, the social and the health sectors or the social sector and youth work, are difficult to create and maintain. A project like the Lahti project can change this by arranging meetings and happenings where the sectoral divisions are overcome. Individuals who share an inspiration can find each other and start cooperation with new kinds of aims and methods.

11 Outcome Evaluation
Marja Holmila and Jussi Simpura

1. VISIBILITY OF THE LAHTI PROJECT IN THE LOCAL NEWSPAPERS

The local media were seen as an important mediator of alcohol-related knowledge, opinions and modes of thinking. For that reason the representatives of the local media were involved in the project intervention as much as possible. Local press-conferences were arranged as a part of each significant happening. All in all, 14 small conferences were arranged. Some individuals from each media channel became familiar to the project group. Media representatives were also involved in the study on key influentials (see Chapter 4).

In order to give an idea of the general alcohol- and drug-related content in the local papers, all alcohol- and drug-related articles were cut out of the two papers during a half-year period, from October 1993 to April 1994. The first one of these papers was *Etelä-Suomen Sanomat*, a politically independent local newspaper, read by 80 per cent of the area's households and 174 000 readers. The other paper, *Uusi Lahti*, appears weekly, free of charge, and is financed by advertisements. It is distributed to 54 220 households.

The articles were coded according to their main content. The size of each article in column millimetres was measured, and the average size for each category was counted. The frequency of each category was weighed by the average size of this category. The articles were also coded according to their degree of locality. The results of the coding are presented in Table 11.1. A quarter of all the articles had a primary reference to Lahti, two-thirds described a national issue, and every tenth dealt with a primarily international issue. Articles with a preventive message and, to a lesser extent, descriptions of alcohol use, were an exception; they were more often local than other articles. The Lahti project influenced this, as will be shown.

The largest part, a fifth of the volume of the newspaper content, dealt with economic news on production and sales of

Table 11.1   The content of drug- and alcohol-related articles in two local newspapers in Lahti, October 1993–April 1994

Content	Weighted %[1] (474)	Articles with local content, % of all articles
Production and sales of alcohol	20	29
Alcohol use as a problem	15	38
Alcohol policy	15	7
Use of illegal drugs, harms and policy related to them	14	18
Articles with a preventive message	14	74
Crimes with alcohol involvement	10	27
Description of drinks or drinking	9	20
Recipes and instructions of serving drinks	3	–
All	100	30

[1] The weighted percentages are calculated on the basis of the average length in column millimetres of articles in each category.

alcohol. A great part of the economic news dealt with the brewery industry, probably because Lahti has a big brewery.

Articles on alcohol policy dealt almost solely with the preparation of the new national alcohol law, which the parliament passed in December 1994. The law meant a considerable change in Finnish legislation, and its preparation was closely linked with the most important political issue of that year: Finland joining the European Union in January 1995. Only a few articles dealt with local alcohol-policy issues.

The majority of the news or articles on illegal drugs were reports on crimes, often of foreign origin. Crimes with alcohol involvement were a numerically large group. These stories were short without any comments or wider discussions. More than half dealt with assaults, homicides or murders. News on crimes were more common during the week than weekends. They are likely to be filler material, which is not used during the weekends when more important articles take precedence.

Light, entertaining stories about parties, social events and life-styles (9 per cent of the volume) can to some extent be seen as promoters of drinking or drink-related fashions, especially when one bears in mind that during the period of this study, only medium beer was allowed to be advertised in Finland.

Articles coded as 'preventive' are of special interest here. These stories were written in such a way that they contained an educational or informative message about the effects of alcohol or drugs, for instance, 'Heavy use of alcohol increases blood pressure' or 'The immediate costs of alcohol use have increased rapidly'. They also gave information on preventive activities in such articles as, 'The benefits of the Lahti project', 'A guide for those who want to cut down their drinking' or 'The nice Crazy Girls project ended in a photograph exhibition'. These articles were generally large, on average 600 millimetres, so that even if their number was much lower than the number of the crime news, for instance, their share of the published material when measured by size was 14 per cent.

In order to follow up on the possible effects of the Lahti project in the newspapers' content, a longer period was covered. During the period between January 1993 and December 1994 all articles except the news on crimes, news on sales and production of alcohol and recipes, which were not likely to be affected by the project, were coded.

How often and in what kinds of articles was the project mentioned? Only six articles on alcohol problems, and two on alcohol policy referred directly to the project, but in the group of preventive articles the project had a noticeable impact: one-third of such articles mentioned the project. In other words, it seems that the project had an important impact on local writing about prevention, but not on other types of alcohol-related articles. Without the project, the local papers' preventive writing would have been much less, though not absent.

It seems that the project lost some of its visibility in the media during the second year, though the total number of preventive articles was nearly the same during both years (61 and 67). However, there was a shift away from the project's visibility so that in the second year direct reference to the project or the individuals involved in the project was less common (17) than during the first year (28). In particular, the researchers (guest speakers) were mentioned less often.

During the first year, the project was new and interesting as a novelty. Also, the key informant interviews were carried out in 1993, and as the journalists were involved in these groups, this may have had an impact on the media's activity. But in both years, all major educational events caused a small peak in local newspaper writing.

2. REACHING THE AUDIENCE

Three telephone surveys (February 1993, March 1994 and December 1994) were conducted in Lahti. The sample size was 700 each time, and the samples were representative according to sex, age and social status. The respondents were asked in December 1994, had they seen or heard of several of the major happenings and forms of activity in the project. The results show that many of the activities were well remembered (Figure 11.1). Especially the 'On the Wagon' Weeks and the Drink Driving Campaigns attracted the attention of the majority of the population. When the survey was conducted, some time had passed since the Liquor Weeks, but many remembered them too. The local media information had gained the attention of almost half of the population. The results also show that the types of activities were in a logical relationship as to which groups of the population they had best reached, thus strengthening the relevance of the findings. For instance, awareness ads (in the form of a rhythmic poem) on the local radio had best reached young men and working-class men, presumably listening to the radio when driving their cars, while the Crazy Girls project was best remembered by white-collar women and young women whom one could expect to be most interested in issues of female identity and drinking.

The educational Liquor Weeks in the public library were remembered by middle-class women (62 per cent) and middle-class men (50 per cent), while the 'On the Wagon' Weeks, which took place in the shopping mall and the streets, were best noticed by working-class women (69 per cent) and working-class men (68 per cent), and by young women (74 per cent) and young men (63 per cent). This probably reflects the fact that middle-class people visit the library more often than the working class, and the shopping mall and the streets of the city

187

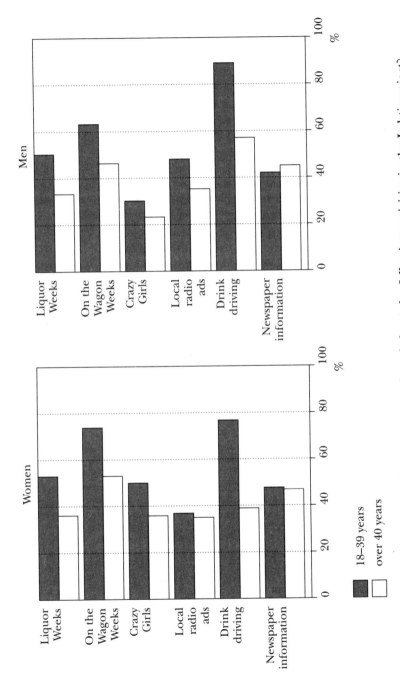

Figure 11.1 Do you recall having seen or heard about the following activities in the Lahti project?

are used by all social groups equally. The drinking and driving campaign was best remembered by the young (89 per cent of men and 77 per cent of women) and those who drink frequently. One could expect cars, intoxication and accidents to be most important in this age group. Women paid more attention to the meetings for drinkers' intimate others than men.

Importantly, the frequent drinkers had been reached as well as those drinking less often. The campaigns had in that sense reached their most important target group. Newspaper information on the limits of risky drinking, which was specifically targeted at heavy drinkers, was best remembered by them. Sixty-seven per cent of the frequently drinking women and 48 per cent of the frequently drinking men remembered having seen the message.

The effect of campaigns diminishes rapidly. March 1994 was the 'high time' of the project and since then its visibility and also impact in the media and people's minds has decreased. In the March 1994 telephone survey, 42 per cent of the respondents knew about the Lahti project and in December 1994 the corresponding figure was only 30 per cent.

3. CHANGES IN PERCEPTION OF ALCOHOL AS A SOCIAL PROBLEM

The proportion of those citizens who considered drinking to be a serious social problem increased during the project (Figure 11.2). In the 1993 and 1994 surveys, the respondents were asked to evaluate the seriousness of 11 potential social problems on a four-point scale. The share of those who had classified alcohol problems as a serious social problem showed a continuous upward trend (among men, from 16 to 21 per cent, and among women, from 29 to 37 per cent). The trend was even more visible when one includes the alternative 'somewhat serious' in the examination. Among men, the share of those who said that alcohol problems were at least a somewhat serious social problem rose from 63 to 75 per cent and among women from 79 to 86 per cent in 18 months. This change also affected the ranking of social problems, so that alcohol rose two steps closer to the top, to fall back one step in autumn 1994. At each poll,

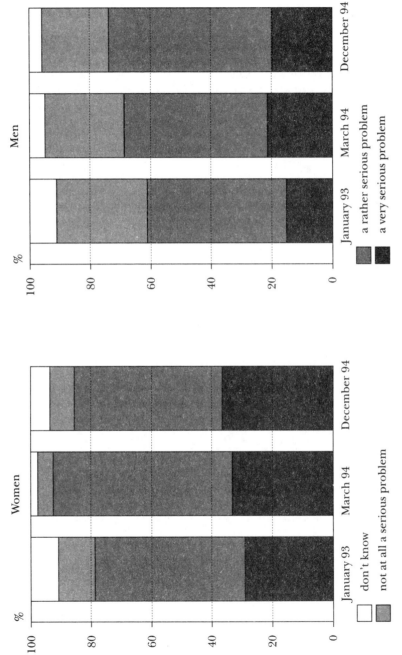

Figure 11.2 Do you consider alcohol use to be a serious, rather serious or not at all serious problem in Lahti?

unemployment was considered to be overwhelmingly the most important social problem in Finland.

A majority of Lahti citizens also gave their consent to using public funds for prevention projects. When asked 'Is it sensible to use public money on prevention projects like the Lahti project?', 87 per cent (90 per cent of women and 84 per cent of men) answered yes. The oldest respondents were less enthusiastic (73 per cent of those over 65 supported the prevention projects) and also the private entrepreneurs were more reluctant than people in other professions.

4. CHANGES IN PUBLIC KNOWLEDGE ABOUT ALCOHOL

Although no consensus seems to exist about 'what everybody ought to know about alcohol', three areas that have been of interest to researchers were in this context chosen as areas where 'objective' needs of information may exist. Therefore survey items focusing on knowledge about the alcoholic content of different drinks, on consumption levels perceived to be harmful for health, and on perceptions of the nature of adverse health effects of drinking were included in the three telephone surveys conducted in the city of Lahti (Montonen 1995c).

The media campaigns arranged in Lahti focused on two topics: on the relative strength of alcoholic drinks, and on risky levels of alcohol consumption. Results from the first telephone survey suggested that there was, indeed, room for improvement in public knowledge about these topics. The telephone surveys also included questions on two additional topics: the nature of adverse health effects of drinking, and knowledge about the time required for alcohol to leave the body. Information on these topics was also was disseminated without, however, giving them special prominence.

The rule of thumb concerning the relative strength of alcoholic drinks is that one bottle of Finnish medium beer and one shot of spirits contain an equal amount of alcohol. This rule is used in a variety of alcohol information materials. In each survey less than half of the respondents were aware of the equivalence. The majority thought that one bottle of medium beer contains less alcohol than one shot of vodka. During the

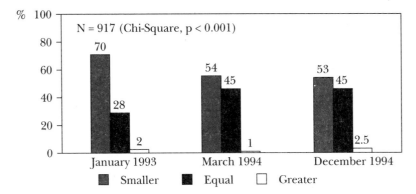

Figure 11.3 Alcohol content: one portion (estimates by frequent drinkers) of alcohol content in one bottle of medium beer versus one portion (4 cl) of vodka

period covered by the surveys a significant change occurred in the distribution of answers: the share of correct answers increased from approximately 30 per cent to approximately 40 per cent, and the share of answers reflecting underestimation of the strength of medium beer decreased from above 60 per cent to above 50 per cent.

The increase of correct answers occurred primarily among frequent drinkers and between the first and the second survey (Figure 11.3). While improvements in answers given by frequently drinking women, and by frequently drinking younger respondents (aged 18–39) are dramatic, improvements among frequently drinking men, and among frequently drinking older respondents fail to reach statistical significance.

Two other survey items asked respondents to estimate how many bottles of medium beer would be needed for the blood alcohol content to reach the level that would result from the consumption of one standard bottle (50 cl) of Koskenkorva, or one standard bottle (75 cl) of table wine. Improved knowledge about the relationship between single portions of beer and spirits seems not to have carried over to these calculations. The only significant difference across the three surveys is that the share of respondents who left these questions unanswered was halved, but even if more respondents thus ventured to give an estimate, the distribution of the estimates remained unaltered.

The question focusing on perceptions of unhealthy alcohol

consumption asked how many bottles of medium beer per week would entail a health risk for an adult person of the respondent's own gender (Montonen 1995c). For the purposes of the present analysis, 16–25 bottles per week has been considered as a 'correct' answer for men, and 11–17 bottles per week for women. In certain information and self-help materials, popular for instance in the Liquor Weeks exhibition arranged in Lahti, these ranges were characterized as levels where 'the occurrence of some problems is likely'. Materials produced for the intervention programme carried out in the health-care centres provided information about risky 'heavy consumption' levels, defined as 16 or more bottles of medium beer per week for women, and 24 bottles or more per week for men.

Among female respondents the share of those who left the consumption-level question unanswered dropped significantly from over 20 per cent to over 10 per cent in the two later surveys. Among males the share of respondents who left the question unanswered remained unchanged. During the time between the two first surveys the perceptions of unhealthy alcohol consumption levels became significantly more realistic among frequent drinkers. Among frequent drinkers, female and male alike, the share of answers above the 'correct' range diminished, while the share of 'conservative' estimates increased. When both 'correct' and 'conservative' answers are taken into account, the share of estimates 'on the safe side' increased among frequently drinking women from around 50 per cent to over 70 per cent, and among frequently drinking men from around 60 per cent to over 70 per cent (Figure 11.4).

Respondents' perceptions of the nature of drinking-related health effects were mapped with a single question asking what kind of adverse health consequences heavy or prolonged drinking will entail (Montonen 1995c). During the Lahti project a variety of channels were used to disseminate general information about the health effects of drinking, as well as information about specific topics, such as effects on the brain or heart, the calory content of alcoholic beverages, or riskiness of drinking during pregnancy. The range of health-related aspects on which materials were available for instance during the Liquor Weeks exhibition was quite extensive. No specific health effects were highlighted more than others, and no major efforts were made to improve the public's knowledge in any specific area.

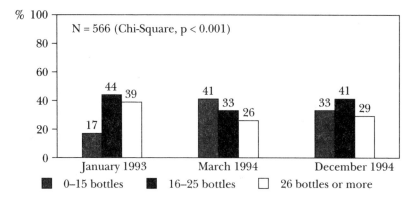

Consumption by an adult man: bottles of medium beer per week

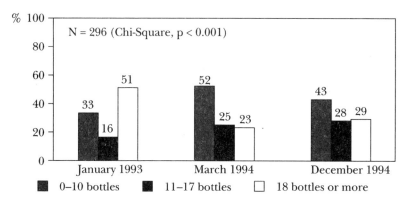

Consumption by an adult woman: bottles of medium beer per week

Figure 11.4   Harmful level of consumption (estimates by men and women who drink frequently)

No significant differences were observable across the three surveys in the answers given to the open-ended questions on adverse health effects. The majority gave one or two examples of adverse health effects, and in addition, approximately one out of ten respondents mentioned examples of social or societal effects, most often problems related to human relationships, particularly within the family, or problems related to working life. In each survey, the six most widely known health effects accounted for more than 70 per cent of all mentions, with the order of 'familiarity' unchanged. Liver damage was by far the most familiar adverse health effect associated with alcohol use, mentioned by well over half of respondents in each survey. Approximately one-third of respondents mentioned examples of damage to the brain or to the central nervous system. Around a quarter, or just under one-third, referred to general deterioration of health. Various sorts of psychic problems, most often anxiety or depression, were mentioned by around one out of five respondents. Alcohol dependency or alcoholism were mentioned by approximately one out of ten. Although the list of health effects mentioned spontaneously by the respondents was extensive, no other type of effect reached 10 per cent of the mentions.

Information about blood alcohol concentration and about the time it takes for alcohol to break down was disseminated in Lahti in driving schools, in special events arranged in conjunction with yearly anti-drink-driving campaigns, and in other major public education events; no specific media information campaigns were arranged around these issues.

Another area of knowledge in which no significant changes occurred in spite of the information given was knowledge about the time it takes for alcohol to leave the body. Respondents were asked how long it would take for the amount of alcohol contained in one bottle of medium beer, consumed by a person weighing 65 kilos, to break down.

Taking into account both individual and situational variation, answers ranging from one to two hours can be considered as acceptable. In all surveys the share of acceptable answers was around 60 per cent. Most of the non-acceptable answers were overestimates (more than two hours): severe underestimation (less than one hour) was extremely rare.

In summary, the public's knowledge improved with respect to two areas that were specifically focused in mass media campaigns. The public's knowledge about the levels of alcohol consumption likely to damage health and the relative strength of single portions of beer and spirits increased.

The improvements in alcohol-related knowledge occurred particularly among frequent drinkers (i.e. respondents who reported using alcohol at least once a week). The changes in alcohol-related knowledge occurred during the first active year of the community project. The improved levels were maintained throughout the second year.

In contrast to these positive changes, no significant changes occurred in areas of knowledge on which some information was disseminated, but with no special emphasis. The public's knowledge about the time it takes for the amount of alcohol contained in one portion of alcohol to break down in the body was initially on a quite satisfactory level, and showed no significant changes. Also, no significant shifts occurred in the public's perceptions of possible adverse health effects of drinking.

5. CHANGES IN DRINKING BEHAVIOUR: STATISTICS ON ALCOHOL CONSUMPTION AND ALCOHOL-RELATED HARM

The quantitative evaluation aimed at measuring the short-term changes in alcohol use and harm. The data were based on varying sets of statistical indicators and on a series of surveys. In order to specify the project impact, a comparison site was used, and parts of the data were gathered there as well. In a small country, it happened that no exact comparison was to be found, and therefore three smaller towns were selected. They were all in southern Finland, industrialized and with the same ethnic tradition as Lahti. In the 1990s, the number of inhabitants in Lahti has been between 93 000 and 94 000. One of the three comparison sites is a city with 40 000 inhabitants, the other two having around 20 000 each. Altogether, the number of inhabitants in the three towns has varied between 88 000 and 89 000 in the 1990s.

The most striking common denominator in all of the towns is the dramatic increase of unemployment. Lahti was hit the hardest by the recession, because its industrial structure has been dependent on domestic demand for consumer goods, and on exports of consumer goods to the former Soviet Union. Both of these branches have suffered severe drawbacks during the 1990s. During the years of the Lahti Project (1992 to 1995) the city of Lahti has experienced unemployment rates heretofore unseen. The highest monthly rates exceeded 30 per cent of the labour force in December 1994. The other three towns have suffered less, partly because of their more favourable industrial composition. Towns Y and Z are dominated by paper and pulp industries exporting to the West, and town X has a remarkable share of inhabitants who commute to work in the capital region.

Measuring the short-term changes of alcohol-related harm is prone to lead to specific problems. Many of the changes remain unobservable merely because of the relatively modest changes. In smaller communities events recorded in official statistics may be so rare that the analysis of changes is practically impossible because there is so much random variation. Typically in a community of 100 000 inhabitants, like the city of Lahti, deaths due to alcohol-related diseases are rare, and irrespective of the accuracy of diagnoses, such figures provide little basis for outcome evaluation. Some other official statistical records are subject to changes in activity and resources of public authorities. For instance, in Finland there is a planned reduction in the involvement of police in public drunkenness, destroying the usefulness of statistics on arrests for drunkenness as a harm indicator. Similarly, in the Lahti project the economic recession may have influenced the provision of health and social services as savings in public expenditure have been sought, thereby deteriorating the before-and-after comparisons of statistics of clientele in various units. Finally, changes in statistical recording practices (definitions, categorizations, ways of producing and reporting data) are a frequent problem in time-series analysis.

The estimation of the community level of aggregate alcohol consumption on the basis of official statistics also faces some problems. A share of the consumption is unrecorded, that is, sold and bought through other than public or legal channels, or produced at home, or imported from trips abroad. In Finland, for instance, more than 20 per cent of the actual alcohol consumption is presumably unrecorded (see Österberg 1995). Another difficulty is that official statistics on community alcohol consumption are mostly based on sales, but all alcohol is not necessarily bought only by the residents of the local community. And vice versa, local residents may buy a remarkable share of their alcohol consumption from other localities. Both of these problems can be omitted, if there is no reason to believe that the share of unrecorded consumption has changed radically or that the buying practices of inhabitants has changed. It is, however, likely that the economic depression has led to an increased share of unrecorded consumption (Österberg 1995, p. 167).

In the present study, a most unwelcome surprise was that the response rates in the basic before-and-after survey on alcohol consumption fell to levels previously unseen in Finland (50 per cent of men and 63 per cent of women in Lahti, and 45 per cent of men and 61 per cent of women in comparison sites who responded to the after-survey). Moreover, this decline was selective in that the response rates fell most in the group of males between 25 and 40 years of age. Since these respondents are the heaviest drinkers in the Finnish population, and therefore a central target group in the community action project, this drop of response rates introduces a serious difficulty in the analysis. All these methodological problems limit the possibilities of accurate measurement of community changes in drinking habits and harms. The following interpretation of the data presented attempts to take these problems into account.

The economic recession of the 1990s had a strong diminishing effect on aggregate alcohol consumption measured as registered consumption. In this study it is assumed that the development of the unregistered consumption has been similar in all the towns and similar to that suggested for the whole country. The decline was stronger in the city of Lahti than in the three comparison sites and in the country as a whole (Figure 11.5). The differences in consumption development are largely parallel to the differences in changes of unemployment rates (Appendix 1). On this level it is very difficult to attribute any of the decreases in alcohol consumption in Lahti to the efforts of the Lahti project. True, the decline in alcohol consumption in Lahti in 1994 was slightly larger than in the comparison sites, but this again may be only an indication of slower economic recovery in Lahti.

In the long run and with larger populations, the incidence of various alcohol-related diseases by and large follows the variation of aggregate alcohol consumption (see e.g. Edwards *et al.* 1994). The results from Lahti do not allow any clear conclusions to be drawn in this respect, because the number of cases each year is too small for exact analysis. The random variation in occurrences per year is very large, as is evident in Table 11.2. It does not make very much sense to compare the figures from Lahti with those from the control sites.

Table 11.3 gives a collection of the most frequently used alcohol-related harm indicators. Starting with arrests for drunkenness, there has been a conscious nationwide aim to reduce

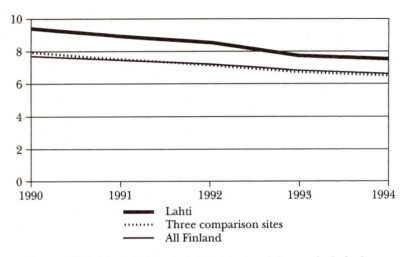

Source: *Alcohol Statistical Yearbook*; Municipal statistics on alcohol sales,
the Finnish Alcohol Company

Figure 11.5   Aggregate alcohol consumption (litres 100 per cent
alcohol per capita), Lahti and three comparison sites, 1990–94

the number of arrests with better collaboration between the police and the health and social welfare system. As a consequence,
there is a clear declining trend in arrests both in Lahti and in
the whole country. Second, the use of A-clinics (special offclinic
services for problem drinkers and drugtakers) in Lahti has been
stable, whereas national figures show a downward trend. This
indicator is largely dependent on local arrangements, and the
national figures are probably influenced by economic difficulties in many of the smaller communities, leading to savings in
the use of services for problem drinkers in particular. Third,
the declining trend in the use of detoxification centres in Lahti
is similar to that in the whole country. And fourth, the decline
in cases of drink-driving can be explained by the economic
recession, leading to weaker enforcement by the police due to
lack of resources, decreasing alcohol consumption and a decline
in the number of kilometres driven each year. Together these
factors have multiplicative effects. The difference between Lahti
and the national figures could be interpreted as an indication
of the more severe effects of the recession in Lahti than in the
country as a whole.

For an outcome evaluation, the review of standard official

Table 11.2   Incidence of various alcohol-related diseases in Lahti,
1990–94: in-patients treated in somatic hospitals

	1990	1991	1992	1993	1994
Liver cirrhosis /100 000 over 15 yrs	19	5	8	27	23
Alcoholism /100 000 over 15 yrs	72	71	35	34	74
Alcohol psychosis /100 000 over 15 yrs	19	23	23	14	18
Alcohol poisoning /100 000 over 15 yrs	14	4	9	5	5

Source: Lahti City Social and Health Care Administration

Table 11.3   Selected alcohol-related harm indicators, Lahti and
all of Finland

	1994	% change in 1990–94
Arrests for drunkenness		
Lahti	3 399	−30
Finland	92 560	−35
Clients at A-clinics		
Lahti (citizens of Lahti)	879	−2
Finland	35 354	−8
Clients at detox centres		
Lahti	415	−17
Finland	8 755	−17
Cases of drink-driving		
Lahti	489	−41
Finland	20 390	−32

and semi-official statistics has provided meagre results. Only
standard statistical material was used here, without any effort
to collect specific information related to the project. All in all,
it is evident that a strict outcome evaluation is very difficult to
produce within a short-term perspective without specific and

detailed collection of non-standard statistical materials. Such materials could allow the use of advanced statistical techniques such as time series analysis or dynamic modelling (cf. Holder and Howard 1992).

6. CHANGES IN DRINKING HABITS: THE SURVEY DATA

The second data set for outcome evaluation consists of questionnaire data collected before, after and during the course of the project. Some of these concerned drinking patterns and personal experiences of problem drinking, other attitudes and opinions on various alcohol-related issues. The most extensive ones in these studies were identical questionnaires conducted before and after the active project period, in the spring of 1992 and 1995. These mailed questionnaires were sent as an appendix to a national study on health behaviour of adult population to samples in Lahti and the three comparison towns. The questionnaire consisted of questions about drinking patterns by beverage type, indicators of problem drinking, attitudes toward alcohol and opinions concerning alcohol-control policies. The samples (495 in 1992 and 500 persons in 1995) were picked separately for each year from the national population registers, using a standardized random sampling procedure.

The basic indicator of drinking patterns was based on a question of the respondent's typical drinking frequency. In Table 11.4 abstainers are those who 'never drink', and frequent drinkers those who drink 'four times a week or more often'. No statistically significant changes could be found when comparing the distributions of respondents by their self-reported drinking frequencies (chi-square tests between years, separately in each of the four groups by gender and site). However, there was a decline in the proportion of male heavy drinkers in Lahti from 11 to 5 per cent, while the decline was smaller in the comparison sites.

Other basic indicators of changes in drinking patterns are the level of aggregate alcohol consumption and the frequency of high alcohol intake per occasion (Table 11.5 and Table 11.6). Both of these are, unfortunately, heavily influenced by the presence or absence of the heaviest drinking groups among the respondents. So, although the results in these tables provide at

Table 11.4   Abstainers and frequent drinkers in Lahti and three comparison sites, 1992 and 1995, percentages

| | Abstainers | | Drinkers who drink 4 times a week or more often | |
	1992	*1995*	*1992*	*1995*
Men				
Lahti	9	11	11	5
Three towns	6	10	6	5
Women				
Lahti	21	16	4	3
Three towns	18	15	3	–

Table 11.5   Frequency of heavy drinking: proportion of those drinking 6 drinks or more per session, Lahti and three comparison sites, 1992 and 1995, percentages

| | Never > 6 drinks per session | | Once a week or more often > 6 drinks per session | |
	1992	*1995*	*1992*	*1995*
Men				
Lahti	17	29	22	19
Three towns	25	27	20	17
Women				
Lahti	59	53	4	1
Three towns	52	53	3	5

face value some indication of declining heavy drinking among men in Lahti, the result may be misleading. An analysis of variance explaining the variation of annual alcohol consumption did not reveal any significant site-specific changes.

The prevalence of self-reported problem drinking was measured by a 10-item index producing the AUDIT scale (see Saunders *et al.* 1993 and Holmila 1995). In Table 11.7, the cutoff points have been set to 8 and 11 points on the scale. The

Table 11.6   Mean values of estimated annual alcohol
consumption, Lahti and three comparison sites,
1992 and 1995 (cl 100 percent alcohol)

| | Men | | Women | |
	1992	*1995*	*1992*	*1995*
Lahti	778	547	249	238
Three towns	698	538	205	205

Table 11.7   The proportion of respondents exceeding certain
limits on the AUDIT scale, Lahti and three control sites,
1992 and 1995, percentages

| | *AUDIT* > = 8 | | *AUDIT* > = 11 | |
	1992	*1995*	*1992*	*1995*
Men				
Lahti	34	31	24	18
Three towns	34	30	23	20
Women				
Lahti	12	8	5	4
Three towns	7	8	3	4

proportion of those exceeding 11 points was 22 per cent of
males and 5 per cent of females in the 1992 Finnish national
drinking habit survey (Holmila 1995), which is very close to the
levels in Lahti and the comparison sites. From 1992 to 1995 the
relative number of men with AUDIT scores exceeding 11 points
reduced more in Lahti than in the comparison towns, and the
same can be noticed among women with scores exceeding 8
points. Analysis of variance explaining the variation of the
AUDIT measure, did not, however, reveal any statistically significant site-specific changes.

To sum it up, the questionnaire responses did not show
any clear changes in drinking patterns and problem drinking
that could have been attributed to the Lahti project. Some decline in heavy drinking could be detected. These results were

not statistically significant, but were systematically in the same direction when using different sources of information. Given that drinking patterns generally change slowly, unless fairly dramatic changes in living conditions and alcohol sales take place (see e.g. Simpura 1995), the results are as expected.

7. CHANGES IN SOCIAL RESPONSE TO ALCOHOL PROBLEMS

The project created a few new forms of social response to alcohol problems in Lahti. The health care intervention of heavy drinkers was carried out as an experimental study, first in a few health care centres, and then spreading to all centres in the city. The goal was to make such action a permanent part of the health-care centres' normal work, and it seems likely that at least some aspects of the intervention will be continued after the project has finished.

Consultation and support for alcoholics' family members was developed and given new resources. A series of open consultation meetings, usually attended by about 30 to 40 persons, was organized with the help of the city's funding. A part-time nurse was then appointed to organize and run the services. This service has continued after the project, and there seems to be continuous demand for this type of help.

The vocational school for restaurant personnel in Lahti arranged two consecutive courses on responsible serving for those working in bars and restaurants. The two-day course was well received, and about 120 waiters and waitresses participated. There is a plan to continue arranging these courses, and the second course took place in the autumn of 1995 (Haavisto 1995).

The city's alcohol policy group had been nominated before the project started. Its position was clarified and strengthened by the project. The group will monitor changes in drinking and related harms, make suggestions to the city council and act as a coordinator for various groups within the city (Alcohol and Drug Policy Plan of the City of Lahti 1992). The experience of arranging several large educational happenings together with new local partners has created a favourable ground for continuous educational activity in the city.

8. DISSEMINATION OF THE PROJECT EXPERIENCE

The project experience has been widely disseminated among different professional groups interested in local prevention of alcohol problems in the whole of Finland. Often the information has come from the local actors in Lahti rather than from the researchers; the former have been telling about their work within the project in their own network meetings. On 16 May 1995 a national seminar was held in Lahti to discuss the project. This meeting gathered 200 participants from all over the country, and produced a seminar report with preliminary research results. In addition to the overall project approach, the health-care centre intervention among heavy drinkers, the Liquor Weeks, the Crazy Girls and the Server Training Course have interested other cities, and Liquor Weeks have actually been arranged in nine locations (Montonen 1995b).

9. CONCLUDING THE OUTCOME EVALUATION

The outcome evaluation of the project showed several changes or processes in the community, which can be seen as results of the prevention work. People's awareness of alcohol-related issues had been at least briefly improved in the sense that the various activities of the project had attracted the attention of the inhabitants of Lahti irrespective of age, gender and drinking style. People's knowledge of the alcohol content of medium beer and their knowledge of the limits of risky drinking increased.

Attitudes toward alcohol problems changed: the proportion of those citizens who considered drinking to be a serious social problem grew during the project. There were system-level changes among the municipality's employees and the voluntary groups in the community in the ways of seeing the prevention of alcohol problems as a part of ordinary daily work and changes in the community's response to alcohol problems were achieved. Mini-intervention for heavy drinkers spread from a few experimental centres to include all the primary health care centres in the city. The street service Mono, for young people, developed its activities. Consultation and support for alcoholics' family members was given more resources and attention.

Changes in drinking habits or measurable harms related to

drinking were not significant. The project stressed the message of risky drinking and various activities underscored the message, including health-care intervention, media campaigns, educational happenings and the family members' support groups. Heavy drinkers noticed the information and were able to recall it. Some decline in heavy drinking could be detected through survey measures and using comparison sites. The results were not statistically significant, but were systematically in the same direction when using different sources of information.

The value of quantitative measures is that they help one not to lose sight of subjective bias or chance. The difficulty in assessing the meanings of the quantitative outcome results are however various. In order to analyse short-term changes in behaviour, harms, attitudes and opinions, standard procedures of data collection may prove insufficient. Even in a country with an internationally exceptionally extensive statistical system, and also with positive attitudes among the population toward scientific data collection, the researcher may have to admit that the effects of a community action project are elusive. With tailored data collection alongside official statistical recording, or with extensive general population surveys, the changes could be better reached. This, of course, means considerable additional costs. Cost-effectiveness is a question that should be raised when discussing outcome evaluation in community action against alcohol problems.

Part IV
Conclusions:
Local Community in
Preventive Action
Marja Holmila

1. THE COMMUNITY AS THE FOCUS OF PREVENTION

This book is aimed at increasing knowledge on two interlinking issues: local community as a system of preventing alcohol problems and the art of planning and implementing community prevention projects. The community perspective means that the local community is the director of the story, the main hero and the most cumbersome villain.

The historic development of alcohol policies in the Nordic countries stresses universalism, but also unity within the scope of the nation-state. Now this almost monolithic structure is slowly eroding, and indeed in two directions. The nation-state as a sovereign actor is losing its powers to international agencies and networks with increasing globalization. At the same time, the nation-state is turning into a set of fragmented local actors and units, often geographical by nature but also consisting of other kinds of network structures. This bifurcation of nation-state politics both upward and downward is a consequence of more general structural changes in world economics, production and information flows (see Chapter 3). For community action, the assumed bifurcation provides a double role. It is an opportunity for new community structures and action patterns to arise, but community action may also be used instrumentally to adapt state-centred operations into changed social conditions. Local communities have an important role in social policy and health politics. The state organizations may still take precedence over localities in decision-making over many issues, but they need to implement their decisions on the local level. The local agents are central actors in this process.

The novelty of community approach in the Nordic context lies first in its implicit assumption of a new kind of community thinking, introducing a strong element of local initiative. It is possible to say that the Nordic traditions, although establishing a strong system of local political democracy, do not necessarily emphasize local initiative. Rather, the localization has meant a well-defined place in the centralized system and a guarantee of equal treatment of localities in the central administration. The new community action is novel also in its approach to civil movements. The mobilization expected in the approach resembles the 'new social movements' that should produce new consciousness and forms of knowledge, rather than the often class-based interest of traditional social movements.

Civil mobilization activated by the Lahti project can be seen as mobilization introduced 'from outside', but it relied on pre-existing orientations and activism. The project experience stresses the fact that it would actually be very difficult to create any voluntary action unless one built it on existing forms of local interests.

A difficulty facing community action projects is that alcohol problems are not novel as social problems. Nor do alcohol problems appear as a symbolic crisis gaining remarkable media coverage and requiring a specific effort on the problem construction, as compared to some other more dramatic or broadly distributed problems such as unemployment, the environment or illegal drugs. For that reason, without a push from health advocates and professionals, local civil action around alcohol issues runs the risk of remaining very weak.

2. IDEOLOGY AND OPINIONS

Prevention of alcohol problems faces a particular contradiction or challenge, which in this book has been called the public health predicament. The contradiction is based on the fact that consumers in postmodern society on the one hand need protection against health risks, which are being increasingly recognized by experts, and that they, on the other hand, construct their basic identities as independent decision-makers opposing any outside regulation or manipulation. While modern societies have reached an unforeseen degree of manageability and technical competence in maintaining healthy life, new risks appear as life becomes more complex. Preventive alcohol policy is thus a paradox. Alcohol as a risky substance differs from many other substances also in its cultural richness. It is enveloped in a symbolic shroud too thick to surrender unconditionally to a simple calculation of risks and benefits.

The questions posed in any reflections, public or private, on alcohol as a social problem are of the kind: what type of society would it be that deprived one of the right to sell, buy or consume anything at any time? or: what public good comes from the sacrifice of freedom to choose and control oneself, and how is each individual expected to benefit from it?

The reflexive intervention among the Lahti influentials was aimed at creating discussion on these issues among the key local persons (see Chapter 4). The intervention brought forward the interactional positions the speakers took, and their values. Three main views on handling the alcohol question in the discussions were found: classical liberalism, neoliberalism and the welfare-state view.

The welfare-state view is to a large extent tantamount to the total consumption theory, according to which alcohol problems can be prevented by limiting availability, and thus the overall consumption of alcohol. The municipal administrators and experts in local health and social affairs preferred this line.

The neoliberal idea entails that everybody should be responsible for him or herself and the general public should not be burdened with external controls. The local journalists' definition of themselves as cultural intermediaries was illuminated through their neoliberal attitudes.

The classical liberal view is based on the idea that normal people are not mature enough to handle alcohol without moral supervision. There should be control, but the control should be returned from state to the (patriarchal) family. The group in which classical liberal understanding of the role of the state was most uniformly represented consisted of influential local businessmen.

The influentials took positions within and between the three outlooks on alcohol policy either arbitrarily or in the context of their specific roles in society, as functionaries, journalists, employers and so on. They were flexible, and their alcohol policy views were not linked systematically with any wider ideological or political orientations. This is in accordance with the theme of mass society theory, which claims that political doctrines have become inconsistent and commitment to them becomes weak. That alcohol is not on the political agenda proper does not mean that people are indifferent toward the problem. They are often confused about the way the problem should be understood and treated but they engage in discussions about it eagerly, even with some passion. They agree that there is a public health predicament – the need to keep social health costs within bearable limits through preventive policy, which, however, tends to contradict the concept of individual responsibility and freedom of choice. Among the Lahti influentials, the universalistic preventive approach that focuses on total consumption and general availability was accepted with difficulty, and mostly by those who could identify themselves as administrators or specialists with professional responsibilities to defend the public good.

3. FLEETING COMMUNITIES AND TRANSIENT NETWORKS

In the process of postmodern disintegration, individuals' significant memberships become less automatic and more a matter of choice. We are not so much thrown into communities, but decide which communities we shall throw ourselves into. New, often temporary memberships by choice are replacing the old ones.

The traditional sociological division of communities in to *Gemeinschaft* and *Gesellschaft* has often led to insisting that the concept of community is outdated. In order to understand the forms of social ties between people in present-day societies, the concept of community has to be approached from a different angle. Communities do not form a single unity, but are formed by several elements. The totality of community life is a combination of various transient and partial communities. Some of them are more enduring, like kinship and family ties, others consist of seemingly superficial and passing social ties, like friendships in the local pub, or the social contact between a patient and a doctor, or the feeling of intimate belonging with hundreds of other spectators in a ski-jump competition. In an individual's everyday life and in his/her experience of being a member of a society, some of these fleeting or invented communities can be very important.

The importance of different forms of community life are not the same for all people, and the importance can change during one's lifetime. Children's and adolescents' social worlds are more likely to be limited to the geographical locality than the adults' worlds. Persons with health or social problems need the local contacts more than, for instance, a company executive in an international firm.

It is also possible to distinguish the surface and the deep structure of community life from each other. The surface consists of all those institutions, services, social groups and organizations that structure the social ties between people. The deep structure is carried by culture, traditions and people's emotional commitment and feelings of belonging.

4. THE NEUTRAL LANGUAGE OF EVALUATION

What was the Lahti project all about? What happened and how can one summarize its lessons? Evaluation is a natural part of a demonstration project. It is important to assess the utility of the action, and rationale of spending the required resources. The research tradition available in doing this is the tradition of evaluation research. Carrying out a quantitative outcome measurement of changes in Lahti and in the three comparison sites showed that the three years of action had managed to increase the public's awareness of alcohol problems, their knowledge on some facts about alcohol and related harms, and the project had gained good visibility and reached its target groups. Measurable changes in drinking habits and alcohol-related harms could not be detected. However, there was some indication that the heaviest drinking groups in Lahti may have reduced their drinking more than was the case in the comparison sites.

The quantitative evaluation aims at a normative neutral language and objective measurable indicators of change. That is its strength but also its limitation. Other types of sociological analysis are necessary in bringing out what happened in the project. Analysing the community and describing the practical know-how, and the ritualistic and emotional aspects of the process are important. In this task, qualitative methods provide the best tools.

5. THE RELEVANT SURFACE COMMUNITIES

A rich network of potentially active local agents was found during the process of Lahti project. The main group was from the municipal structure, that is, the health and social professionals employed by the city. Their importance in the process is, to some extent, a particular feature of Finnish society. There are strong traditions of organized local democracy linked to the centralized state, and any civil action in the health and social sector, even if born spontaneously, usually becomes tied to the professional structures to ensure continuity and universalism.

The project created some new permanent forms of social response to alcohol problems, like the health-care intervention of heavy drinkers, courses on responsible serving for those working in bars and restaurants, consultation and support for alcoholics' family members, youth work among the girls and other youth work activities. It created waves of information in the local media, thus taking part in the agenda-setting of alcohol and drug problems in Lahti. It developed problem management by increasing skills and motivation both in individuals and in organizations. The intervention also changed, at least temporarily, the self-understanding of the social system as far as the responsibility of alcohol prevention and drug-related harms are concerned: the major preventive happenings (e.g. Liquor Weeks, On the Wagon Weeks, Youth theatre) opened up the dividing walls between the different sectors of the municipality structure, and linked professional and voluntary resources.

One of the problems in developing municipal prevention work is the strong tradition of sectoral specialization, which sometimes hinders the municipality's professionals from cooperating locally. In spite of the fact that Lahti is rather a small town, one of the most common positive remarks made by the participants in the feedback interview was that the project had helped them to find new contacts for carrying out prevention work.

Voluntary organizations and interest groups – of which the various sport clubs are among the most important – often have a crucial role in the everyday life of their members. If such organizations even sporadically take part in some preventive event as was the case during the On the Wagon Weeks, an important anchorage into the basic community network has been achieved.

In the early teenage years, young people distance themselves from organized or home-centred leisure and start loitering about to explore the potentials of the public space and their own social identities within it. Finnish cities are relatively safe, and young people from ordinary homes are allowed to spend evenings, even late nights downtown, hanging around, drinking and socializing. Activities and discos are arranged in youth houses and young people often go to the libraries. The parks, play-grounds and sports fields provide meeting places during the summer. The voluntary organization Mono had adapted its action along these patterns of young people's use of time; its members patrolled the city during Friday nights helping youngsters in immediate trouble and providing counselling to those whose drinking was beginning to get out of hand.

The Lutheran Church is by far the biggest religious community in Lahti. The citizens do not go to church often but it nevertheless has influence in their moral and social life. Nearly all 15-year-olds take part in Confirmation schools, and these are often arranged as summer camps including various group activities in natural surroundings, by a lakeside. During this special week, issues related to growing up are discussed in groups, and the problems of alcohol and drug use have now become a permanent part of the agenda.

During the Lahti project, the church took the role of the 'moral voice' in the sense that it formulated a set of normative rules on how parents should relate to their children's drinking: a controversial attempt in a community that strongly underlines individualism and each family's own autonomy in children's upbringing.

For the ordinary citizen of Lahti, as for the citizens of other towns and cities, the most convenient and accessible social meeting place is the local pub. It is always open, it is easy to enter, and one knows what to do there. The number of alcohol outlets had grown fast in Lahti, and at the same time their standards of good practice had deteriorated as the competition had become more severe. Service to drunken persons, violence, noisy and disorderly behaviour are common phenomena. As was demonstrated during the project, a lot can be achieved by joint efforts between the restaurant personnel, the patrons and the health advocates in developing these central social meeting places so they will be less of a risk for individual health or public order.

The media represent one of the public voices in the community. Routine, everyday information on local events, services and decisions requires use of the media. The local media maintains the community feeling, and the voice of the local reporter creates domesticity. The local newspaper reporters see themselves as independent commentators and mediators of knowledge as 'pure' as possible. They want to view their readers and listeners as autonomous respondents capable of making their own interpretations. The commercial local radios strive to emphasize the personalities of their commentators. Their most important task is to produce popular entertainment, using non-fictitious material from the immediate local environment. Lahti has two local newspapers, and two radio channels. Their role in the Lahti project was substantial: the local media published research reports, and covered the major happenings as news items. They made it very clear, however, that they were not willing to take the role of an active advocate of health promotion or any other educational message.

There seems to be a tendency toward more unified media content from centralized and often international sources. Respectively, editorial input on local issues and also the newspapers' own interpretation of ready-made material is diminishing. The study of the local newspapers in Lahti found a remarkable shift during eight years. Earlier, positive welfare-state thinking was dominant, and the public good was an acceptable basis for action in most issues. During the 1990s when deep economic crisis and mass unemployment took place, the welfare state framework weakened and was replaced partly by arguments that emphasized the economic necessities instead of the public good. Interest in the problems of the marginalized population groups decreased. This change of framework was reflected also in writings on alcohol issues, albeit weakly.

Family and other intimate relationships represent the most lasting social ties in the world of transient and multiple communities. In the case of alcohol problems, the strength of these ties is a resource, but also a source of painful contradictions. Accepting this pain and handling it seem to form a difficult dilemma in our culture, which so strongly stresses individual liberty and responsibility. The family members of heavy drinkers have a pressing need to change their personal lives. In terms of prevention, it is also important to change the cultural values and images that label family members and increase their stress. In Lahti, the family members' support and counselling groups succeeded very well, and have now become a permanent part of the community services. Public discussion around family issues was also, to some extent initiated.

6. CREATIVE, RITUALISTIC AND EMOTIONAL

The deep structure of community life is based on the ideal or the dream of belonging to a group, of acceptance, reciprocity and mutual gifts. As Simmel remarks: 'social equilibrium and cohesion could not exist without the reciprocity of service and return service', and 'all contacts among men rest on the schema of giving and returning the equivalence' (Simmel 1950, p. 387). This reciprocity is constantly violated, but the expectation is not destroyed.

The emotional investment in belonging to a community is to a great extent an individual choice, and does not in any way reflect objective facts like the number of social contacts or social status. The feeling of belonging probably also varies during one's lifetime, and people in different stages of their lives invest in differing degrees in their local environment.

Belonging is basically a feeling, a decision and an orientation. It can be strengthened by rewards and reciprocity, or personal history, but is not dependent on them. Most local people identify with some of the most important symbols of their local community. In the case of Lahti these symbols are Top of the World winter sports, especially ski-jumping, and the famous city orchestra.

One can argue that in spite of individual differences, collective changes in the intensity of community feeling take place in time. The deep economic recession that started at the beginning of the 1990s was at deep shock to Finns who, for 30 years, had been used to continuous economic growth and prosperity.

It is very likely that the Lahti project, with its strong emphasis on community values and optimism, would not have been similarly welcome had it been launched five years earlier, during the times of busy moneymaking and competing. During a time of bankruptcies, cuts in social welfare and high unemployment, just working together as a community suddenly began to seem like a good idea.

The project years in Lahti taught us that symbols, emotions and rituals are very important. Science-based information and fact-based rational argumentation alone are not enough to create action to better people's lives. Feelings of togetherness and fun are essential elements. One of the working rules during the project was that only when people seemed to enjoy themselves or had passionate views on the issue, was it worth pursuing the idea any further. Artistic and creative abilities were in high demand, but caring and networking was also given an important role. If anyone in the process of community action feels to be an object of action rather than an active subject, the outcome is not likely to be very good. In this context, it may be also useful to remember that projects are short-lived butterflies which come and go, but the localities must build permanent structures in which the artisan skills of preventive work can permanently nest.

The years in Lahti filled most of us who were involved in it with a feeling of contentment: efforts in developing local preventive action can be rewarding. It is possible to create modern, communicative community action around such difficult and private issues as alcohol use, and to do it in a way that is likely to increase people's well-being within that community. The main lesson from the project can, perhaps, be formulated in the following way: the type of community prevention that really works and creates sustainable changes is neither value-neutral nor given from above; rather, it is ritualistic, emotional and requires subjective involvement of the people in the community. This is not to say that prevention needs to be irrational, but its rationality should not be of the limited kind.

Appendix 1 Unemployment Rates

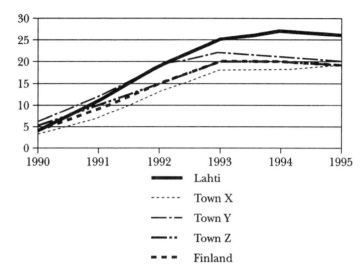

Source: The Ministry of Labour and Employment. The figures are annual means of the percentages of those officially registered as unemployed from the total working force.

Figure A.1   Unemployment rates in Lahti, three comparison sites and all of Finland, 1990–95

Appendix 2 A Guidebook for Controlled Drinking

This guide is made for you, to help you learn to control your own alcohol use better or give it up altogether. Perhaps you have been drinking quite a lot for a few years now, or once in a while it has got out of hand. You have had hangovers or suffered interminable stomach aches. You may have had trouble sleeping. Or alcohol may have caused some other problems.

With the help of this guide you can estimate whether you are a heavy drinker and see how you will be able to change your drinking habits.

Even if you were using alcohol because of its positive effects, heavy drinking creates many harmful effects as well. The more you drink the more likely you are to have an accident, end up in trouble either at home or at work, and have health problems.

Did you know that only a few tens of thousands of us Finns are true alcoholics? There are, however, several hundreds of thousands of heavy drinkers, according to some estimates as many as 600 000. As many as one out of five Finns in some age groups is a heavy drinker.

Clarify Your Own Situation

Few of us have stopped to think about the amount of alcohol we consume or, whether it would be wise to stop drinking. Make an honest estimate of your weekly alcohol consumption and compare the result with the following heavy drinking limits. If your average alcohol consumption consistently surpasses the limits described in the list, then you are a heavy drinker and alcohol may be endangering your health.

218

Limits for heavy drinking:

MEN   24 units per week   (24 bottles of beer (less than 4.6% alcohol), $3\frac{1}{2}$ bottles of wine, or $1\frac{3}{4}$ bottles of spirits)

WOMEN 16 units per week   (16 bottles of beer, $2\frac{1}{3}$ bottles of wine, or $1\frac{1}{5}$ bottles of spirits)

In changing your drinking habits, consider whether you wish to drink less or quit drinking altogether.

Drinking less is sufficient if
- you want to learn to control your drinking
- you have been drinking heavily for only a few years
- you have no withdrawal symptoms after drinking

Quit drinking if
- you have been diagnosed with a sickness or injury that can be aggravated by alcohol
- you are not able to stick to the limits set beforehand but continue to drink once having started
- you know that alcohol does not agree with you because you become unpleasant or prone to violence when you drink
- you are pregnant – there is no excuse for using alcohol during pregnancy
- you feel you're an alcoholic

What are the Benefits of Decreasing Drinking?

- The risk of accidents is decreased, as is the risk of getting high blood pressure or liver disease.
- The chances of being overweight decrease
- The ability to concentrate improves
- There are fewer hangovers, headaches, and stomach aches
- There is less feeling of tiredness and sleep is more peaceful
- There is an increasing general feeling of well-being
- There is more time and energy to spend on other things besides drinking
- Relationships with family members and friends improve
- Sex may be more enjoyable
- If you are pregnant, quitting alcohol drinking may enhance your child's chances to be born healthy
- You have more money to spend. Calculate how much money you spent last week on alcohol.

Learn to Calculate Portions

It is easier to keep track of drinking if you learn to calculate the
amount of alcohol in a drink as portions. Basically, a portion
is 12 grams of pure 100 proof alcohol. A portion of a particular
beverage thus varies in volume depending upon how strong the
drink is.

1 unit = 12 grams   (1 bottle (0.33 l) beer ('medium' beer in
                     Finland with less than 4.6 per cent alcohol
                     by volume), a 12 cl glass of red, or white
                     wine, a small 8 cl glass of fortified wine,
                     a 4 cl shot of strong spirits (e.g. whiskey,
                     cognac, rum))

Similarly you can count that:

One bottle (0.33 l) of strong (over 4.6%) beer	= 1.3 units
One pint of middle beer (0.5 l)	= 1.5 units
One pint of strong beer (0.5 l)	= 2 units
One bottle (0.75 l) of wine	= 6 units
$\frac{1}{2}$ bottle wine	= 3 units
1 bottle (0.5 l) spirits	= 13 units
$\frac{1}{2}$ bottle spirits	= 6.5 units

Set your Goal, Choose Your Means

1. Make a Decision about a Long-Term Plan
Only you can choose between abstinence and decreased drinking. After having made the decision it is worthwhile thinking
about how you will reach your goal.

You can strive for your goal, for example,
• by quitting right away and remaining abstinent from then on
• by immediately drinking less and sticking to this limit
• by gradually decreasing your drinking either to moderate
  level or to zero

2. Begin with a Few Abstinent Weeks
A well-tested way to start controlling drinking is to remain abstinent for at least a fortnight and after that start aiming for
the final goal.

3. Define Your Goal, Recognize Your Own Drinking Habits
Setting an upper limit for how much you drink at a time may
help you reach your goal. Remember, however, that this is a
matter of reducing risks, not eliminating them. There are always
risks involved in drinking alcohol, but the risks do increase
rapidly if your blood alcohol level is higher than 0.1 per cent. It
is hard to estimate the amount you've consumed while you are
drunk. Therefore, it is good to practise new drinking habits:

- Always measure your drinks so you know how much you
  have drunk
- Dilute strong drinks
- Don't drink it at once, but sip it slowly
- Drink non-alcoholic beverages every now and then
- Drink no more than one unit per hour
- Eat while you are drinking
- Recognize the situations in which you grab a bottle (for
  example, alone at home or with friends who imbibe a lot).

Upper limit for one occasion:
MEN   7 units (7 bottles of beer, or 1 bottle of wine, or $\frac{1}{2}$
         bottle of spirits)
WOMEN   5 units (5 bottles of beer, or $\frac{2}{3}$ bottle of wine, or $\frac{1}{2}$
         of a bottle of spirits)

4. Learn to Cope in Company
Before you go to places where alcohol is being served, prepare
yourself by deciding whether you will be drinking at all, or if
so, how much; are you going to take the car; and what time will
you be leaving.

- A couple of days in advance, imagine how you will succeed
  in sticking to your goal.
- Don't surpass your set limit with excuses ('one more won't
  hurt – this is a party').
- Think ahead of reasons for leaving early in case you feel
  you are not be able to cope with the situation.
- Learn to say no. You can refuse a drink by saying, for
  example:

Thanks
  – but no more
  – but none now
  – but not yet

   because I decided to drink less
   tonight
   because I'm drunk already
   because I have an important
   meeting tomorrow
   because I won't be able to sleep
   because I want to be awake
   tomorrow
   because I have decided to cut
   down drinking

5. *Alcohol Does Not Help*

Drinking does not solve problems even if it offers a temporary feeling of relief. Ask yourself whether you have personal problems that make the decision to cut down or quit drinking feel difficult. Everyday problems are best solved immediately and, if necessary, with professional help.

Alcohol does not help, if
- you lose your job or your spouse
- you feel disgusted, restless, angry, or frustrated
- when you feel guilty about something
- when you want to manage a difficult situation
- when you want to sleep well.

6. *How to Replace Alcohol*

The easiest way to become a teetotaller or a moderate drinker is to find something else to do instead of drinking. Try to invest time in relationships and things
- that you consider important
- that bring you joy
- things you have neglected because of drinking.

Spend time with your family, go to a library, exercise, take hikes, visit cultural events, do voluntary work, attend knitting clubs, take on adult education, paint, build, take a cooking class, study. There are unlimited possibilities to learn and do. The most important thing is to seek company where drinking is not an item.

Keep Track of Your Drinking

Drinking diary:
When you have decided to decrease your alcohol drinking or stop completely, start keeping a drinking diary. It is the best way to observe your own drinking and see your progress. A drinking diary shows you in which situations and with whom you drink more than usually. With this information, it is possible to think up ways to avoid difficult situations in the future.

Whether your goal is abstinence or moderate use, mark down daily
- abstinent days
- how many drinks you had on days you used alcohol
- how you were able to say 'no' in a tempting situation

In addition to keeping a drinking diary, it is helpful
- if you decide in advance how much you will drink during a week and then stick to the decision
- if you have at least a few days each week when you don't drink at all
- if you drink, drink slowly and less
- if you come up with other things to do besides drinking

How You Succeed

Plan Your Drinking Ahead
- Don't drink out of habit: make a conscious choice before every drink.
- Don't drink daily: it is good to have a break even if you had only one drink a day.
- Don't drink in order to cope: alcohol does not solve problems – it creates them.
- Decide in advance how much you will drink during the week and then stick to your decision.
- Have at least a few alcohol-free days each week and at least one alcohol-free month a year.
- If you don't succeed, start again, think what went wrong, and learn from your mistakes.
- Decide at what time of day you stop drinking.
- For some people, a strictly held drinking time-table works

well: for example, no drinking before 20.00 and none after 24.00.

DO YOU WANT A DRINK? DECIDE:
- on which days of the week you drink alcohol
- how many drinks you will allow yourself
- how many drinks you are going to have in one week

AND STICK TO YOUR DECISION!

References

Aaro, L.E., 'Research and Evaluation in Health Promotion'. A paper presented at a meeting on Health Education in the 90s. Helsinki, Finland, 7 August 1992.

Aasland, O.G., Bruusgaard, D. and Rutle, O., 'Alcohol Problems in General Practice', *British Journal of Addiction*, 82 (1987) 197–201.

Ahlström, S., 'Nuorten alkoholijuomien hankinta' (The adolescents' ways of acquiring alcohol), *Alkoholipolitiikka*, 56 (1991) 178–86.

Ahlström, S. *et al.*, 'Nuoret alkoholin käyttäjinä' (Young People's Drinking), Reports from the Social Research Institute of Alcohol Studies 187 (Helsinki: The Social Research Institute of Alcohol Studies, 1994).

Albrecht, G., 'Introduction: Evaluation Strategies', in G. Albrecht and H.-U. Otto (eds), *Social Prevention and the Social Sciences. Theoretical Controversies, Research Problems, and Evaluation Strategies* (Berlin: Walter de Gruyter, 1991) 3–13.

Alcohol Statistical Yearbook 1994 (Helsinki: The Finnish State Alcohol Company, 1995).

Alcohol and Drug Policy Plan of the City of Lahti. The Alcohol Policy Team 1992.

Alcoholic Beverages and European Society. Report with 4 annexes (London: Amsterdam Group, 1994).

Allamani, A., Ammannati, P. and Sani, I.B., *Early Experiences of the Alcohol Community Project in Florence, Italy*. A Paper presented at the 1995 Kettil Bruun Society Thematic Meeting, Third Symposium on Community Action Research, Greve in Chianti (Florence) Italy, 25–29 September 1995.

Albrecht, G., 'Methodological Dilemmas', in Albrecht, G. and Otto, H.-U. (eds), *Social Prevention and the Social Sciences. Theoretical Controversies, Research Problems, and Evaluation Strategies* (Berlin: Walter de Gruyter, 1991) 397–428.

Anderson, P., *Management of Drinking Problems*. WHO Regional Office for Europe, Regional Publications, European Series, no. 32, Denmark 1990.

Anderson, P., 'Alcohol as a Key Area', *British Medical Journal*, 303 (1991) 766–9.

Anderson, P., 'The Evidence for the Effectiveness of General Practice Interventions for Individuals with Hazardous Alcohol Consumption'. A paper presented at the WHO Regional Office for Europe's Working Group on the role of general practice settings in the prevention and management of the harm done by alcohol use. Vienna, 19–22 October 1992.

Anderson, P. and Davey, K., 'Communitarism: Import Duties'. *New Statesman & Society*, 3 March 1995.

Anderson, P. and Scott, E., 'The Effect of General Practitioners' Advice to Heavy Drinking Men', *British Journal of Addiction*, 87 (1992) 891–900.

Appel, C., *Alkohol und Gesellschaft. Zur Relevanz und Aktualität der amerikanischen Temperenzbewegung* (Freiburg im Breisgau: Lambertus, 1991).

Argyris, C., 'Participatory Action Research and Action Science Compared. A Commentary', *American Behavioral Scientist*, 32 (1989) 612–23.

225

Asher, R.M., *Women With Alcoholic Husbands. Ambivalence and the Trap of Codependency* (Chapel Hill: University of North Carolina Press, 1992).

Babor, T.F., Ritson, E.B. and Hodgson, R.J., Alcohol-Related Problems in the Primary Health Care Setting: A Review of Early Intervention Strategies', *British Journal of Addiction*, 81 (1986) 23–46.

Babor, T.F., 'Background to the Study', in *World Health Organization; Project on Identification and Management of Alcohol-Related Problems, Report on Phase II; A Randomized Clinical Trial of Brief Interventions in Primary Health Care* (Geneva: WHO/PSA/91.5, 1992).

Babor T. and Grant, M. (eds), *Project on Identification and Management of Alcohol Related Problems, Report on Phase II: A Randomized Clinical Trial of Brief Interventions in Primary Health Care* (Geneva: World Health Organization, 1992).

Bales, R., 'Cultural Differences in Rates of Alcoholism', *Quarterly Journal of Studies on Alcohol*, 6 (1946) 480.

Barrows, S., 'Parliaments of the People. The Political Culture of Cafés in the Early Third Republic', in Barrows, S. and Room, R. (eds), *Drinking, Behavior and Belief in Modern History* (Berkeley and Los Angeles: University of California Press, 1991) 87–97.

Bauman, Z., *Postmodern Ethics* (Oxford: Basil Blackwell, 1993).

Beck, U., *Risk Society: Towards a New Modernity* (London: Sage Publications, 1992).

Bell, D., 'The World and the United States in 2013', *Daedalus*, 116 (1987) 1–31.

Bien, T.H., Miller, W.R. and Tonigan, J.S., 'Brief Interventions for Alcohol Problems: A Review', *Addiction*, 88 (1993) 315–36.

Biernacki, P., *Pathways from Heroin Addiction. Recovery without Treatment* (Philadelphia: Temple University Press, 1986).

Blair, P., 'Trends in Local Autonomy and Democracy: Reflections from a European Perspective', in R. Batley and G. Stoker (eds), *Local Government in Europe. Trends and Developments* (London: Macmillan, 1991).

Bracht, N., *Health Promotion at the Community Level* (Newbury Park, California: Sage Publications, 1990).

Boje, T. and Olsson Hort, S.E. (eds), *Scandinavia in a New Europe* (Oslo: Scandinavian University Press, 1993).

Brennan, T., *Public Drinking and Popular Culture in Eighteenth Century Paris* (New Jersey: Princeton University Press, 1989).

Bruun, K. Edwards, Lumio *et al.*, 'Alcohol Control Policies in Public Health Perspective' (Helsinki: The Finnish Foundation for Alcohol Studies vol. 25, 1975).

Bruun, K. and Frånberg, P. (eds), *Den svenska supen. En historia on brännvin, Bratt och byråkrati* (Drink in Sweden. A History of Alcohol, Bratt and Bureaucracy) (Stockholm: Prisma, 1985).

Casswell, S. and Gilmore, L., 'An Evaluated Community Action Project on Alcohol', *Journal of Studies on Alcohol*, 50 (1989) 339–46.

Casswell, S., 'Alcohol and Public Policy. Efforts to Influence Demand'. Unpublished paper 1992.

Christensen, E., *When Mother or Father Drinks . . . Interview with Children and Parents in Families with Alcohol Misuse* (Kobenhavn: Socialforskningsinstituttet, 1994, Rapport 94:2) (In Danish).

Christie, N. and Bruun, K., *The Good Enemy: Drug Policy in the Nordic Countries* (Stockholm: Rabén & Sjögren, 1985).

Collier, J., 'United States Indian Administration as a Laboratory of Ethnic Relations', *Social Research*, 12 (1945) 275–86.

Collins, R.L., Leonard, K.E. and Searles, J.S. (eds), *Alcohol and the Family. Research and Clinical Perspectives* (New York: The Guilford Press, 1990).

Cook, T.D. and Campbell, D.T., *Quasi-Experimentation: Design and Analysis Issues for Field Setting* (Boston: Houghton Mifflin Company, 1979).

Corey, S.M., *Action Research to Improve School Practices* (New York: Columbia University, 1953).

Cork, R.M., *The Forgotten Children: A Study of Children with Alcoholic Parents* (Toronto: Alcoholism and Drug Addiction Research Foundation of Ontario, 1969).

Cornel, M. and van Zutphen, W.M., 'Recognition of Problem Drinking and the Role of the General Practitioner', *Canadian Family Physician*, 35 (1989) 167–9.

Coulehan, J.L. *et al.*, 'Recognition of Alcoholism and Substance Abuse in Primary Care Patients', *Archive of International Medicine*, 147 (1987) 349–52.

Crespi, F., *Social Action and Power* (Oxford: Blackwell, 1992).

Denzin, N.K. (book review), 'Women With Alcoholic Husbands: Ambivalence and the Trap of Codependency'. By Ramona M. Asher. *American Journal of Sociology*, 98 (1993) 952–4.

Duignan, P., Casswell, S. and Stewart, L., 'Evaluating Community Projects: Conceptual and Methodological Issues Illustrated from the Community Action Project and the Liquor Licensing Project in New Zealand'. A paper presented at the Second International Research Symposium on Experiences with Community Action Projects for the Prevention of Alcohol and Other Drug Problems in San Diego, 29 January–2 February 1992.

Duignan, P. and Casswell, S., 'Evaluating Community Development Programs for Health Promotion: Problems Illustrated by a New Zealand Example', *Community Health Studies*, 13 (1989) 74–81.

Edwards, G. *et al.*, *Alcohol Policy and the Public Good* (New York: Oxford University Press, Oxford Medical Publications, 1994).

Elden, M. and Chisholm, R.F., 'Emerging Varieties of Action Research: Introduction to the Special Issue', *Human Relations*, 46 (1993) 121–42.

Elmeland, K. and Nygaard, P., 'A Community Action Project in Denmark'. An unpublished research plan, 1995.

Eskola, K. and Hammerton, P., *Thinking about Action. The Role of Research in Cultural Development. Project No 5: 'Your Town, Your Life, Your Future.'* (Strasbourg: Council for Cultural Cooperation, 1983).

Esping-Andersen, G., *The Three Worlds of Welfare Capitalism* (Cambridge: Polity Press, 1990).

Etzioni, A., *The Spirit of Community: Rights, Responsibilities and the Communitarian Agenda* (New York: Crown, 1993).

European Alcohol Action Plan (Copenhagen: WHO Regional Office of Europe, 1994).

European Social Policy – A Way Forward for the Union. A White Paper, COM, 33 (Brussels: Commission of the European Union, 1994).

Ewing, J.A., 'Detecting Alcoholism: The Cage Questionnaire', *Journal of the American Medical Association*, 252 (1984) 1905–7.

Eyerman, R. and Jamison, A., *Social Movements. A Cognitive Approach* (Oxford: Polity Press, 1991).

Falk, P. and Sulkunen, P., 'Drinking on the Screen. An Analysis of a Mythical Male Fantasy in Finnish Films', *Social Science Information*, 22 (1983) 387–410.

Farquhar, J.W. *et al.*, 'Effects of Communitywide Education on Cardiovascular Disease Risk Factors: The Standford Five-City Project', *Journal of the American Medical Association*, 264 (1990) 359–65.

Featherstone, M., *Consumer Culture and Postmodernism* (London: Sage Publications, 1991).

Flora, J.A. and Cassady, D.C., 'Roles of Media in Community Based Health Promotion', in N. Bracht, *Health Promotion at the Community Level* (Newbury Park, California: Sage Publications, 1990).

Foucault, M., 'The Political Technology of Individuals', in L.H. Martin, H. Gutman and P.H. Hutton (eds), *Technologies of the Self: A Seminar with Michel Foucault* (London: Tavistock, 1988).

Gamson, W.A. and Modigliani, A., 'Media Discourse and Public Opinion on Nuclear Power: A Constructionist Approach', *American Journal of Sociology*, 95 (1989) 1–37.

Gamson, W. *et al.*, 'Media Images and the Social Construction of Reality', *Annual Review of Sociology*, 18 (1992) 373–93.

Gerner, K., 'Gorbatshovin Neuvostoliitosta Gorbatschowin Venäjäksi' (From Gorbachev's Soviet to Gorbacher's Russia), *Alkoholipolitiikka*, 60 (1995) 98–107.

Giddens, A., *The Consequences of Modernity* (Cambridge: Polity Press, 1990).

Giesbrecht, N. *et al.* (eds), *Research, Action and the Community: Experiences in the Prevention of Alcohol and Other Drug Problems*. OSAP Prevention Monograph 4 (Rockville, Maryland: US Department of Health and Human Services, 1990).

Giesbrecht, N. *et al.*, 'Community Action Research Projects: Integrating Community Interests and Research Agenda in Multicomponent Initiatives'. A paper presented at the 36th International Institute on the Prevention and Treatment of Alcoholism, Stockholm, Sweden, 2–7 June 1991.

Gilbert, N. and Mulkay, M., *Opening Pandora's Box. The Sociological Analysis of Scientific Discourse* (Cambridge: Cambridge University Press, 1984).

Goffman, E., *Forms of Talk* (Oxford: Basil Blackwell, 1981).

Goode, E. and Bem-Yehuda, N., 'Moral Panics: Culture, Politics and Social Construction', *Annual Review of Sociology*, 20 (1994) 149–71.

Goodstadt, M., 'Addressing the Problems of Action Research in the Community: Lessons from Alcohol and Drug Education', in N. Giesbrecht *et al.* (eds), *Research, Action and the Community: Experiences in the Prevention of Alcohol and Other Drug Problems*. OSAP Prevention Monograph 4, 1990, 225–38.

Graham, K., La Rocque, L., Yetman, R., Ross, T.J. and Guistra, E., 'Aggression and Barroom Environments', *Journal of Studies on Alcohol*, 41 (1980) 277–92.

Graham, K., Saunders, S. and Flower, M., 'Approaches and Agenda of Researchers or Evaluators versus Those of Community Developers: Perspectives of the Program Developers, the Program Manager and the Program Evaluator', in Giesbrecht, N. *et al.* (eds), *Research, Action and the Community: Experiences in the Prevention of Alcohol and Other Drug Problems.* OSAP Prevention Monograph 4, 1990.

Gramsci, A., *Selections from the Prison Notebooks*, ed. and trans. Q. Hoare and G. Smith (London: Lawrence & Wishart, 1971).

Greenfield, T.K. and Zimmermann, R. (eds), *Experiences with Community Action Projects: New Research in the Prevention of Alcohol and Other Drug Problems.* CSAP Prevention Monograph 14 (Rockville, MD: US Department of Health and Human Services, 1993).

Greenwood, D.J., Whyte, W.F. and Harkavy, I., 'Participatory Action Research as a Process and a Goal', *Human Relations*, 46 (1993) 175–92.

Gundelach, G., 'Communities, grassroot movements and substance abuse problems', *Nordic Alcohol Studies*, 11 (1994) 5–12 (English Supplement).

Gundelach, P., 'Graesrodsbevegelser, lokalsamfund og rusmiddelproblemer' (Grassroots movements, local communities and problems of abuse), *Nordisk Alkoholtidskrift*, 10 (1993) 14–22.

Gusfield, J., *Symbolic Crusade: Status Politics and the American Temperance Movement*, 2nd edn (Urbana: University of Illionis Press, 1986).

Haatanen. P., 'Suomalaisen hyvinvointivaltion kehitys' (The Development of the Finnish Welfare State), in O. Riihinen, *Sosiaalipolitiikka 2017* (Social Policy 2017) (Porvoo: WSOY, 1992), pp. 31–68.

Haavisto, K., *Lahden peruskoulujen 8.luokkalaisten alkoholin käytöstä keväällä 1993* (Use of Alcohol among the 8th Grade Students of the Secondary Schools of Lahti in the Spring of 1993), Lahti Project Working Papers 6 (Helsinki: Social Research Institute of Alcohol Studies, 1993).

Haavisto, K., Nurminen, R. and Tommola, S., *Lahtelaisissa lukioissa ja ammatillisissa oppilaitoksissa opiskelevien päihteiden käytöstä keväällä 1993* (Use of Alcohol and Drugs among the Students of the Colleges and Vocational Schools in Lahti in the Spring of 1993). Lahti Project Working Papers 3. (Helsinki: Social Research Institute of Alcohol Studies, 1993).

Haavisto, K., 'Vastuullisen anniskelun edistäminen'. Lahtiprojektin arviointiseminaari 16.5.1995. Onnistuuko päihdehaittojen vähentäminen paikallisesti? (Promoting responsible service. In: The evaluation seminar on Lahti Project 16 May 1995. Can alcohol related harms be reduced locally?) (Helsinki: Alko Group, Alcohol Policy Planning and Education Unit, 1995).

Hämeen lääninhallitus, 'Ehkäisevä päihdetyö yksilö- ja yhteisötasolla väestön hyvinvointia lisäämässä. Tutkimus ehkäisevässä päihdetyössä huomioon otettavista väestön tavoista, asenteista ja odotuksista' (The District Government of Häme, Preventive Action as a Method of Increasing Public Well-Being. Research on Habits, Attitudes and Expectations). A Report (Hämeenlinna: 1990).

Hamilton, M., Barber, J. and Banwell, C., 'Alcohol and Other Drugs – a Family Business', Editorial, *Drug and Alcohol Review*, 13 (1994) 371–4.

Hands, M. and Dear, G., 'Co-Dependency: A Critical Review', *Drug and Alcohol Review*, 13 (1994) 437–46.

Hanhinen, S., 'Sosiaalisten ongelmien, erityisesti päihdeongelmien, määrittely lehdistössä valtakunnallisella, paikallisella ja lähipaikallisella tasolla' (The Definition of Social Problems, in Particular Alcohol and Drug Problems in the National, Local and Neighbourhood Press). Master's thesis (Helsinki: University of Helsinki, Department of Social Policy, 1994).

Hannibal, J.U. *et al.*, 'Responding to Alcohol Problems'. Report on an International Collaborative Study on Community Response to Alcohol-Related Problems. Draft publication, April 1992.

Hannibal, J.U. *et al.*, 'Alcohol and the Community'. Report on an International Collaborative Study on Community Response to Alcohol-Related Problems (Copenhagen: World Health Organization, Regional Office for Europe, 1995).

Hanson, B.S., Larsson, S. and Lindbladh, E., 'Experiences from the Kirseberg Public Health Project in Malmö, Sweden: An Alcohol Prevention Campaign', in Greenfield, T.K. and Zimmermann, R. (eds), *Experiences with Community Action Projects: New Research in the Prevention of Alcohol and Other Drug Problems*. CSAP Prevention Monograph 14 (Rockville, MD: US Department of Health and Human Services, 1993), pp. 147–57.

Haranne, M., *Community Power Structure Studies. An Appraisal of an Ever-Green Research Tradition with a Finnish Example* (Helsinki: University of Helsinki, Research Group for Comparative Sociology, 1976).

Harrison, B., *Drink and the Victorians. The Temperance Question in England 1815–1978* (London: Faber & Faber, 1971).

Healther, N. *et al.*, 'Interpreting the Evidence of Brief Interventions for Excessive Drinkers: The Need for Caution', *Alcohol & Alcoholism*, 30 (1995) 287–96.

Hein, R. and Somervuori, A., 'Alkoholijuomien kulutus, haitat ja alkoholipolitiikka' (Use of Alcohol, Harms and Alcohol Policy), in K. Kiianmaa and M. Salaspuro (eds), *Alkoholi. Biolääketieteellinen käsikirja* (Alcohol. A Biomedical Handbook) (Keuruu: Otava, 1993).

Heiskanen, M.K. *et al.*, *Tapaturmat ja väkivalta 1988* (Accidents and Violence in 1988). Oikeus 7 (1990) Statistics on Criminality 7 (Helsinki: The Central Statistical Bureau, 1990).

Hilgartner, S. and Bosk, C.L., 'The Rise and Fall of Social Problems: A Public Arenas Model', *Americam Journal of Sociology*, 94 (1989) 53–78.

Hendry, L.B., 'The Influence of Adults and Peers on Adolescents' Lifestyles and Leisure-Styles', in K. Hurrelmann and U. Engel (eds), *The Social World of Adolescents* (Berlin: Walter de Gruyter, 1989).

Holder, H. and Wagenaar, A., 'Mandated Server Training and Reduced Alcohol-Involved Traffic Crashes: A Time Series Analysis of the Oregon Experience', *Accident Analysis and Prevention*, 26 (1994) 89–97.

Holder, H.D. *et al.*, 'Potential Consequences from Possible Changes to Nordic Retail Alcohol Monopolies Resulting from European Union Membership', *Addiction*, 90 (1995) 1603–18.

Holder, H. and Wallack, L., 'Contemporary Perspectives for Preventing Alcohol Problems. An Empirically Derived Model', *Journal of Public Health Policy*, 7 (1986) 324–39.

Holder, H. and Howard, J. (eds), *Community Prevention Trials for Alcohol Problems: Methodological Issues* (Westport: Praeger, 1992).

Holmila, M. 'Alkoholipoliittisen ajattelun pulmakohtia. Vaikuttajien mielipiteitä alkoholipolitiikasta' (Problems in Alcohol Policy Thinking. The Opinions of Key Persons). Report from the Social Research Institute of Alcohol

Studies 148 (Helsinki: The Social Research Institute of Alcohol Studies, 1981).

Holmila, M., *Wives, Husbands and Alcohol. A Study of Informal Drinking Control within the Family* (Helsinki: The Finnish Foundation for Alcohol Studies, vol. 36, 1988).

Holmila, M., Ahtola, R. and Stenius, K., 'Asiakkaiden mielipiteitä juoppouden hoidosta' (Heavy Drinkers' Opinions of Social and Health Services). Report from the Social Research Institute of Alcohol Studies 182 (Helsinki: Social Research Institute of Alcohol Studies, 1989).

Holmila, M., 'Problems of Action Research: Some Practical Experiences', in N. Giesbrecht *et al.* (eds), *Research, Action and the Community: Experiences in the Prevention of Alcohol and Other Drug Problems.* OSAP Prevention Monograph 4 (Rockville, Maryland: US Department of Health and Human Services, 1990).

Holmila, M., 'Lokalsamhället som projekt inom alkohol- och drogpreventionen' (Conducting and Researching Community Action Projects to Prevent Alcohol- and Drug-Related Problems), *Nordisk Alkoholtidskrift,* 9 (1992) 145–51.

Holmila, M., 'Proposal for a Demonstration Project for a Comprehensive Community Alcohol Programme to Prevent the Harm Done by Alcohol Use'. WHO, Regional Office for Europe. Working Group on Community and Municipal Action on Alcohol. Warsaw, 18–20 November 1992.

Holmila, M., *Lahtelaisia mielipiteitä alkoholin tarjonnasta* (Public Opinions on Alcohol Supply in Lahti). Lahti Project Working Papers 2 (Helsinki: Social Research Institute of Alcohol Studies, 1993).

Holmila, M. and Haavisto, K., *Alkoholinkäytön liittyminen poliisin väkivaltatoimiston tutkimiin tapauksiin Lahdessa* (Cases of Alcohol-Related Violence Examined by the Lahti Police). Lahti Project Working Papers 9 (Helsinki: Social Research Institute of Alcohol Studies, 1994).

Holmila, M., 'Excessive Drinking and Significant Others', *Drug and Alcohol Review,* 13 (1994) 431–6.

Holmila, M. and Haavisto, K., 'Häiriöt ja kontrolli lahtelaisissa ravintoloissa' (Disturbances and control in three restaurants in Lahti), *Alkoholipolitiikka,* 59 (1994), 210–18.

Holmila, M., 'Lahti-projekti. Paikallistoimintaa ja tutkimusta päihdehaittojen ehkäisemiseksi' (Lahti Project. Community Action and Research for Prevention of Alcohol Problems), *Janus,* 2 (1994) 393–8.

Holmila, M., 'Community Action on Alcohol', *Health Promotion International,* 10 (1995) 283–91.

Holmila, M., 'Intoxication and Hazardous Use of Alcohol: Results from the 1992 Finnish Drinking Habits Study', *Addiction,* 90 (1995) 785–92.

Holmila, M. 'Lahti-projektin saavutusten arviointia', in Lahti-projektin arviointiseminaari 16.5.1995. 'Onnistuuko päihdehaittojen vähentäminen paikallisesti?' (Evaluating the Lahti Project', The Evaluation Seminar on the Lahti Project 16.5.1995. 'Can alcohol related harms be reduced locally?) (Helsinki: Alcohol Policy Planning and Education Unit, Alko Company 1995).

Holstein, J. and Miller, G. (eds), *Perspectives on Social Problems,* vol.1 (London, 1989).

Homel, R., Tomsen, S. and Thommeny, J., 'Public Drinking and Violence: Not Just an Alcohol Problem', *Journal of Drug Issues*, 22 (1992) 679–97.

Hoole, F.W., *Evaluation Research and Development Activities*. Sage Library of Social Research, vol. 68 (Beverly Hills, California: Sage, 1978).

House, E.R., *Evaluating with Validity* (Beverly Hills/London: Sage, 1980).

Hunter, F., *Community Power Structure: A Study of Decision Makers* (USA, 1953).

Institute of Medicine, 'Prevention and Treatment of Alcohol-Related Problems: Research Opportunities'. Committee to Identify Research Opportunities in the Prevention and Treatment of Alcohol-Related Problems, *Journal of Studies on Alcohol*, 53 (1992) 5–16.

Jacobs, D.R., 'Community-Wide Prevention Strategies: Evaluation Design of the Minnesota Heart Health Program', *Journal of Chronic Disease*, 39 (1986) 775–88.

Janowicz, M., 'Professional Models in Journalism: The Gatekeeper and the Advocate', *Journalism Quarterly*, 52 (1975) 618–62.

Järvinen, M. and Stenius, K., 'En karl lyder mycket bättre! Restaurangkontrolen och kvinnan' (A Man Sounds Much Better! Control of Public Drinking Places and Women) *Alkoholpolitik*, 2 (1985) 46–50.

Jensen, Ø. and Kjærnes, U., 'Designing the Good Life. Nutrition and Social Democracy in Norway', in P. Sulkunen (eds), *Constructing the New Consumer Society* (London, Macmillan, 1996).

Johnson, C.A., 'Objectives of Community Programs to Prevent Drug Abuse', *Journal of School Health*, 56 (1986) 364–8.

Johnson, J.L. and Rolf, J.E., 'When Children Change: Research Perspectives on Children of Alcoholics', in R.L. Collins, K.E. Leonard and J.S. Searles (eds), *Alcohol and the Family, Research and Clinical Perspectives* (New York: The Guilford Press, 1990).

Jordan, S. and Yeomans, D., 'Critical Ethnography: Problems in Contemporary Theory and Practice', *British Journal of Sociology of Education*, 16 (1995) 389–408.

Julkunen, R., *Hyvinvointivaltio käännekohdassa* (The Turning-Point of the Welfare State) (Tampere: Vastapaino, 1992).

Juntto, A., *Asuntokysymys Suomessa Topeliuksesta tulopolitiikkaan* (The Housing Policy Question in Finland from Topelius to the Present Day) (Helsinki: Sosiaalipoliittisen yhdistyksen tutkimuksia, 1990).

Kämäri, L., 'Mistä on kreisit tytöt tehty?' (What are Crazy Girls Made Of?), *Sosiaaliturva*, 23 (1993) 29–31.

Kämäri, L. and Pyykkö, J., *Kreisit tytöt sekoilevat selvinpäin. – Nuorten päihdekasvatuksen toimintaprojekti* (Crazy Girls are Crazy without Drinks. An Action Project on Young Girls' Drug Education). Lahti Project Working Papers 10 (Helsinki: Social Research Institute of Alcohol Studies, 1994).

Kamerow, D.B., Pincus, H.A. and Macdonald, D.J., 'Alcohol Abuse, Other Drug Abuse, and Mental Disorders in Medical Practice', *JAMA*, 255 (1986) 2054–7.

Kantola, L. and Montonen, M., *Drokeja ja drinkkejä. Taikui Oz – draama päihdevalistuksen muotona* (Drugs and Drinks. The Wizard of Oz – A Drama as a Method of Alcohol and Drug Prevention). Lahti Project Working Papers 7 (Helsinki: Social Research Institute of Alcohol Studies, 1993).

Kasvio, A., 'Työelämän muutos ja toimintatutkimus' (Changes in the Work Life and Action Research), *Sosiologia*, 31 (1994) 24–34.

Kickbusch, I., 'Health Promotion and Disease Prevention; the Implications for Health Promotion', in C.E. Normand and P. Vaughan (eds), *Europe without Frontiers* (New York: John Wiley & Sons, 1993).

Klingemann, H., 'The Motivation for Change from Problem Alcohol and Heroin Use', *British Journal of Addiction*, 86 (1991) 727–44.

Koepsell, T.D. *et al.*, 'Selected Methodological Issues in Evaluating Community–Based Health Promotion and Disease Prevention Programs', *Annual Review of Public Health*, 13 (1992) 31–57.

Kokeny, M. *et al.*, 'The Role of Health Promotion in Preventive Policy against Cardiovascular Diseases in Hungary', *Health Promotion*, 1 (1986) 85–92.

Kornhauser, W., *The Politics of Mass Society* (Glencoe, Illinois, 1959).

Koski-Jännes, A., *Alcohol Addiction and Self-Regulation. A Controlled Trial of a Relapse Prevention Program for Finnish Inpatient Alcoholics* (Helsinki: The Finnish Foundation for Alcohol Studies, vol. 41, 1992).

Kosonen, P., *Eurooppalaiset hyvinvointivaltiot* (European Welfare States) (Helsinki: Gaudeamus, 1995).

Krestan, J.A. and Bepko, C., 'Codependency: The Social Reconstruction of Female Experience', *Journal of Feminist Family Therapy*, 3 (1991) 49–66.

Kuusi, P., *Social Policy for the Sixties. A Plan for Finland* (Helsinki: Finnish Social Policy Association, 1964).

Lagerspetz, M. (ed.), *Social Problems in Newspapers. Studies around the Baltic Sea.* NAD Publication 28 (Helsinki: Nordic Council for Alcohol and Drug Research, 1994).

Lash, S. and Urry, J., *Economies of Signs and Spaces* (London: Sage, 1994).

Levine, H., 'The Good Creature of God and the Demon Rum: Colonial American and 19th Century Ideas about Alcohol, Crime and Accidents', in R. Room (ed.), *Alcohol and Disinhibition: Nature and Meaning of the Link* (Rockville, Md.: US Department of Health and Human Services, 1983).

Lindbladh, E. and Hanson, B.S., 'Alkoholprevention i lokalsamhället. Totalkonsumtionsmodellen i ett vardagsperspektiv' (Alcohol Prevention in a Local Community. Total Consumption Model in an Everyday Perspective), *Nordisk Alkoholtidskrift*, 10 (1993) 256–264.

Lupton, D., *The Imperative of Health: Public Health and the Regulated Body* (London: Sage, 1995).

Maffesoli, M., *The Time of the Tribes: The Decline of Individualsim in Mass Society* (London: Sage, 1994).

Magnusson, L., 'Orsaker till det förindustriella drickandet. Supandet i Hantverkets Eskilstuna' (Reasons for pre-industrial drinking. The craftsmen of Eskilstuna), *Alkoholpolitik*, 2 (1985) 23–9.

Mäkelä, K., Sulkunen, P. and Österberg, E., 'Drink in Finland: Increasing Availability in a Monopoly State', in E. Single, P. Morgan and J. de Lint (eds), *Alcohol, Society and the State 2. The Social History of Alcohol Control Policy in Seven Countries* (Toronto: Addiction Reserch Foundation, 1981).

Mäkelä, K., 'State Alcohol Monopolies in Finland, Norway and Sweden', in *The Role of Alcohol Monopolies.* Report from a conference in Skarpö, Sweden, January 1987. Stockholm 1988.

Mäkelä, K., 'Suomi ja sen hyvinvointivaltio, valtio ja sen Suomi' (Finland and Its Welfare State, the State and its Finland), *Tiede & edistys*, 13 (1988) 88–96.

Mäkelä, S.L. and Teräväinen, R., *Nuorten päihteiden käytön ehkäisy ja vähentäminen Lahdessa. Tavoite- ja toimenpideohjelma* (Preventing and Reducing the Use of Alcohol and Drugs in Lahti. Goals and Plans of Action). Lahti Project Working Papers 12 (Helsinki: Social Research Institute of Alcohol Studies, 1994a).

Mäkelä, S.L., *Katsaus Lahden päihdeoloihin vuodesta 1982–1993* (Statistical Review on Alcohol and Drug Issues in Lahti in the Years 1982–1993). Lahti Project Working Papers 11 (Helsinki: Social Research Institute of Alcohol Studies, 1994b).

Mathrani, S., 'Community Public Policy: A Balanced Alcohol Strategy for Oxford – A Case Study', in Greenfield, T.K. and Zimmermann, R. (eds), *Experiences with Community Action Projects: New Research in the Prevention of Alcohol and Other Drug Problems*, CSAP Prevention Monograph 14 (Rockville, MD: US Department of Health and Human Services, 1993) 95–101.

Mayfield, D., McLeod, G. and Hall, P., 'The CAGE Questionnaire: Validation of a New Alcoholism Screening Instrument', *American Journal of Psychiatry* 131 (1974) 1121–3.

McCombs, M.E. and Shaw, D.L., 'The Evolution of Agenda-Setting Research: Twenty-Five Years in the Marketplace of Ideas', *Journal of Communication*, 43 (1993).

McCrady, B. and Hay, W., 'Coping with Alcohol Problems in the Family', in J. Orford and J. Harwin (eds), *Coping with Disorder in the Family* (London: Croom Helm, 1982).

McGraw, S. *et al.*, 'Methods in Program Evaluation. The Process Evaluation System of the Pawtucket Heart Health Program', *Evaluation Review*, 13 (1989) 459–83.

McGuire, W.J., 'Attitude Change: The Information Processing Pradigm', in C.G. McClintock (ed.), *Experimental Social Psychology* (New York: Reinhart and Wishart).

McKnight, A.J. and Streff, F.M., 'The Effect of Enforcement upon Service of Alcohol to Intoxicated Patrons of Bars and Restaurants', *Accident Analysis and Prevention*, 26 (1994) 79–88.

Mills, C.W., *The Power Elite* (New York: Oxford University Press, 1959).

Mishra, R., *The Welfare State in Capitalist Society* (New York: Harvester, 1990).

Montonen, M., 'Viinaviikot kirjastossa' (Liquor Weeks in Library), *Kirjastotiede ja informatiikka*, 12 (1993) 3–19.

Montonen, M., 'Drokeja ja drinkkejä teatterissa' (Drugs and Drinks in Theatre), *Alkoholipolitiikka*, 59 (1994) 440–8.

Montonen, M., *Alcohol and the Media* (Copenhagen: WHO Regional Publications, European Series No. 62, 1995a).

Montonen, M., 'The Liquor Weeks: Local Cooperation to Inform the Public about Alcohol'. Kettil Bruun Society Thematic Meeting. Third Symposium on Community Action Research. 24–29 September 1995, Greve in Chianti, Italy, 1995b.

Montonen, M. 'The Public's Knowledge about Alcohol'. An unpublished manuscript, 1995c.

Moores, S., *Interpreting Audiences. The Ethnography of Media Consumption* (London: Sage Publications, 1993).

Morgan, D.L., *Focus Groups as Qualitative Research* (Newbury Park, California: Sage, 1988).

Morgan, D.L. (ed.), *Successful Focus Groups. Advancing the State of the Art* (Newbury Park, California: Sage, 1993).

Moser, H., *Aktionsforschung als kritische Theorie der Sozialwissenschaften* (Munchen: Kösel-Verlag GmbH & Co, 1978).

Mosher, J. 'Server Intervention: A New Approach for Preventing Drinking Driving', *Accident Analysis and Prevention*, 15 (1983) 483–97.

Mosher, J.F. and Jernigan, D.H., 'New Directions in Alcohol Policy', *Annual Review of Public Health*, 10 (1989) 245–79.

Moskowitz, J.M., 'The Primary Prevention of Alcohol Problems: A Critical Review of the Research Literature', *Journal of Studies on Alcohol*, 50 (1989) 54–88.

Murphy, H.B.M., 'Hidden Barriers to Diagnosis and Treatment of Alcoholism and Other Misuse', *Journal of Studies on Alcohol*, 41 (1980) 417–28.

Naisiin kohdistuva väkivalta. Väkivaltajaoston mietintö (Violence against Women. Report of a Committee on Violence). Sosiaali-ja terveysministeriö, Tasa-arvojulkaisuja, Sarja B: Tiedotteita 5/1991 (Helsinki: Social and Health Ministry, 1991).

Neuman, R.W., 'A Threshold of Public Attention', *Public Opinion Quarterly*, 54 (1990).

Nilssen, O., 'The Tromso Study: Identification of and a Controlled Intervention on a Population of Early-Stage Risk Drinkers', *Preventive Medicine*, 20 (1991) 518–28.

Norton, A., 'Western European Local Government in Comparative Perspective', in R. Batley and G. Stoker (eds), *Local Government in Europe. Trends and Developments* (London: Macmillan, 1991).

Nutbeam, D., 'Health Promotion Glossary', *Health Promotion*, 1 (1986) 113–27.

Nutbeam, D. and Crawford, J., 'The Welsh Heart Programme Evaluation Strategy: Progress, Plans, Possibilities', *Health Promotion*, 2 (1987) 5–18.

Ojanen, A., 'Pahoinpitelyjen vähentäminen Lahdessa. Erityiskohteina ravintolat ja niiden edustat' (Reducing Violence in Lahti. Targeting on the Restaurants and Their Environment). A Memo (Lahti: Lahden poliisilaitos, 1993).

Olsson, S., *Social Policy and the Welfare State in Sweden* (Lund: A Arkiv Förlag, 1990).

Onikki, E. and Ranta, H. (eds), *Suomen laki II* (The Finnish Law) (Helsinki: Lakimiesliiton kustannus, 1995).

Orford, J., 'The Prevention and Management of Alcohol Problems in the Family Setting: A Review of Work Carried Out in English-Speaking Countries', *Alcohol and Alcoholism*, 19 (1984) 109–22.

Orford, J., 'Control, Confront or Collude: How Family and Society Respond to Excessive Drinking', *British Journal of Addiction*, 87 (1992) 1513–25.

Orford, J., 'Empowering Family and Friends: A New Approach to the Secondary Prevention of Addiction', *Drug and Alcohol Review*, 13 (1994) 417–30.

Österberg, E., 'Country Profiles. Finland', pp. 107–56, in T. Kortteinen (ed.), *State Monopolies and Alcohol Prevention*. Report from the Social Research Institute of Alcohol Studies 181 (Helsinki: The Social Research Institute of Alcohol Studies, 1989).

Österberg, E., 'Would a More Liberal Control Policy Increase Alcohol Consumption?' *Contemporary Drug Problems*, Winter (1990) 545–73.

Österberg, E., 'Implication for Monopolies of the European Integration'.

236   *References*

Paper prepared for the Symposium on Alcohol Monopolies and Social and Health Issues, Toronto, Ontario, Canada, 27–30 October 1992.

Österberg, E., 'The Alko Strikes and their Effect on Crime', in E. Österberg and S.-L. Säilä (eds), *Natural Experiments with Decreased Availability of Alcoholic Beverages. Finnish Alcohol Strikes in 1972 and 1985*, vol. 40 (Helsinki: The Finnish Foundation for Alcohol Studies, 1991) 105–15.

Österberg, E., *Alkoholin kulutus ja juomatavat Helsingissä 1990-luvun alussa*, Helsingin kaupunki ja Alkoholipoliittinen tutkimuslaitos (Helsinki: Helsingin kaupungin hankintakeskus, 1995).

Österberg, E., 'Kotivalmisteisen alkoholin käyttö tasaantui vuonna 1994' (Consumption of Home-Made Alcohol Stabilized in 1994), *Alkoholipolitiikka*, 60 (1995) 161–7.

Ottawa Charter for Health Promotion, *Health Promotion*, 1 (1986) iii–v.

Parsons, T. and Shils, E., *Toward a General Theory of Action* (Cambridge, Mass.: Harvard University Press, 1951).

Partanen, J., *Sociability and Intoxication: Alcohol and Drinking in Kenya, Africa and the Modern World* (Helsinki: The Finnish Foundation for Alcohol Studies, vol. 39, 1991).

Partanen, J. and Montonen, M., *Alcohol and the Mass Media*, EURO Reports and Studies 108. (Copenhagen: World Health Organization. Regional Office for Europe, 1988).

Patton, M.Q., *Qualitative Evaluation Methods* (London: Sage Publications, 1980).

Peltonen, M., *Viinapäästä kolerakauhuun* (From the 'Finnish Booze' to Fear of Cholera) (Helsinki: Hanki ja jää, 1988).

Pentz, M.A. *et al.*, 'A Multicommunity Trial for Primary Prevention of Drug Abuse', *Journal of the American Medical Association*, 261 (1989) 3259–66.

Pernanen, K., *Alcohol and Human Violence* (New York: The Guilford Press, 1991).

Perry, C.L.,'Community–Wide Health Promotion and Drug Abuse Prevention', *Journal of School Health*, 56 (1986) 359–63.

Pietilä, M., 'We Set Out as Crusaders and Realized that it is Impossible – Journalists' Opinions on Alcohol Policy and on their Professional Roles in Interview Talk'. Master's thesis in Sociology, University of Helsinki 1995.

Piispa, M., 'Mistä puhumme kun puhumme alkoholiongelmasta. Alkoholiongelman ja alkoholipolitiikan konstruktiot Suomessa 1950–1990' (Alcohol problems and alcohol policy as social constructions), *Janus*, 2(1994) 249–66.

Pirie, P.L.,'Evaluating Health Promotion Programs', in N. Bracht, *Health Promotion at the Community Level* (Newbury Park, California: Sage Publications, 1990).

Pittman, D., 'International Overview: Social and Cultural Factors in Drinking Patterns, Pathological and Nonpathological', in D. Pittman (ed.), *Alcoholism* (New York: Harper & Row, 1967).

Pokorny, A.D., Miller, B.A. and Kaplan, H.B., 'The Brief Mast: A Shortened Version of the Michigan Alcoholism Screening Test', *American Journal of Psychiatry*, 129 (1972) 342–5.

Posavac, E.J. and Carey, R.G., *Program Evaluation. Methods and Case Studies* (New Jersey: Prentice-Hall, 1992).

Potter, J. and Wetherell, M., *Discourse and Social Psychology. Beyond Attitudes and Behaviour* (London: Sage, 1987).

Pringle, M. and Laverty, J., 'A Counsellor in Every Practice', *British Medical Journal,* 306 (1993) 2–3.

Puska, P., *Large Scale Demonstration Projects for National Chronic Disease Prevention: Concepts of the WHO Cindi Programme.* World Health Organization Working Groups on CINDI Programme and Community Action on Alcohol, Dublin, 28–29 October 1993.

Puska, P. *et al.*, *Community Control of Cardiovascular Diseases – The North Karelia Project: Evaluation of a Comprehensive Community Programme for Control of Cardiovascular Diseases in 1972–77 in North Karelia* (Copenhagen: WHO/ EURO, 1981: Monograph series).

Puska, P. *et al.*, 'The Community Health Strategy to Prevent Coronary Heart Disease: Conclusions from the Ten Years of the North Karelia Project', *Annual Review of Public Health,* 6 (1985) 147–93.

Puskala, K. and Miettinen. S., 'Ravintolahenkilökunnan näkökulma humalatilan kohtaamisesta ja vastuullisesta anniskelusta' (Restaurant Personnel's Opinions on Responsible Service). An unpublished paper, Fellmanni-instituutti, Lahti 1995.

Rapoport, R.N., 'Three Dilemmas in Action Research', *Human Relations,* 23 (1970) 488–513.

Reese, S.J., 'Setting the Media's Agenda: A Power Balance Perspective', in J.A. Anderson (ed.), *Communication Yearbook 14* (Newbury Park, California: Sage Publications, 1991).

Reid, A.L.A. *et al.*, 'Detection of Patients with High Alcohol Intake by General Practitioners', *British Medical Journal,* 293 (1986) 735–7.

Report of a Committee on Violence, *Violence against Women,* Publications on Equality, Series B: Bulletin 5 (Helsinki: Social and Health Ministry, 1991 (in Finnish).

Reuter, S. and Tigerstedt, C., 'Alkoholpolitiken i Norden sedan 1980' (Alcohol policy in the Nordic countries from 1980 onwards), *Nordisk Alkoholtidskrift,* 9 (1995) 59–72.

Reynolds, R. and Holder, H., 'A Community Approach to the Prevention of Alcohol Problems: A Case Study from the San Diego County Alcohol Program', 1988.

Riesman, D., *The Lonely Crowd* (New Haven: Yale University Press, 1950).

Ritson, E.B., *Community Response to Alcohol Related Problems. Review of an International Study.* Public Health Papers no. 81 (Geneva: World Health Organization, 1985).

Robertson, R., *Globalization. Social Theory and Global Culture* (London: Sage, 1992).

Roman, P., (book review) *The Other Half: Wives of Alcoholics and their Social-psychological Situation,* by Jacqueline P. Wiseman, *Deviant Behavior,* 14 (1993) 266–70.

Romelsjö, A., Andren, A. and Borg, S., 'Design, implementation and evaluation of a community action program for prevention of alcohol-related problems in Stockholm City: Initial Experiences', in T. Greenfield and R. Zimmerman (eds), *Experiences with Community Action Projects: New Research in the Prevention of Alcohol and Other Drug Problems.* OSAP Prevention

Monograph 14 (Rockville: US Department of Health and Human Services, 1993).

Room, R., 'Community Action and Alcohol Problems: The Demonstration Project as an Unstable Mixture', in N. Giesbrecht *et al.* (eds), *Research, Action and the Community: Experiences in the Prevention of Alcohol and Other Drug Problems*. OSAP Prevention Monograph 4 (Rockville, Maryland: US Department of Health and Human Services, 1990).

Room, R., Greenfield, T. and Weisner, C., 'People Who Might Have Liked You to Drink Less: Changing Responses to Drinking by U.S. Family Members and Friends, 1979–1990', *Contemporary Drug Problems*, 18 (1991) 573–96).

Rothman, J., 'Three Models of Community Organization Practice, Their Mixing and Phasing', in F.M. Cox *et al.* (eds), *Strategies of Community Organization*, 1970.

Russ, N.W. and Geller, E.S., 'Training Bar Personnel to Prevent Drunken Driving: A Field Evaluation', *American Journal of Public Health*, 77 (1987) 952–4.

Rutman, L., *Planning Useful Evaluations, Evaluability Assessment* (Beverly Hills, California: Sage Publications, 1980).

Rychtarik, R.G., 'Alcohol-Related Coping Skills in Spouses of Alcoholics: Assessment and Implication for Treatment', in R.L. Collins, K.L. Leonard and J.S. Searles (eds), *Alcohol and the Family, Research and Clinical Perspectives* (New York: Guilford Press, 1990).

Säilä, S.L., 'Readiness of Service Units to Treat Alcohol and Drug Problems' (Palvelupisteiden valmius käsitellä päihdeongelmia), Reports from the Social Research Institute of Alcohol Studies 185 (Helsinki: The Social Research Institute of Alcohol Studies, 1991).

Sairanen, S., 'Paikallistason sosiaalipolitiikka ja päihdeongelmat' (Local Social Policy and Alcohol and Drug Problems). Manuscript for a Master's Thesis, University of Helsinki, Department of Social Policy, 1995.

Saltz, R.F., 'Research in Environmental and Community Strategies for the Prevention of Alcohol Problems', *Contemporary Drug Problems*, 15 (1988) 67–81.

Saunders, J.B. *et al.*, 'Development of the Alcohol Use Disorders Identification Test (AUDIT): WHO Collaborative Project on Early Detection of Persons with Harmful Alcohol Consumption II', *Addiction*, 88 (1993) 791–804.

Schneider, J.W., 'Social Problems: The Constructionist View', *Annual Review of Sociology*, 11 (1985) 209–29.

Seppä, K., Koivula, T. and Sillanaukee, P., 'Drinking Habits and Detection of Heavy Drinking among Middle-Aged Women', *British Journal of Addiction*, 87 (1992) 77–81.

Seppä, K. and Mäkelä, R., 'Alkoholin suurkuluttajat sairaalapotilaissa' (Excessive Drinkers among Hospital Patients), *Suomen Lääkärilehti*, 8 (1993) 684–6.

Sillanaukee, P., *A Guide for Controlled Drinking*. Alcohol Policy Planning and Media Department. Alko, No. 033, 1993.

Sillanaukee, P. *et al.*, 'Alkoholin suurkulutuksen kriteerit' (The Criteria for Excessive Use of Alcohol), *Suomen Lääkärilehti*, 47 (1992) 2919–21.

Sillanaukee, P., 'Lahti-project: Reducing Alcohol and Drug Problems at the Community Level – Focus on Primary Health Care'. Lahti Project. Working Papers 8 (Helsinki: Social Research Institute of Alcohol Studies, 1993).

Simmel, G., *The Sociology of Georg Simmel* trans., ed. and with an introduction by Kurt H. Wolff (Glencoe, Illinois: The Free Press, 1950).

Simpson, R. *et al.*, 'A Guide to The Responsible Service of Alcohol' (Toronto: Addiction Research Foundation, 1986).

Simpura, J., *Vapaan viinan aika. 50 vuotta suomalaista alkoholipolitiikkaa.* (The Era of Free Liquor. 50 Years of Finnish Alcohol Control Policy) (Helsinki: Kirjayhtymä, 1982).

Simpura, J. (ed.), *Finnish Drinking Habits. Results from Interview Surveys Held in 1968, 1976 and 1984,* The Finnish Foundation for Alcohol Studies, 35 (Jyväskylä: Gummerus Oy, 1987).

Simpura, J., 'Alcohol-Related Caseload of Social Welfare System, Off-Clinic Health Services and Police: a Study in Three Finnish Towns'. A paper presented at the 17th Annual Alcohol Epidemiology Symposium of Kettil Bruun Society in Sigtuna, 10–14 June 1991.

Simpura, J. and Tigerstedt, C., 'Theoretical Perspective and Historical Context: Introduction to a Comparative Study', in J. Simpura and C. Tigerstedt (eds), *Social Problems around the Baltic Sea.* NAD Publication No. 21 (Helsinki: Nordic Council for Alcohol and Drug Research (NAD), 1992).

Simpura, J., 'Suomalainen viinapää tänään' (Finnish Boozing Today), *Duodecim,* 109 (1993), 2065–73.

Simpura, J., 'Alkoholi sosiaalisena ongelmana Lahdessa. Lahti-projektin arviointiseminaari 16.5.1995. Onnistuuko päihdehaittojen vähentäminen paikallisesti?' (Alcohol as a Social Problem in Lahti), in The Evaluation Seminar on Lahti Project 16 May 1995. Can Alcohol Related Harms be Reduced Locally? (Helsinki: Alcohol Policy Planning and Education Unit, Alko, 1995).

Simpura, J., Paakkanen, P. and Mustonen, H., 'New Beverages, New Drinking Contexts? Signs of Modernization in Finnish Drinking Habits from 1984 to 1992, Compared with Trends in the European Community', *Addiction,* 90 (1995), 673–83.

Single, E., 'International Perspectives on Public Drinking: Results of an Informant Survey. Report of the WHO Project on Public Drinking', *Contemporary Drug Problems* (forthcoming).

Smythe, C., Jeffries, J. and Tessier, C., 'Evaluation of a Community Coalitions's Implementation of the Server Intervention Program'. A paper presented at the 21st Annual Alcohol Epidemiology Symposium of the Kettil Bruun Society of Social and Epidemiological Research on Alcohol, Porto, Portugal, 5–9 June 1995.

Spector, M. and Kitsuse, J.I., *Constructing Social Problems* (New York: Aldine de Gruyter, 1987 (1977)).

Stallings, R.A., 'Media Discourse and the Social Construction of Risk', *Social Problems,* 37 (1990) 80–95.

Steiner, C., *Games Alcoholics Play. The Analysis of Life Scripts* (New York: Ballantine Books 1978).

Stockwell, T., Lang, E. and Rydon, P., 'High Risk Drinking Settings: The

Association of Serving and Promotional Practices with Harmful Drinking', *Addiction*, 8 (1993) 1519–26.

Stoker, G. (eds), *Local Government in Europe. Trends and Developments* (London: Macmillan).

Suhonen, P., *We, Media and the Environmnent* (Mediat, me ja ympäristö) (Helsinki: Hanki ja jää, 1994).

Sulkunen, I., 'Temperance as a Civic Religion', *Contemporary Drug Problems*, 12 (1985) 267–85.

Sulkunen, P., 'Alcohol Consumption and the Transformation of Living Conditions. A Comparative Study', *Research Advances in Alcohol and Drug Problems*, 7 (1983) 247–97.

Sulkunen, P., 'Logics of Prevention. Mundane Speech and Expert Discourse on Alcohol Policy', in P. Sulkunen, J. (ed.), *Constructing the New Consumer Society* (London: Macmillan, 1996).

Sulkunen, P., 'The Conservative Mind. Why Does the New Middle Class Hate Alcohol Control?', *Addiction Research*, 1 (1994) 295–308.

Sulkunen, P., *The European New Middle Class. Individuality and Tribalism in Mass Society* (Avebury: Aldershot, 1992).

Sulkunen, P., 'Agent, thief, guerilla and critic' (Agentti, varas, sissi ja kriitikko), *Alkoholipolitiikka*, 56 (1991) 419–20 (in Finnish).

Sulkunen, P., 'De stora projektens död', *Nordisk alkoholtidskrift*, 8 (1991) 208–20.

Sulkunen, P., 'Mythical Images of Drinking Revisited', A Paper presented at the Fourth International Conference on the Study of Consumption, SISWO, Amsterdam, 9–11 September 1993.

Sulkunen, P., 'Problems of Prevention. Mundane Speech and Expert Discourse on Alcohol Policy', in P. Sulkunen *et al.*, (eds), *Constructing the New Consumer Society* (London: Macmillan, 1996).

Sulkunen, P. and Törrönen, J., 'Constructing Speaker Images. The Problem of Enunciation in Discourse Analysis'. *Semiotica*, forthcoming/b.

Sulkunen, P. and Törrönen, J., 'The Production of Values. The Concept of Modality in Textual Discourse Analysis'. *Semiotica*, forthcoming/a.

Sulkunen, P. *et al.*, *Lähiöravintola* (The Suburban Pub) (Helsinki: Otava, 1985).

Sulkunen, P. and Kekäläinen, O., *WPindex 1.0. A Light Solution to the Problems of Heavy Work. A Programme for Qualitative Analyses. A User's Guide* (Helsinki: Gaudamus, 1992) (in Finnish).

Tarschys, D., 'The Success of a Failure: Gorbachev's Alcohol Policy, 1985–1988', *Europe-Asia Studies*, 45 (1993) 7–25.

Tester, K., *Media, Culture and Morality* (London and New York: Routledge, 1994).

Tigerstedt, C. and Roseqvist, P., 'The Fall of a Scandinavian Tradition? Recent Changes in Finnish Alcohol Policy'. A Paper presented at the 21st Annual Alcohol Epidemiology Symposium, Porto, Portugal, 5–9 June 1995.

Titmuss, R., *The Philosophy of Welfare* (London, 1987).

Tones, K., Tilford, S. and Robinson, Y., *Health Education. Effectiveness and Efficiency* (London: Chapman and Hall, 1990).

Törrönen, J., 'Reading Newspaper Editorials on Alcohol Policy'. Paper for pre-symposium on Issues in Qualitative Research in connection with the

References 241

20th Annual Alcohol Epidemiology Symposium of the Kettil Bruun Society
for Social and Epidemiological Research on Alcohol, Ruschlikon, Switzer-
land, 4–5 June 1994.
Törrönen, J., 'Liberal versus Welfare-State Type Rhetoric. Decision Makers'
Interpretations of two editorials', *Alkoholipolitiikka*, 60 (1995) 308–22.
Tossavainen, K., *Health Education in Schools to Encourage Good Health Habits.*
(Nuorten terveyskäyttäymistä tukeva koulun terveyskasvatus). Evaluation
of Preventive Health Education Concerning the Use of Tobacco and Alco-
hol (Helsinki: The Social and Health Research and Development Center,
Vapk, 1993).
Touraine, A., *The Voice and the Eye, An Analysis of Social Movements* (Cam-
bridge: Cambridge University Press, 1981).
Touraine, A., *La voix et le regard* (Paris: Seuil, 1978).
Touraine, A., *Critique de la modernité* (Paris: Fayard, 1992).
Trist, E. and Murray, H., 'Historical Overview – The Foundation and Devel-
opment of the Tavistock Institute', in E. Trist and H. Murray (eds), *The
Social Engagement of Social Science: A Tavistock Anthology, Volume I: The Socio-
Psychological Perspective* (Philadelphia: University of Pennsylvania Press, 1990).
Troyer, R.J., 'Are Social Problems and Social Movements the Same Thing?',
pp. 41–58 in J.A. Holstein and G. Miller (eds), *Perspectives on Social Problems.
A Research Annual*, vol. 1 (New York and London: JAI Press, 1989).
Wallace, P.G., Brennan, P.J. and Haines, A.P., 'Are General Practitioners
Doing Enough to Promote Healthy Lifestyle'? Findings from Medical
Research Council's general practice research framework study of lifestyle
and health, *British Medical Journal*, 294 (1987) 940–2.
Wallack, L.M., 'Mass Media Campaigns: The Odds against Finding Behavior
Change', *Health Education Quarterly*, 8 (1981) 209–60.
Wallack, L.M., 'Social Marketing and Media Advocacy: Two Approaches to
Health Promotion', *World Health Forum*, (1990) 143–54.
Warsell, L., 'The Tasks and Possibilities of Education in Local Prevention'.
In the evaluation seminar on the Lahti Project 16 May 1995. Can alcohol
related harms be reduced locally? (Valistuksen tehtävät ja mahdollisuudet
paikallisessa päihdetyössä. Lahti-projektin arviointiseminaari 16.5.1995.
Onnistuuko päihdehaittojen vähentäminen paikallisesti? (Helsinki: Alco-
hol Policy Planning and Education Unit, Alko, 1995) 17–23 (in Finnish).
Whyte, W.F., 'Introduction' in W.F. Whyte (ed.), 'Action Research for the
Twenty-First Century: Participation, Reflection, and Practice, *American
Behavioral Scientist*, 32 (1989).
Williams, R., *Towards 200* (London: Chatto & Windus, 1983).
Williams, R.H., 'Constructing the Public Good: Social Movements and Cul-
tural Resources', *Social Problems*, 42 (1995) 124–44.
Wiseman, J., *The Other Half. Wives of Alcoholics and their Social-Psychological
Situation* (New York: Aldine de Gruyter, 1991).
Woolgar, S. and Pawluch, D., 'Ontological Gerrymandering. The Anatomy
of Social Problems Explanations', *Social Problems*, 32 (1985) 216–17.
Yin, R.K., *Case Study Research. Design and Methods*, Second edition. Applied
Social Research Methods Series, vol. 5 (London: Sage, 1994).

Index